GOODS, POWER, HISTORY

Why do we acquire the things we do? Behind this apparently ingenuous question are several answers, some straightforward and others more interesting. To feed ourselves, might be the first response, for it is obvious that we expend much energy in the quest for food. Clothing and shelter would also seem to constitute our basic needs. Yet we can easily see that even in the Garden of Eden, people wanted more than they needed. This simple impulse has created the ever mounting abundance we call progress and nearly all of the subsequent trouble on our planet.

Four main interwoven themes run through this exploration of material culture in Latin America over the past five centuries: supply and demand; the relationship between consumption and identity; the weight of ritual, both ancient and modern, in what we acquire; and the importance of colonial and postcolonial power in the practice of consumption.

Arnold J. Bauer is Professor of History at the University of California, Davis. He has lived, worked, and studied in Mexico, Chile, and Spain and has held visiting professorships at Catholic University in Santiago, Chile, and Universidad Iberoamericana in La Rábida, Spain. Professor Bauer is the author of *Chilean Rural Society* (1975) and editor of *La iglesia en la economía de América Latina* (1986) and has published several articles in the *American Historical Review*, the *Hispanic American Historical Review*, the *Cambridge History of Latin America*, *Historia*, and various Latin American publications.

NEW APPROACHES TO THE AMERICAS

Edited by Stuart Schwartz, *Yale University*

Also published in the series

Noble David Cook, *Born to Die: Disease and New World Conquest,
1492–1650*
Herbert S. Klein, *The Atlantic Slave Trade*
Robert M. Levine, *Father of the Poor? Vargas and His Era*
Susan Socolow, *The Women of Colonial Latin America*

Forthcoming in the series

Alberto Flores Galindo (translated by Carlos Aguirre and Charles
Walker), *In Search for an Inca*
Sandra Lauderdale Graham, *Slavery in Nineteenth-Century Brazil*
Gilbert Joseph and Patricia Pessar, *Rethinking Rural Protest in Latin
America*
John McNeill, *Epidemics and Geopolitics in the American Tropics*
Eric Van Young, *Popular Rebellion in Mexico, 1810–1821*

Goods, Power, History

Latin America's Material Culture

Arnold J. Bauer
University of California, Davis

CAMBRIDGE
UNIVERSITY PRESS

PUBLISHED BY THE PRESS SYNDICATE OF THE UNIVERSITY OF CAMBRIDGE
The Pitt Building, Trumpington Street, Cambridge, United Kingdom

CAMBRIDGE UNIVERSITY PRESS
The Edinburgh Building, Cambridge CB2 2RU, UK
40 West 20th Street, New York, NY 10011-4211, USA
10 Stamford Road, Oakleigh, VIC 3166, Australia
Ruiz de Alarcón 13, 28014 Madrid, Spain
Dock House, The Waterfront, Cape Town 8001, South Africa

http://www.cambridge.org

First published 2001

Printed in the United States of America

Typeface Goudy Regular 10.5/13 pt.   *System* QuarkXPress [BTS]

A catalog record for this book is available from the British Library.

Library of Congress Cataloging in Publication data

Bauer, Arnold J.
Goods, power, history: Latin America's material culture / Arnold J. Bauer.
p.   cm. – (New approaches to the Americas)
Includes bibliographical references and index.
ISBN 0-521-77208-7 – ISBN 0-521-77702-X (pb)
1. Consumption (Economics) – Latin America – History.   2. Material culture –
Latin America.   I. Title.   II. Series.

HC130.C6 B38 2001
339.4'7'098 – dc21   00-064143

ISBN 0 521 77208 7   hardback
ISBN 0 521 77702 X   paperback

For
Rebecca, Lucy, Colby, Colton, Jonah,
and
Macarena Gómez-Barris

CONTENTS

Maps and Figures

Maps

Figures

Preface

Some two thousand years ago a well-known collection of books and letters warned that it was easier for a camel to pass through a needle's eye than for a rich man to enter heaven; worse yet, the volume's main protagonist even drove the money changers from the temple. At the beginning of the third millennium, we pay no heed to such distressing admonitions while money and goods are firmly enshrined in our emporia of consumption.

During the intervening two thousand years, not to mention the previous millennia, most people waged a daily battle, often unsuccessfully, to acquire the bare rudiments of food, clothing, and shelter that might enable them to reproduce their life. They adapted plants to the environment, fashioned tools, and tried to produce a little more as a hedge against misfortune. Only a relative handful of people got lucky, invented a better mousetrap or, more commonly, managed to persuade or force others to yield up a surplus that might create greater comfort or luxury. More recently, a larger but still small share of the planet's population is able to fill house and garage with consumer goods, while scrambling to pay off the mortgage and the Master Card bill.

On the eve of the year 2000, computers calculated that the planet's living population had reached six billion and, barring global disaster, will increase to around nine billion in the next fifty years. Unless we undergo an improbable change in values, our descendants will not be content with rice and homespun cotton cloth; more likely they will aspire to the high-energy, intensive consumerism so eagerly promoted in North America and Europe. Most people will probably want a wide range of goods, including a television, radio, and refrigerator, processed food and drink, maybe even a car, the single most destructive consumer good we've yet produced. The bad news is that if we get them, the environmental impact will probably be devastating; if we don't, or if goods continue to be so unequally distributed, one can imagine unprecedented class or ethnic conflict. Such prospects may help explain the outbreak of a rash of studies on consumption. Although the present book will solve no global problems, it may provoke readers to think a bit more about why we – or, more properly, why Latin Americans – acquired the things they did over the past five hundred years or so.

If pressed to explain, most of us would probably say we buy things because they're useful and we buy more when we have more income. That explanation is straightforward enough, and largely accurate, but the closer we look, the more we see that almost all goods are fraught with all kinds of meaning. The most humble gruel, as well as the prince's cape, are rather more than nourishment and clothing, and the explanation for acquiring them involves more than a conventional sense of utility.

Nor have we been unambivalent in the way we feel about our own acquisitions; of course, about the possessions of others we can become even more agitated and often condemnatory. At various times, people in the West, at least, have been both ecstatic and tormented about the possession of material objects. We also have the wit to see, and consequently to fear, that wealth, unequally divided, is a source of social upheaval. It's not just that some have possessions and others don't, or that egregious display or a sense of deprivation has led to envy, resentment, contempt, or warfare. Those who manage to acquire clothes and carriages, a Lambourghini or an Internet company, have at times felt uncomfortable and even guilty about the goods they've accumulated. Reflecting, perhaps, the influence of the two-thousand-year-old teachings mentioned earlier, the ambivalence between the propriety of restrained "decency" on one side and the desire to flaunt spectacular wealth on the other runs right through European history and its transatlantic extensions.

A random tour, through time and place, reveals this ambivalence. *Fifteenth-century Tuscany:* When the Franciscan monk Giralomo Savonarola tells the people of Florence that they ought to tear off their jewels and silk and sacrifice them to God, they praise him as a saint and offer him a cardinal's hat; when he insists they actually do it, they have him burned as a public nuisance. *Twentieth-century Mexico:* When certain members of the community of Tzintzuntzan acquire more animals and land than others, they are elected to stage the annual fiesta.

In a week-long display of food, drink, and fireworks, their excess wealth is burned off and the village returns to a relatively egalitarian harmony. *Present-day Rio de Janeiro:* When white Brazilians sniff at the excesses of the poor inhabitants of the hillside *favelados* who spend nearly their entire annual income on the extravagant use of sequins and costumes for Carnival, they are mocked by one Joaozinho Trinta, a samba float designer: "only intellectuals like misery, what poor people go for is luxury."[1] *The industrialized West:* These days, one of the luxuries that people in the high-consuming industrial countries give ourselves, out of high moral or aesthetic impulse – and, even more passionately, because of environmental concerns – is to lament the efforts made by less fortunate people in poorer countries to attain the standard of living, or, more precisely, the consumption patterns, of the West.

These and many other issues and a great many fascinating stories, hover around the history of material culture. Goods, commodities, things, are present in a thousand books, pictures, and paintings, but in regard to that part of the world imperfectly called Latin America, there are actually very few attempts to explain why people acquire the things they do or to follow out the implication of certain patterns of consumption.[2] This book does not attempt to plug one of those gaps we historians are forever trying to fill, but rather to tiptoe around the cracks in the record. The examination of what and why we acquire things, is, of course, a vast and fascinating subject that can hardly be resolved – indeed, barely introduced – here. But there are a few stories to be told, and I have tried to do that in a way that might provoke the interested reader to take up the subject of material culture more profoundly.

The present book emphasizes the core items of material life – food, clothing, shelter, and the organization of public space – in both their

---

[1] In the biting interpretation of George Bernard Shaw, *Androcles and the Lion*, in *Collected Plays with Their Prefaces* (London: Max Reinhardt, 1972), 4:467; George Foster, *Tzintzuntzan: Mexican Peasants in a Changing World* (Boston: Little Brown, 1967); Alma Guillermoprieto, *Samba* (New York: Random House, 1991), p. 90.

[2] Sidney Mintz, *Sweetness and Power* (New York: Viking Penguin, 1985), which shows how a European taste for sweetness is connected to the enslavement of millions of workers on Caribbean plantations; Eric Van Young's essay, "Material Life," in Louisa Shell Huberman and Susan Socolow, eds., *The Countryside in Colonial Latin America* (Albuquerque: University of New Mexico Press, 1996), pp. 49–74; and Benjamin Orlove, ed., *The Allure of the Foreign: Imported Goods in Postcolonial Latin America* (Ann Arbor: University of Michigan Press, 1997), are exceptions.

rudimentary and elaborate manifestations. It begins with pre-Columbian practice and then takes up the effect of the European invasion from the sixteenth century onward; the consequence of the first wave of classical liberalism from the 1870s to the 1920s; the inward turn toward a kind of consumer nationalism from the 1930s to the 1970s; and the present neoliberal epoch.

Four main interwoven explanatory schemes run through the narrative: supply and demand, or relative price; the relationship between consumption and identity; the importance of ritual, both ancient and modern, in consumption; and the idea of "civilizing goods." This last refers to the relationship between colonial and postcolonial power and consumption. "Power" means not only, say, royal directives regarding clothing, the tax and tariff policy of the modern state, the dominance of knowledge, or the naked force of capital, but also the attraction exercised by external reference groups or the power of fashion set by the powerful at home and abroad. All of these brought forth imitation, resistance, negotiation, and modification, and out of the resultant mix we can see – or I hope, at least, that this book helps the reader see – the ongoing practice of Latin America's material culture.

A Note on Terminology

The terms people use to describe geography or themselves and others are laden with meanings that betray, sometimes unconsciously, cultural prejudices or suggest a point of view offensive to current sensibilities. "Naming" implies power, and because we are dealing with a colonial world, many terms we have were originally imposed by the conquerors or invaders of what is now Latin America. Columbus, indifferent to the fact that places had names before he came on the scene, claimed that he "named" more than two hundred islands and settlements during the first days of the Northern Hemisphere autumn of 1492. He extended the practice to human beings. His first mistake, to call the native inhabitants "Indians," was continued by colonial Europeans and by the "Indians" themselves, and it is still with us. Spanish-speaking people also used *naturales* or, later, *gente indígena*, but these are awkward in translation. Because many teachers and students in the Native American studies programs in North American universities today often self-describe themselves with Columbus's original misnomer, "Indian" is used in this book to signify those people who thought of themselves as such or were considered by others to have been Indians. Neither usage is unproblematic.

Other terms such as black, white, mestizo, cholo, and mulatto have often been employed pejoratively, but their use is inescapable for a modern writer. Designations for specific native people are no less troublesome. When Hernán Cortés met Moctezuma on the main road to Tenochtitlan in November 1519, his translators described the native people as "Culhua," "Mexica," or "Nahua." The term "Aztec" only came into popular usage three centuries later. Yet, we are stuck with it, and I use it. "Inca" in the sixteenth century referred to a specific social class among the inhabitants of the central Andes; "Quechua," to a topographical stratum. Today, the term "the Incas" commonly describes the people present in Peru at the time of the European entry.

Generally I try to use the terms spoken or written by the people who lived in the period I write about in order to avoid jarring anachronisms. Thus I use "the Indies," the words used by many Europeans in the sixteenth, seventeenth, and eighteenth centuries to designate what is now "Latin America" because that (still imaginary place) did not yet exist. Englishmen during the same centuries, following the lead of German geographers, preferred "America" for the entire Western Hemisphere, as Latin Americans did and some still do today. "Our America," for example, in the mind of the great nineteenth-century Cuban writer, José Martí, stretched from the Rio Grande to Patagonia. But this is confusing for some students in the United States because in recent years, again, quite unthinkingly, our leaders have arrogated the term "America" to apply just to this country.

For the two great pre-Columbian high-culture regions in the Western (another loaded term) Hemisphere, there is no entirely satisfactory vocabulary. I use Mesoamerica or Mexico for one high-culture area and the Andes or the Andean zone for the other where perhaps I should use Anáhuac and Tawantinsuyo. But I use the currently popular terms because I imagine they are more familiar to my readers than the Náhautl or Quechua terms, which in any case apply only to specific regions within the larger core areas. Because I almost entirely (and shamefully) ignore Brazil, I often generalize with "Spanish America" but sometimes, if Brazil *is* included, I try to use the more inclusive adjective "Iberian" or "Latin" America.

The names for the invaders themselves present a certain problem. We usually think, and I usually write, that "Spaniards," or "Portuguese," conquered and colonized Latin America. But, in fact, a small number of people from all around the Mediterranean – from Crete, Genoa, France, Tuscany – as well as from Holland, the Atlantic Islands, and, of course, Africa, all participated.

"Latin America" was invented by the devilish French in the 1850s, who also came up with the unhelpful, "Third World" a century later. This became conventional usage only toward the end of the nineteenth century. It is an unsatisfying, grossly inaccurate term, but hard to ignore. When appropriate, after the new republics emerge in the early nineteenth century, I write of Chileans, Colombians, Mexicans, Cubans, and so forth.

Apologia pro Vita Sua

In this discussion of tastes and values that are inevitably subjective, I should, perhaps, try to make clear the origin and quirky development of my own. I was brought up on a proper Kansas farm in the rolling, wooded country five miles east and ten north of the intimidating metropolitan hub of Clay Center. On Saturday nights in the summer, my family would "go to town"; my mother and sisters browsed in the Five and Ten, while my father, down the street, leaned on the new harvestors in the farm machinery stores and talked solemnly with other farmers about the weather and soils. Now and then we'd be treated to nickel hamburgers in a little corner niche by the gas station, a welcome change from fresh, fried chicken and tender ears of corn, which was the daily fare at home. I wouldn't go near a Big Mac today, but the smell and taste of those five-cent burgers and the feel of the torn plastic covers on the counter stools still call out to me. I'm glad that no cultural critic in those years condemned my indescribable pleasure as vulgar.

Several years later as a young man, I went for two years to study economics in Mexico City. Finding a room with a respectable Mexican family, I was gently and seriously checked out by student friends of the older son. In due course I met with their approval and was then asked to weekend house parties to dance, badly, with chaperoned girls. I was invited to the annual formal ball for engineering students in the old Minería Building on Tacuba Street and to listen to the first Cuban chachacha bands in the heart of the old city. We ate tacos and grilled onions in streetside stands and bought bread and olives from the abrupt Catalans, who seemed to own all the delicatessens in town. There was no Wal-Mart or Costco, not a single Burger King, whole districts of the city without ketchup. Returning in subsequent years, what I had imagined to be the "real Mexico" had mostly disappeared.

Having lived two years outside of Casablanca, I was not unaccustomed to unusual places, but, even so, Mexico in the mid-1950s was decidedly a foreign country. Having had the great fortune to live there, I thought, naively of course, that I had experienced at least a hint of what Guillermo Bonfil Batalla later called "México profundo" or the deep, authentic Mexico. The Mexico of recent years, by contrast, seemed drained of its uniqueness, Americanized, like any other place. I know, of course, that every serious visitor, from Hernán Cortés onward, must think that he or she has seen the real thing. When those writers and artists who lived through the heady years of the 1920s returned, they surely must have found my "authentic" Mexico of the 1950s unbearably superficial. And I'm sure that young people today find the great capital fascinating. I don't defend my conceit, but rather warn that any lingering crankiness about Big Macs, the Colonel and his chickens, the Cowboys, or MTV on a friend's cable television out in Tacubaya might be explained by a sense of loss.

The Cuban Revolution and Berkeley in the 1960s fed my anti-imperialism and outrage against United States policy toward Latin America; living in Chile before and after the disaster of the Popular Unity had a sobering effect. The subsequent twenty-five years have made me more circumspect and, probably, more boring.

I recognize that private property and material incentives generate wealth, but I can't bear the constant hammering, on all sides, to consume, as if shopping were our only reason for being alive. I like good plain food, particularly the *pollo deshuesado al ajo arriero* in the Casa Vieja, an honest restaurant in Santiago. I believe canned and bottled soft drinks should be banned from the planet. I became impatient with the inability of socialists in Chile, Nicaragua, and Cuba to create an adequate material life for their citizens, but if Fidel were to pass on, I'd feel it as I would a death in the family. I understand that the present capitalist global market makes available thousands of things previously unimagined to millions of people, but I think the system in its present workings is disastrous to the environment, spiritually deadening, and probably not sustainable. But "there are more things in Heaven and Earth than are dreamt of" in our present philosophy. I hope the present student generation will be able to find a balance between its humane and material culture.

Acknowledgments

My interest in material culture was first provoked by my anthropology colleague, Benjamin Orlove, who has been a continuing source of ideas and gentle admonition. Marcello Carmagnani of the University of Turin invited me to write an earlier version of a portion of this book for the volume *Para una historia de América* (Mexico: Fondo de Cultura Economica, 1999) and gave me the benefit of his global knowledge. I want to thank my dear friends David Sweet, Louis Segal, Richard Curley, Ted and Jo Burr Margadant for critical comment and warm encouragement. M. Merker of San Francisco gave me a lifetime of loving support. Charles Walker, an incomparable colleague, read every word and offered, in his seemingly effortless manner, smart and constructive observation. Christopher Rodríguez was an exemplary research assistant; Sebastián Araya at California State University at Humbolt made the maps, and I am grateful to him and to Professor Mary Cunha for their kind assistance. Gabriel Unda provided his expert knowledge in working up the illustrations. Mr. Tobiah Waldron made the index.

Stuart Schwartz at Yale suggested that I write the present volume. The anonymous readers for the Press offered acute and informed opinion. Frank Smith and Brian MacDonald at Cambridge University Press have been patient, keen-eyed, and helpful editors. I should also like to thank the Committee on Research at the University of California at Davis, the Dean of Letters and Science, and the Office of Research for financial assistance.

Finally, what began as cultural wars ended in warm harmony, and in the course of this struggle, Danielle Greenwood managed to pry open my hard head so that two or three new ideas might rush into the vacuum. Her influence is present throughout the book.

CHAPTER 1

INTRODUCTION

Why do we acquire the things we do? Behind this apparently ingenuous question are several answers, some straightforward and others rather more interesting. To feed ourselves, might be the first response, for we can easily see that we expend nearly as much energy in the quest for food as we do for sex, both as a rule required for our reproduction. Clothing and shelter, too, would be high up on the list of the most basic material requirements, although these are less urgent in the lower elevations of the tropics than in the higher latitudes. Food, clothing, and shelter, then, would seem to constitute the basic *needs* of human existence and these are the fundamental categories of goods, in their increasing complexity, that we will follow in the course of this book. But wait. Economists are inclined to talk about "wants," which are universal and limitless, rather than "needs," which are in fact almost impossible to define. We shall quickly see that from the very beginning, even in the Garden of Eden, people "want" more than they "need." This simple impulse created the ever mounting material abundance, which we are accustomed to call progress, and nearly all of the subsequent trouble on our planet.

In the beginning of our story, particularly before the European invasion in the sixteenth century brought an unanticipated range of new goods to what is now Latin America, the quantity and quality of food, clothing, or shelter for ordinary people were determined by a family's ability to produce, and the choice among goods was limited by transport costs or simple availability and, no doubt, by a modest conception of what constituted needs or were felt as wants. Further up the social scale, specialized artisans or those who organized trade acquired more elaborate cloth or pottery, while above these strata ruled the pre-Columbian elite, which managed to command labor services or tribute to acquire a surplus of goods that mightily impressed the early Spaniards.

With only ordinary tools or knowledge, people work within the restraints of a given economic and political environment to produce a range of goods, which, of course, affects what they consume. This, among the most simple groups, may run from the prickly pear of the cactus to a coarse stone tool or simple sandals. So a "geography of production" influenced choice.[1] Even had a fifteenth-century Mexica warrior been able to dream of a steel blade, none was available at any price. Later, in colonial Latin America, the high transportation costs to import European wine or wheat flour put those commodities out of reach of all but the wealthy. Consequently, demographic change, transportation and transaction costs, markets and merchants are all fundamental in determining what we eat, drink, and wear.

All things on our planet, and for that matter even extraterrestrial "moon rocks," come to have value under certain circumstances. A hand-sized pounding stone worn smooth in a river bed or a sliver of razor-sharp obsidian was prized in regions where such tools were scarce. For a long time in the Old World and the New, these ordinary things and more sophisticated goods such as sheep's wool or baskets of maize were directly exchanged for salted fish or roofing poles. No doubt people were quick to establish relative value and inclined to haggle out of their own self-interest. But, at the same time, a great many things or objects have no exchange value until a demand or a market arises for them. The Algonquin, for example, could not imagine a price tag on the forests of tall trees until they saw English shipbuilders eyeing them for masts. Spaniards driving cattle and sheep into the Indies immediately placed a value on previously idle grasslands, which now became a commodity, to be bought, grabbed, leased, or rented. Time itself, today a prized commodity bought and sold at every moment, had a very different value to societies that organized their work around the task to be done rather than the hours, or hourly pay, required to do it.

During the last several centuries the notion of "price" (a reward paid for goods or services) and that even more abstract and symbolic marker called "money" have come to stand for the value of everything and everyone: there are "no free lunches," and, as we abundantly know,

---

[1] Fernand Braudel, *The Structures of Everyday Life*, trans. Sian Reynolds from the French (New York: Harper and Row, 1981), p. 324.

every man "has his price." Among pre-Columbian native Americans, however, price and money were still rudimentary concepts, whereas the invading Europeans could hardly think of anything else. But if many cultural features of contact societies were mutually incomprehensible, the inhabitants of both worlds quickly figured out the cost of one object, say, a Castilian shirt, in relation to cacao beans, and then smoothly adopted the *symbolic system* of money even where coins were not commonly used. And so, in this first approach to our question of why people acquire things, let's always keep in mind that over the past five hundred years or so in Latin America the economists have a fundamental point: relative price and supply and demand *are* important in explaining why people acquire the goods they do. But embedded in the code we call "price" are several elements that help determine our acquisition of goods. Otherwise it would be hard to explain why today, "when you offer two identical cappuccinos for sale on opposite sides of the same street, one for six dollars and the other for two, you will see people knock each other down as they flock to pay the six."[2]

A quick look around, at a teenager's jeans or an executive's yacht – or, closer to the concerns of this work, say, an Inca's spondylus ornaments or a French-style mansion in belle epoque, Rio de Janeiro – reminds us of the commonplace that many people acquire goods for display, as markers of identity and a boost to self-esteem. Some people (not everyone, not at all times) self-consciously consume food, clothing, or live in certain dwellings to express individuality or identity. Even the *way* we consume a certain dish or drink or wear a specific hat or uniform may be designed to produce a sense of uniqueness, or group, or even national, solidarity.

To complicate the matter even further, the value we attribute to an object may be largely determined by what *it means to us* – by the degree to which it "resonates with associations and meanings in our own minds." More complicated yet, we, and the historical consumers in this book, often unconsciously accept an objective "price" for certain goods when in fact our own subjective desires have established the price in the first place. We are inclined to believe that the objects or commodities we buy "dropped from heaven or sprang from the skull of Zeus fully formed," their price tags already dangling from them "like an original appendage," when in fact "the whole idea of a thing being worth,

---

[2] Adam Gopnik, *New Yorker*, April 26, 1999.

or equal to, two ounces of gold, or forty bucks, or a loaf of bread, is strictly a human conceit layered onto the object in question."[3]

When a Spanish woman in sixteenth-century Mexico beseeches her brother to bring with him on the next fleet to a country teeming with hogs "four cured hams from Ronda," or when a dissolute Franciscan posted to a remote village in the Amazon headwaters pleads for the Bourbon governor to send him specifically some Bramante cloth, we have evidence of the way people endow specific goods with subjective meaning.[4] We can easily imagine that once the good priest passes on, his treasured piece of cloth will lose the value he imbued it with and lie dusty and ignored in the mission church, just as the incalculable value of the narrow bed in my study, made with lathe and plane by my own hands from walnut planks sawed in my father's mill, will no doubt end up in a garage sale for a few paltry dollars. There is nothing more objectively real about the value of either cloth or bed than there is about the venerated bits of rudely carved wood hanging around the necks of the people the Portuguese found along the coast of West Africa for which they used the term *feitico*, the origin of our word "fetish."[5]

With this said, it must also be true that for many Mexicans or Peruvians, Cubans or Chileans over the past five hundred years, the rudimentary objects of daily use must hardly have been seen as reflections of one's identity or, for that matter, not given much thought at all. The ordinary hoe, a clay pot, a common woolen shawl were usually not offered for sale or their price even contemplated. They were simply used and replaced, often by home manufacture, when broken or worn out. Let's recognize that it's difficult to gauge the attitudes of ordinary people toward ordinary goods. Was an Andean herder indifferent toward his llama flock? Did a sixteenth-century blacksmith feel a greater degree of attachment to his homemade tools than does, for example, a present-day suburban husband toward his? Perhaps the easily knocked together adobe and thatch-roofed dwellings of people throughout Mexico and

---

[3] Thorstein Veblen, *The Theory of the Leisure Class* (1899; reprint, New York: Penguin, 1994), set out the classic view on "conspicuous consumption." For a modern and often poetic reflection on current practice, see Leah Hager Cohen, *Glass, Paper, Beans: Revelations on the Nature and Value of Ordinary Things* (New York: Doubleday, 1997), pp. 205–7.

[4] James Lockhart and Enrique Otte, eds., *Letters and People of the Spanish Indies* (Cambridge: Cambridge University Press, 1976), p. 136; Archivo general de Indias, Charcas, leg. 623.

[5] Cohen, *Glass, Paper, Beans*, pp. 208, 199.

the Andes mattered less to their inhabitants than do our "homes" today.[6] Or maybe not. Perhaps the layered associations of love and death, birth and the memory and joy of children's play imbued dwellings with a value not captured by the cold-eyed calculation of square footage in the modern housing market.

There are other, perhaps even less obvious, explanations for the acquisition of goods than the need for subsistence or relative price or even for display or identity. A third observation of everyday life shows that goods have other important uses. They provide, for example, the material substance in rituals that help to create and maintain social relationships – or, put another way, goods "fix public meanings." But what is "meaning"? Social meaning, in the words of a brilliant anthropologist, "flows and drifts, it is hard to grasp . . . but as in tribal society so too for us: rituals serve to contain the drift of meaning." Mary Douglas goes on to say that "more effective rituals use material things and the more costly the ritual trappings, the stronger we can assume the intention to fix the meanings to be." Human rationality presses us to make sense of the world. For example, the social universe needs to be marked off in temporal dimensions, "the calendar has to be notched for annual, quarterly, monthly, weekly, daily and shorter periodicities . . . so the passage of time can then be laden with meaning." Thus we commemorate a new year, birthdays and first Communion, weddings, a silver jubilee, a millennium, "a time for living, a time for dying, a time for loving."[7] Indeed, in recent years, our clever salesmen have made it easy for us by suggesting materials – paper, glass, silver, gold – appropriate to certain wedding anniversaries. And, as we are all acutely aware, consumption goods, including even the everyday ritual of morning coffee, are indispensable to celebrate these moments that punctuate our social universe and draw the lines of social relationships.

Moreover, our often unconscious adherence to ritual or convention with its consequent effect on *the way* we consume, can be seen in our private as well as public actions. Mary Douglas asks us to consider, for example, a solitary diner, casually standing at the fridge door reaching in for his supper. "He unthinkingly adopts the sequential rules and categories of the wider society. . . . he would never reverse the

[6] Van Young, "Material Life," pp. 51–2.
[7] Mary Douglas and Baron Isherwood, *The World of Goods* (New York: Basic Books, 1979), pp. 60–4.

conventional sequence, beginning with pudding and ending with soup, or eat mustard with lamb and mint with beef."[8] Even in the most rudimentary adobe and thatch dwellings in colonial Mexico and Peru, ordinary people adhered to their forms of the "rituals of dinner."

The consumption of goods is also interwoven with rule. The state, for example, can endeavor to shape consumption through sumptuary laws, an insistence on uniforms for soldiers or schoolchildren, the imposition of tariffs or the proscription of certain goods, or, say, through the control of grain prices in sixteenth-century Lima or a subsidy paid until recently to tortilla producers in Mexico. There is also a reciprocal feature in material politics. People consume their way into citizenship in the new nineteenth-century nations through the acquisition of goods such as imported, or urban or "western" clothing or food; by participating in public ceremonies such as the *fiestas patrias*; or by acquiring private property – often a requirement for voting. These purchases bring people into local and national markets or, because they're taxed, enmesh them in the new fiscal machinery, place them on property or tax rolls, make them, in the eyes of the state, "legible."[9] All this helps construct new identities that make previously marginal people socially and politically acceptable as citizens.

I also hope that this brief excursion into material culture will encourage readers to see the objects and commodities we consume today not as disembodied tools or tiles stacked on the shelves of hangar-like Home Depots or apathetic polyesters from God knows where, lying in unruly piles in the new outlet stores, but rather to imagine the makers of all these things, perhaps – at the very best – as the poet imagines the builders of Machu Picchu, "the tiller of fields, the weaver, reticent shepherd, the mason high on his treacherous scaffolding, the jeweler with crushed fingers, the farmer anxious among his seedlings."[10] For much of our story most people, in fact, produced their own foot plows or hoes, put up their own shacks or huts, wove their own cloth. Others usually bought directly from the seller, examined the farmer's onions in their own hands, scolded the underpaid construction workers, looked over the seamstress's shoulder. So the link between local goods and

[8] Ibid. (A colleague pointed out that students in a rush might constitute an exception to this statement.)

[9] James Scott, *Seeing Like the State: How Certain Schemes to Improve the Human Condition Have Failed* (New Haven, Conn.: Yale University Press, 1998).

[10] Pablo Neruda, *The Heights of Macchu Picchu*, trans. Nathaniel Tarn from the Spanish (New York: Farrar, Straus and Giroux, 1974), canto xii.

local producers was obvious in a way literally unimaginable today. With long-distance trade and the emergence of a world market, which began with a trickle of goods in the sixteenth century, expanded unevenly in the nineteenth, and now floods anonymously into our markets from the most distant corners of the planet, the rupture between producer and consumer has become nearly complete.

Our examination embraces those parts of the world, now known conventionally but imperfectly as Latin America, over the past several centuries with special attention, particularly in the early colonial centuries, to the core areas of Mesoamerica and the Andes. These were the sites of pre-Columbian high culture, later the centers of colonial regimes, and they remain important today. For the eighteenth, nineteenth, and twentieth centuries, our discussion follows the expansion of European migration into the southern cone of Chile and Argentina, and the forced African diaspora into the Caribbean. Brazil, a fascinating culture on its own, is here dealt with unevenly. Everyone knows that there were – and are – class, gender, and ethnic divisions along with marked regional and even local differences throughout this large time and space. I make no claim for comprehensive treatment and even less for definitiveness. Many specialists may be astonished at my omissions and brutal generalizations.

Like everywhere else on the globe, from the very beginning of human settlement in the hemisphere, more or less discrete groups constantly came into contact with people of other cultures and goods. There is evidence, for example, of the ninth-century A.D. exchange of "thin orange pottery" from the high plateau of Mexico into the tropical lowlands of central America; of turquoise trade across the arid reaches of northern Mexico during the eleventh-century postclassic period; or even perhaps of jade figurines between Mesoamerica and the Andes 2,500 years ago. But from the sixteenth century to the present, the people of what is now called Latin America became subject to the entirely distinct material regimes of the Spanish and Portuguese empires and later, from the early nineteenth century, dependent upon the powerful industrial countries of western Europe and the United States.

Everyone acknowledges the enormous contribution of American silver, maize, chocolate, potatoes, tomatoes, and even sisal, quinine, and cocaine, to global society, but apart from these and other foods, fibers, or minerals, Latin America's contribution to global material culture is scant. Neither the Andean foot plow, *chaquitaclla*, the three-stone sling, fine pottery, the exquisite work of silversmiths or goldsmiths, nor even the truculent llama found its way to western Europe. Later, in the industrial age, the vast array of global manufactures in the nineteenth and twentieth centuries were imported *into* Latin America, none, not even bridles or shoes or woolen capes, went the other way. Nor for that matter have cooked dishes or prepared drinks crossed from west to east. There were not, and still are not, at least until very recently, *papas a la huancaína* or *mole oaxaqueño* in Madrid; no *pulque* in Chicago; no *yerba mate* in Galicia. Nor were there any tamales or enchiladas in the United States outside the population of Mexican descent, until the past forty years or so. Had the ancient Peruvians somehow found their way to Granada and imposed their rule on Ferdinand and Isabella, is it not likely that roast *cuy* (guinea pigs) and frothy *chicha* would have appeared in kitchens from Madrid to Seville? Perhaps llamas and alpacas would now be grazing in Castile alongside merino sheep, the creature the Spaniards were quick to introduce into the Americas.

In the realm of material culture then, the people of Latin America have been presented during the past five hundred years with a more abundant and a far wider range of goods from abroad, particularly manufactures, than those present in their own territories. With few exceptions, the flow of new goods has generally been into, not out of, Latin America. This is not, however, a simple matter of supply and demand or quality of product. The creation of a material regime takes place in a field of power. This is sometimes formal and direct, as in the case, for instance, of colonial sumptuary laws, which aimed (not very effectively) to control consumption, or in the frequent collusion between crown officials and colonial merchants that forced Indian villagers to purchase goods of European provenance. The effect of colonial power can also be seen in the never-ending, informal and voluntary maneuvering for new identities or positions. This took place, and was practiced by everyone, within the framework of new fashions, new "reference groups" or models of consumption, or the need to make visible and stable the categories of culture that seem to emerge with particular importance in colonial and postcolonial societies.

How, then, can one set in motion our stories of the nearly infinite number of transactions that make up the creation of the essentially occidental but still hybrid regime of goods and commodities that we see today in Latin America? Recognizing the importance of price and markets but moving beyond an excessively economistic plot, I have taken a page from the sociologist Norbert Elias who explained changes in European *manners* as part of an inexorable "civilizing process." Here I want to show that changes in Latin American material culture were to a certain degree driven by the imposition and often eager acceptance of "civilizing *goods*" introduced by various colonial and neocolonial regimes over the past five hundred years.

From the beginning of the Iberian intrusion down through the French, English, and present-day United States material regimes, those who endeavored to *impose* consumption in Latin America, as well as those inhabitants of Latin America who *voluntarily* acquired certain goods, often came to think of themselves as part of an occidentalizing process. For the invading Spaniards in the sixteenth and seventeenth centuries this was a matter of imposing *buena policía* in the new colonies; for the eighteenth century they undertook a "civilizing process," and later the nineteenth-century liberals promoted the project of "modernity." The Spanish insistence, for example, that towns be laid out in a strict gridiron pattern or that Indians wear trousers, the various decrees against "scandalous dress," and the practice of forcing Andean and Mexican villagers to buy iron goods, cloth, or mules in the eighteenth century are examples of compulsion in order "to civilize," as well as to make money. Far more important, however, were the shoes in place of sandals, wheat bread instead of maize, Asian silk off the Manila galleon rather than coarse local cotton, a piano, a mansard-roofed mansion, a Dallas Cowboys sweat shirt, and a hundred other choices that people voluntarily made and still make to establish their position in the social hierarchy, and to be seen, depending on the century, as less "barbarous," more "civilized, more "modern," or more *de onda*, more "with it."

None of this practice is unique to Latin America. But the scramble for identity, the need to redraw, or cross over, the lines of social relationships through acts of visible consumption, are perhaps rather more intense in colonial and postcolonial societies where power and the reference for fashion are often established by foreigners, while the status and prestige of people within the colony or country are strongly influenced by the jigsawed-puzzle of class and ethnicity, the negotiation of which is made all the more important because of its ambiguity.

The imposition and acceptance of "civilizing goods" is not, of course, the whole story of Latin America's material culture. In this history, successive waves of outsiders, or small dominant groups within the different countries, have endeavored to squash down upon the mass of people a layer of goods and practices at times not in consonance with the deeper culture. Consequently, throughout these five centuries we see men and women resist the imposition of culture-altering goods. Many elements in ordinary life, in fact, remain remarkably constant over the centuries and form the deep practice of everyday life. Thousands of women continue to pat out, one at a time, the ancient tortilla for the *comal*; coca leaf remains indispensable in the Andes; adobe and thatch still provide shelter. But more commonly, it is true, along with acceptance or resistance we also see innumerable cases of the appropriation, modification, and adjustment of new goods to local conditions. This has gone on ceaselessly but with special intensity since the sixteenth-century European invasion.

The individual tortilla maker or *tortillera* is rare today; country women take their dampened flour to a local mechanical contraption, pay a fee to have the tortillas stamped out, or more commonly buy the *masa* itself, in *supermercados*. Same ancient food, different technique. At the Cuzco airport, coca leaves now show up in Lipton Tea–sized porous bags so that the traveler, gasping for breath at eleven thousand feet, may have at hand hot *mate de coca* in a Styrofoam cup. Everywhere, Mediterranean tiles or corrugated metal sheets have replaced the thatch on adobe shacks. In the end, we have a negotiated, hybrid material culture but one in which imported elements are clearly dominant.

I present six broad stages in the development of Latin America's material culture. The first begins in the centuries just before the sixteenth-century European invasion at a time when a large part of the native population had settled into sedentary agriculture organized around small hamlets, substantial villages, and even, for the age, substantial urban centers. Drawing on the complex history of several millennia, the large mass of the people, perhaps 85 to 90 percent, here as in contemporary Europe or Asia, lived an essentially rural life. With notable exceptions, this was a world of self-sufficiency and the barter of goods and services within a very small radius. Most of the goods available in the so-called postclassic period (ca. A.D. 1000–1492) were in fact present much earlier, perhaps fifteen hundred years before, when the essential elements of Meso-American and Andean diet, clothing, shelter, and tools were established. Pre-Columbian life was neither hermetic nor static. In each archaeological horizon, which is the residue of successive waves of conquest, destruction, and building, archaeologists have found a different mix of goods and evidence of changing diet.

The archaeological record establishes the presence of goods but is less eloquent on the circumstances of their circulation. Although most goods were exchanged locally, it is clear that food, cloth, building material, precious stones, metals, shells, and feathers moved through a tribute system and markets throughout Mesoamerica, and on the backs of men, women, and llamas across wide swaths of the Andes. The use of these goods, of course, was never immutable: men and women modified their diet, dress, and shelter to the environment and accepted new materials and techniques. In both the Mesoamerican and Andean worlds imperial and religious rituals impelled the consumption of goods, as did the need to cement alliances and curry favor. Gift giving was a practice as deeply imbedded in pre-Hispanic culture as it was for the future invaders.

The sixteenth-century European invasion – our second stage – shattered the societies of indigenous America and truncated the organic development of its material culture. During the first decades the relatively few Spaniards engaged in the conquest and its consolidation insisted on their own, familiar, material regime and endeavored to provision their early settlements, bringing wine and wheat flour, dried cod and imported cloth. But the introduction of European plants and animals, together with a precocious development of artisans of all kinds, soon made European commodities available not only to themselves but also to the native population and their descendants who undertook a selective appropriation of foreign goods. The process was gradual. European conquest and settlement affected first the native elites and the more urbanized populations in general, and then new goods and commodities began to spread through towns, missions, mines, and haciendas.

By the 1570s the violence of armed conquest diminished and the impact of the demographic disaster swept through the Americas. The Spaniards undertook a sweeping reorganization of the landscape, congregating the remaining native population into planned villages with Spanish-style government. Almost immediately the first generations of mixed races began to emerge. Within the new hierarchy of colonial power there arose concerns about class and ethnic identity or political and social status, leading to a scramble for survival and position that encouraged the consumption of goods of all kinds. Atlantic convoys, pack mules, and wheeled vehicles brought unimagined goods within reach of local consumers. Plows, draft animals, pulleys, whims, iron tools, and new plants and animals shifted the supply and demand of new and old goods. Usefulness and relative price help explain the adoption or rejection of certain goods, but in the emerging colonial world of uncertain status and ambiguous values, social and cultural determinants of consumption were present as well. But let's not exaggerate. Some things changed not at all or very little. Throughout the colonial period and beyond, native men and women, in diminishing numbers, to be sure, continued to dress in homespun and home-woven cloth and to depend primarily upon the ancestral diet of native foods.

Our fourth watershed, carrying a substantial inundation of goods from abroad, begins with the independence of most of Latin America from Spain (1808–25) and reaches a flood tide in the last third of the nineteenth century when the export of food, fiber, and minerals enabled the Latin American republics to import a wide variety of commodities from the industrial countries of the Atlantic basin. Those with money in the new republics quickly embraced the arts, fashions, and superior manufactures of England and France. Imported machinery, steel rail, and steam engines permitted Latin American political and social leaders to import electric lights, trolleys, engines, rifles, and machinery in order to modernize their countries as well as buy the food, clothes, and architectural services that would set them off from their darker and less cultivated compatriots. In the upper reaches of society, the reference groups for consumption became predominately foreign. Houses built in the style of the French Second Empire lined the new avenues, and English leather and cottons and fine French textiles and wines became the vogue.

Goods, consequently have a relationship with "modernity." This becomes apparent as Latin Americans, in the nineteenth century, retained a tenuous adherence to colonial tradition while longing to be part of the emergent, Western bourgeoisie. The avid consumption of European goods, the journeys to Paris and London, contact with intellectuals, artists, and engineers "was something more than vain posturing or following the latest fashions"; it was to place one's self at the peak of the historical moment, it was to be *modern*.[11] The opera, for example, could be enjoyed by members of the emerging middle classes in similar and familiar circumstances across the board, in La Scala, Covent Gardens, the Met, Manaos, or the Teatro Municipal in Santiago. By entering the larger world of fashion, buying Charles Frederick

---

[11] Sergio Villalobos, *Origen y ascenso de la burguesía chilena* (Santiago: Editorial Universitaria, 1987), pp. 78–9.

Worth gowns or English woolens, the new elites everywhere could *feel* European or, again, feel *modern*. Perhaps a mundane parallel in our own time can be seen in the way people of an older, manual-typewriter generation, not wanting to feel antiquated or "out of it," buy computers, get on the Internet, and can *feel* as up-to-date as the fast-track youth. We notice today, however, as technology outpaces culture, a generational inversion in which adults do not pass on experience to their apprentice children but rather strain to learn from their own offspring.

By the first years of the twentieth century, demographic growth, along with the collapse of the largely artificial belle epoque splendor gradually brought mestizo politics and culture onto center stage in the midst of a raging debate about the appropriate path of modernity. This process, our fifth stage, building from the late nineteenth and early twentieth centuries and inevitably filled with ambiguities, involved a halting turn toward consumer nationalism. This led to the promotion of national values, the formal repudiation (but continued use) of foreign models and goods, the gradual development of import substitution industries, and the promotion of national culture. Under the rubric of *indigenismo*, urban leaders in Mexico in the 1920s, Peru in the 1930s, and Guatemala and Bolivia in the 1940s and 1950s made continued attempts to occidentalize the indigenous populations, to bring people perceived as Indian into a national political and material culture, made more feasible by the accelerating rural-urban migration.

Finally, the present. From the 1970s and continuing today, governments are unceremoniously discarding the previous model and turning back to the nineteenth-century practice, never fully realized, of export-led development and free markets. Imports are restrained only by the capacity of fervent consumers to buy. Although the first wave of liberal capitalism in the last third of the nineteenth century powerfully affected the culture and consumption of Latin American elites, its effect was felt less as one moved out from the cities and into the lower reaches of the social order. During the past two or three decades of the present neoliberal epoch, consumption is still concentrated in the upper reaches of Latin American society where a visibly large share of the new wealth has come to rest. But the new orthodoxy of free trade has also created an ocean of relatively inexpensive new goods, previously unimaginable by ordinary people, that now washes into outlet stores, vast Wal-Marts and Home Depots, and even to the most remote households. For some, the gaudy malls, the grease and stench of

fast-food franchises, the tacky T-shirts, the vulgarity of Hollywood films
must seem as if a global "uncivilizing" process has come round at last,
sweeping away the decency and decorum that often accompanied the
first, less savage, liberalism. For others, long deprived of the most basic
goods, the shelves of tape, tools, steel pans, designer "bluyeanes," cheap
shoes, and the democratizing informality of dress and food must seem
like a consumer's heaven on earth.

CHAPTER 2

THE MATERIAL LANDSCAPE OF
PRE-COLUMBIAN AMERICA

Inique in nahuah mozcalia quicuani motlaque cultiani ahuaque
tlacualeque.[1]

Pasa por aquellos dos pueblos un camino ancho, hecho a mano,
que atraviesa toda aquella tierra y viene desde el Cuzco hasta
Quito que hay más de tres cientas leguas; es tan ancho que seis de
a caballo pueden ir por él a la par sin llegar uno a otro.[2]

THE THINGS OF EVERYDAY LIFE

Everything derives from food production. The extra food that men and
women produce from improved plants or edible creatures or their use
of new tools and hard work enable other people such as potters, war-
riors, priests, or university professors to practice their crafts without
having themselves to grub in the earth or worry about where the next
meal might come from. The fundamental change in global food production began some fourteen thousand years ago when people slowly
began to develop the various cereals that would become the main

---

[1] "These Nahuas were experienced eaters, they had provisions, were owners of
drink, owners of edible things." Quoted in Salvador Novo, *Historia gastronómica
de la ciudad de México* (Mexico City: Editorial Porrua, 1997), p. 4.
[2] "Between those two towns there's a wide road, all hand-made, that cuts through
the entire land from Cuzco to Quito, which is more than three hundred leagues;
it is so wide that six men on horseback can ride side by side without touching."
Eyewitness account (1532) of Francisco de Xerez, *Verdadera relación de la conquista del Perú y provincia del Cuzco, llamada Nueva Castilla* (Seville, 1534),
reprinted in *Cronistas de las culturas precolombinas* (Mexico City: Fondo de
Cultura Económica, 1963), p. 436. A league was a little less than three miles.

source of caloric intake of everyone on the planet, and to tame a handful of animals for domestic use. Cereal crops are fast growing and have fairly high yields. Today, wheat, corn, rice, barley, and sorghum account for over half of all the calories consumed by humans beings on the planet. Eurasia, and especially Mesopotamia, was fortunate because of its particularly rich endowment of natural grasses. There are thousands of wild grass species on the earth but thirty-two of the fifty-six most important from which high-yield cereals could be derived – particularly barley and emmer wheat – were present there.

Mesopotamia was also richly endowed with the wild ancestors of the most practical and easily domesticated animals. There are today, for example, 148 large herbivorous mammals in the world that one might think possible of domestication. Yet, only 14 in fact were domesticated before the twentieth century. The wild ancestors of four of these (sheep, goats, cattle, and pigs) were present from the beginning in Eurasia. Another, the horse, domesticated for both warfare and traction, had an prolonged impact on Eurasian society. According to Jared Diamond's fascinating account, this head start made all the difference in the subsequent uneven development of global societies. Long before the European contact with America, the food surpluses generated in the eastern Mediterranean led to large empires, the inventions of ironwork and wheels, and the use of gunpowder and firearms.[3]

The Western Hemisphere had its own wild grasses. One of them, *teocinte*, now thought to have been present by 6000 to 5000 B.C. in South America as well as Mexico, began its slow development into *zea mays* – or maíz in Spanish, choclo in Quechua, maize or simply corn in American English. It became the fundamental cereal of the Western Hemisphere and the abundant food surplus generated by this plant underlay all the great Andean and Mesoamerican civilizations. In addition, throughout the Andes, from present-day Colombia to Chile, a range of tubers, the ancestors of our potatoes, supplied an even more basic food source as did manioc (or yucca) in the tropical lowlands. Any glance at a market in Mexico or Peru reveals an enormous variety of edible legumes and fruit long ago brought to fruition. Native Americans were accomplished horticulturalists.

Alas, there was only a scant endowment of potentially domesticable large mammals in the Western Hemisphere. The cranky alpacas and

---

[3] Jared Diamond, *Guns, Germs, and Steel: The Fates of Human Societies* (New York: Norton, 1997), pp. 125–42, 158–64.

llamas were fine for wool, yielded some meat, but were useless for traction. Moreover, they refused to carry humans and were reluctant bearers
of cargo. Further north, the buffalo was the best large, local candidate
for meat or milk, but this creature remained feral and, indeed, has only
recently been crossed with cattle to produce the dubious "beefalo." The
prehistoric horse became extinct some thirteen thousand years ago,
before American development really got going. All this meant that in
the fateful encounters following 1492, the European invaders rode
horseback and had steel and firearms. Much worse for the native inhabitants, the invading pigs, cows, and sheep carried deadly pathogens into
a numerous and accomplished people still, however, without sufficiently destructive means to defend themselves. Let us now turn our
attention to the main features of this material world on the eve of the
European invasion as it appears in the archaeological record and in the
inevitably peculiar impressions of the invaders themselves. Food, clothing, and shelter continue to provide the main lines of inquiry.

MESOAMERICA

Forty years ago, Carl Sauer, an original human geographer, sketched
out the broad outline of American food regimes, beginning with a distinction between the seed planters and those who set out cuttings for
vegetative reproduction. His scheme, which new research has slightly
revised, is still useful as a point of departure to understand a pre-
Columbian geography of production, horticultural technique, and some
peculiarities in the gender division of work. Sauer noticed the prepon-
derance of seed planting in agricultural regimes above a line drawn
through the Florida strait, south across the Gulf of Mexico and then
through present-day Honduras. This line separates the present-day
states of Guatemala and Mexico from the West Indies and South
America. Those lands to the south, were characterized by the presence
of vegetative reproduction: manioc in the tropics and several varieties
of tubers in the higher elevations of the Andes.[4]

---

[4] Carl Ortwin Sauer, *Agricultural Origins and Dispersals* (Cambridge, Mass.: MIT
Press, 1952). A different version of these pages and parts of the subsequent chap-
ters were published as Arnold J. Bauer, "La cultura material," in Marcello
Carmagnini, Alicia Hernández Chávez, and Ruggiero Romano, eds., *Para una historia de América: Las estructuras* (Mexico City: Fondo de Cultura Económica,
1999), pp. 404–97.

Map 2.1. Predominant food crops in pre-Hispanic America. *Source:* Courtesy, Sebastian Araya. California State University at Humboldt.

For Mesoamerica (present-day central Mexico, Guatemala, and El Salvador) we can now follow, in more detail than Sauer had available, the long process through which men and women brought to domestication, through seed selection, a wide range of plants, the most important of which were squash, beans, chiles, and, above all, corn. By around 3000 to 2000 B.C., these plants, supplemented by the pulpy leaves and the prickly pear of the nopal, wild fowl, the domesticated dog, deer, and small wild animals, provided the basis for sedentary settlement and population growth. When this system reached maturity in the higher elevations northwest of the Gulf of Fonseca (present-day Nicaragua), a wide swathe of seed planters extended from Guatemala into the present-day southwestern United States. They supported increasingly large numbers of people eating an essentially vegetarian diet of which corn in various forms was an important part of total caloric intake.

By the time we come to the centuries preceding the European invasion, the people of central Mexico had worked out a complex diet of maize, beans, squash, chiles, and amaranth, supplemented with algae from the lakes, honey from the stingless bee, a multitude of ducks, the domesticated turkey, dogs fattened for meat, and a wide range of small mammals, birds, fish, reptiles, amphibians, crustaceans, insects, worms, in fact, anything that could be eaten – a list of foods that made up the basis "for a rich and varied diet."[5] *Pulque*, the fermented sap of the maguey, was a popular alcoholic drink. Although the Mexica state endeavored to control its use, it was no more successful than the contemporary Inca in controlling the corn beer (*chicha*) of the Andes or than many modern states in similar, quixotic efforts to restrict drink or drugs.[6] There were, of course, no draft animals. Stone axes and hoes and the inevitable digging stick or *coa* were the sole farming tools.

The European invaders were understandably astonished that such huge surpluses were obtained through, in their eyes, such primitive methods. The secret was corn, often intensively cultivated in irrigated and mulched fields. This cereal, particularly when made into tortillas,

---

[5] Sherburne F. Cook and Woodrow Borah, "Indian Food Production and Consumption in Central Mexico before and after the Conquest (1550–1650)," in Cook and Borah, *Essays in Population History: Mexico and California* (Berkeley: University of California Press, 1979), 3:134–40.

[6] William Taylor, *Drinking, Homicide and Rebellion in Colonial Mexican Villages* (Stanford, Calif.: Stanford University Press, 1979), pp. 29–72.

Figure 2.1. Two men planting maize, depicted in a mid to late sixteenth-century codex. The first man is using the *coa* or digging stick; the second indigenous man is shown in European-style trousers. *Source*: Codex Florentino. Courtesy, Biblioteca Medicea Laurenziana, Florence.

continues to be a fundamental element in the Mesoamerican diet. Metates and griddles for baking tortillas appear in excavated strata from around 2000 B.C. on, but corn in those early years still occupied a relatively small percentage, perhaps no more than 15 to 20 percent, of the total diet.[7] From then on, as domestication advanced and settlement became more permanent, corn in various dishes became more and more important. People ate it in *atole*, *tamal*, and *pozole*, but the thin corn cakes – or, as the Spaniards called them, tortillas – came to be the most important source of nourishment. Having little grease and no oil in which to fry, the people of Mesoamerica were mainly boilers and griddle cookers. The tortilla was inevitably accompanied with chile and thus "in-chilied" or, in Spanish, *enchilada*, a practice as common in the fourteenth century as in the twentieth, when a woman near Orizaba (Mexico) told an American visitor, Charles Flandrau that "my little boy" – aged three – "won't *look* at a tortilla unless it is covered with chile."[8]

[7] William McNeish, "The Origins of New World Civilization," *Scientific American* 211, no. 5 (Nov. 1964): 10.
[8] Charles Flandrau, *Viva Mexico!* (Urbana: University of Illinois Press, 1964), p. 44.

"The dress of these people," wrote the Anonymous Conqueror, who claimed to have seen Mesoamerican society at the moment of its destruction, "consists of some sheet-like cloaks and . . . they cover their shameful parts both front and rear with pretty towels like big hanker-chiefs." Women's clothing consisted of a cape, skirt and an outer shirt (*huipil*) extending to the knee. Coarse textiles were woven of maguey fiber, the superior ones of cotton, a product of the hot country to the southeast and a highly desired tribute good in the high valley of Mexico. No hats were worn. "They wear nothing on their head except their long hair which is most beautiful."[9] In the absence of abundant leather, some men and women wrapped their feet in deer skin but most in maguey-fiber sandals.

The ordinary Mexican highland dwelling was a one-room adobe hut with a single, small, open doorway; poles with thatch or slab shingles formed the flat roof. Commonly occupied by more than one family, they were mainly places for eating and sleeping; ordinary people spent most of their time outdoors. In preconquest Tepoztlán, just south of present-day Mexico City, for example, "253 out of 490 households . . . were made up of two or more related couples." A wall with a single entrance surrounded the small huts; a number of such compounds made up a hamlet. People slept on mats and ate without chairs or tables. Grinding stones and griddles, a few earthen jars and pots together with baskets and brooms were "the principle furnishing, often the only furnishing, of macegual homes."[10] Few observers failed to notice an unusual profusion of flowers in Mexican life, a feature that continues to the present, not only in decoration but in innumerable place names and song.

THE ANDEAN REGION

Whereas the seed planters and the corn tortilla regime dominated agri-culture and food regimes in Mesoamerica, root crops, mainly manioc

[9] El Conquistador Anónimo, *Relación de algunas cosas de la Nueva España y de la gran ciudad de Temestitan, México* (Mexico City: Editorial América, 1941), pp. 26–7, 47–8; Frederick Hicks, "Cloth in the Political Economy of the Aztec State," in Mary Hodge and Michael Smith, eds., *Economies and Polities in the Aztec Realm* (Austin: University of Texas Press, 1994), pp. 89–90; see also Ross Hassig, *Trade, Tribute and Transportation: The Sixteenth Century Political Economy of the Valley of Mexico* (Norman: University of Oklahoma Press, 1985).

[10] Carrasco citation in Friedrich Katz, *The Ancient American Civilizations* (New York: Praeger, 1972), p. 222.

(yucca) and sweet potatoes, all reproduced vegetatively, were the main food crops of the West Indies and the tropical littoral of South America. This was perplexing to sixteenth-century Europeans because prior to 1492 no root crop in temperate Europe was a major source of calories. Tubers belonged to "the humble and despised category of vegetables."[11] The great staple of the islands was the bitter yucca grown in the lowlands of the Spanish Main as early as 3000 B.C. The islanders "grated, drained off the juice of the poisonous roots," and baked the residue into unleavened flat bread, a procedure common to the American tropics. The bread, tasty and nutritious, can be kept months even in humid weather, without spoiling. Corn was present in the Caribbean at contact, but it was not a major foodstuff in the islands and not ground into flour. Nor was it fermented into alcohol; in fact, the Caribbean people, alone among Central and South American native Americans, apparently had no alcoholic drink.[12] Among the forest people of the Caribbean littoral or in the drainage basins of the Orinoco or Amazon River, fish, turtles, and mollusks supplemented manioc. Their scant clothing was appropriate to the tropics and rather more curious than scandalous to the eyes of cold-weather Europeans.

As one climbs into the higher elevations of the Andes, manioc gives way to a wide range of other root crops that provided the fundamental food for the mass of the population. The potato, domesticated at least seven thousand years ago, was only one of several Andean root crops. Ultimately spread everywhere, the potato today is the most important root crop in the world. Most potatoes could be freeze-dried into *chuño* and preserved, although in the high elevations, the bitter varieties last longer. Root crops remain the fundamental staple of ordinary Andean people.[13] As in Mesoamerica, the Andean diet was overwhelmingly vegetarian. Some plants known in Mexico

---

[11] Sofie Coe, *America's First Cuisines* (Austin: University of Texas Press, 1994), p. 16.

[12] Carl Sauer, *The Early Spanish Main* (Berkeley: University of California Press, 1966), pp. 53–4; see also Irving Rouse, *The Tainos: Rise and Decline of the People Who Greeted Columbus* (New Haven, Conn.: Yale University Press, 1992), pp. 12–13. The Taino word for corn (*maíz*) spread throughout Mesoamerica in the wake of the Spanish conquest.

[13] J. Alden Mason, *The Ancient Civilizations of Peru*, rev. ed. (New York: Penguin, 1968), p. 141; see the expert account by Stephen B. Brush, "Potato," in Barbara A. Tennenbaum, ed., *Encyclopedia of Latin American History and Culture* (New York: Simon and Schuster Macmillan, 1996), 4:459–61.

Figure 2.2. Tukano (Colombian Amazon) woman peeling manioc tubers in the 1980s. Apart from the steel knife, little has changed since the sixteenth century. *Source*: Linda Mowat, *Cassaba and Chicha Bread and Beer of the Amazon Indians* (*Aylesbury, Bucks: Shire Publications, 1989*). Photograph: courtesy, Donald Taylor and Brian Moser.

such as chiles (here called *ají*), squash, several varieties of beans, and *palta* or avocados were present throughout the present-day states of Ecuador, Peru, and Bolivia, but *quínoa* (a cereal rather like millet) *oca*, *ullucu*, *anu*, *mashua*, and lupin as well as the white potato are exclusively Andean.

Once thought to be a late (ca. 1500 B.C.) arrival from Mexico, there is now abundant evidence that maize predated the Chavin period and indeed this cereal already had a certain impact in coastal and inland coastal valleys of Peru by 4000–3000 B.C. Nevertheless, its spread onto terraces in the high intermontane valleys of the Andes apparently was not extensive until accompanied by the state-directed irrigation projects of the Inca period. People ate corn here not in tortillas but still green, on the cob, as toasted kernels, or boiled and made into *humitas*, a form similar to the Mexican tamal. Animal fat was apparently not used for frying; llama meat was dried or occasionally cooked in a kind of stew, as was the odd, dried fish. The Jesuit Bernabé Cobo, who lived in Peru for most of the first half of the seventeenth century, considered the food of the ordinary Andean inhabitant "rustic and coarse" (*rústico i grosero*). The people of the Andes cooked mainly by boiling or by grilling the occasional fish or guinea pig. Above all, corn provided the basis for the fermented chicha, widely drunk, then and now throughout the Andes.[14]

Finally coca. The extent of its use is the subject of long debate going back to the early chroniclers. It now seems clear that growers from the eastern subtropical slope traded coca with communities of highland people before and during the advent of the Incas, so the leaves were not, as once thought, controlled by the Inca state. Chroniclers such as Garcilaso de la Vega (El Inca) who wanted to portray the Incas as wise and moderate leaders, as well as writers such as Huamán Poma who were inclined to condemn the Spanish conquest as a disruption of native order, coincided in the notion that the Incas had established a state monopoly and that coca use consequently was restricted to the royal group. Recent research in ethnographic materials has overturned that view, in fact, as the foremost ethnohistorian of the Andes points out, "there is no evidence whatsoever to substantiate this widely held

---

[14] See Karen Olsenk Bruhns, *Ancient South America* (Cambridge: Cambridge University Press, 1994), pp. 89–96, for a summary of recent research; *Obras del P. Bernabé Cobo*. Biblioteca de Autores Españoles, vol. 92 (Madrid, 1956), p. 245.

belief."[15] With the European occupation, coca chewing continued and probably increased despite occasional complaint and pious denunciation by colonial officials and more than one member of the native elite. Of course, the practice continues today, another element in the material culture of America that has resisted centuries of opposition but continues beneath the overlay of a hybrid material culture.

A major difference from Mesoamerica was the presence in the Andes of camelids. The domesticated llama and alpaca provided meat, wool, and carriage. In the higher elevations their wool provided men and women welcome comfort against the brilliant cold of the Andean night. Just how the fibers were separated from the animal, however, is painful to imagine. Presumably, handfuls of wool were hacked off the creatures with razor-sharp obsidian, or perhaps Andean groomsmen or women combed out the shedding hair. Here the invading Europeans surely brought a welcome device. Metal shears have been present from ancient times in the Old World; in fact, the picture of a Flemish pair in 1500 is almost an exact copy of Roman design. The Spaniards, long familiar with wool and sheep, were quick to bring shears to the Andes; yet, as late as the 1820s, English merchants in the Peruvian central highland believed a substantial market was available because "the natives are unacquainted with the kind of shears used in England."[16] Llamas and alpacas never provided traction in this wheeless and plowless world, but they were able, however reluctantly, to carry goods over long distances. Camelids enabled the Andean inhabitants to bridge difficult arid and mountainous stretches and ultimately to link far-flung ecological "islands" of the Andean archipelago into coherent communities.[17] Pastoral experience also permitted the native people of the Andes to accept with less reservation than their Mesoamerican contemporaries, the unanticipated invasion of European livestock. Sheep, mules, burros, even cattle, were to settle fairly comfortably into the Indian landscape.

---

[15] John V. Murra, "Notes on Pre-Columbian Cultivation of Coca Leaf," in Deborah Pacini and Christine Franquemont, eds., Coca and Cocaine: Effects on People and Policy in Latin America, Cultural Survival Report, June 23, 1986, pp. 49–52.

[16] Thomas Kruggler, "Changing Consumption Patterns and Everyday Life in Two Peruvian Regions: Food, Dress, and Housing in the Central and Southern Highlands, 1820–1920," in Orlove, The Allure of the Foreign, p. 51.

[17] John V. Murra's ideas are developed in many publications, including Formaciones económicas y políticas del mundo andino (Lima: Institute of Peruvian Studies, 1975).

Had a fifteenth-century Mexica been able to peek into a contemporary Peruvian peasant house, she would have found many things
familiar but also, no doubt, been startled by the sudden darting about
of small, domesticated *cuyes*, or what the Spaniards called "little rabbits
of the Indies" (*conejillo de Indias*). Roasted on a spit or boiled in stews,
they provided a meal-sized animal protein source to the Andean household, a convenience unknown in Mexico until the arrival of the European chicken.

The clothing of ordinary people in the Andes was similar to that of
Mesoamerica. Cotton was common on the Peruvian Pacific coast and
appears early in the archaeological record, but in time both wool and
cotton and bast fibers as well were found throughout the highlands.
"The ubiquitous breechcloth," sleeveless tunic, and a simple cloak were
men's dress; women generally wore a one-piece dress, a combined skirt
and blouse, that reached to the ankles and was bound at the waist with
a wide sash. In the absence of shears, "like all garments, this dress was
a large rectangular piece of woven cloth, merely wound around the
body." Where the Mesoamericans, or at least some of them, had deer-
skin, the Andean inhabitants had llama leather for sandals and, of
course, camelid wool for clothing. The Aymara in the coldest elevations wore knitted, woolen caps, "as most of the highlanders do
today."[18] There is scant mention for either sex of underclothes, which
suggests either its absence or leads into uncomfortable speculation.
Before trade brought cotton to the highlands where the bulk of the
people lived, hard to wash and scratchy wool was the alternative to
nakedness. As for more intimate apparel, particularly for women, the
record is silent.

A common Mexica peasant would not have felt out of place in an
Andean highland house. Both were typically one room, made of adobe,
occasionally of rough stone, with thatched roofs. In neither case were
there tables or chairs; ordinary people ate and slept on the floor, a practice the Spaniards would find indecent and even "barbarous." Kurakas,
socially a cut above, threw down a cloth. Every house had a tiny clay
stove, with adjustable fire slots, extremely economical of fuel. Bernabé
Cobo wrote, "The Spaniards burn more in their stoves in one day than
the Indians consume in a month," echoing Garcilaso's remark that
while the Incas "were stingy with fuel, they were astonished at the way

---

[18] Mason, *Ancient Civilizations*, pp. 147–9.

the Spaniards wasted it."[19] Native houses were arranged around a central court where several related families lived.

Here, then, is a partial list of the basic elements in the diet, clothing and shelter of the mass of ordinary inhabitants of America in the decades before the European invasion. People produced most food items locally for local consumption and served them in clay or wooden dishes. Clothing was homemade, the cotton or alpaca wool spun and woven by thousands, indeed millions of peasant hands. The rude houses they constructed from local materials; their stone, wooden, or nonferrous metal tools, also homemade, bore the contours of long wear. These goods, some of them traded within communities or laid out on mats for exchange in innumerable local markets, represent a stratum of ordinary use that lay beneath the flow of tribute goods requisitioned by the Aztecs or the Incas' demands for labor services in the Andes. Before we take up a discussion of these developments, let us notice some striking differences between Mesoamerica and the Andes, especially in the gender division of work in the production of food and cloth, because the early patterns carry through into later centuries. Perhaps in the end these too, were partly shaped by the divisions we have seen between seed planting and vegetative reproduction.

THE FOOD REGIMES OF MESOAMERICA
AND THE ANDES

Most people living today, insulated from the actual production of goods by layers of packages, processing, stores, and advertising, have to remind ourselves that not too long ago, men, women, and children spent a large part of every day occupied in the daily output of their own consumer goods. The ancient European expression, "men work from sun to sun but women's work is never done" was even more appropriate in the peasant worlds of Mexico and the Andes. An examination of food and clothing preparation with attention to the gender division of work reveals interesting differences between Mesoamerica and the Andes.

---

[19] *Obras del P. Bernabé Cobo*, p. 243; *Obras completas del Inca Garcilaso de la Vega*. Biblioteca de Autores Españoles, vol. 133 (Madrid, 1960), p. 134. Garcilaso, the mestizo son of a Spanish conquistador and an Inca princess, was brought up in Cuzco in the early years of the conquest.

As the long march of corn domestication followed its erratic and, no doubt, discontinuous path from the tiny grains of five or six thousand years ago to a more recognizable hand-sized ear some three thousand years ago, the practice of consuming corn in the form of the maize cake or tortilla apparently spread throughout a wide area of present-day Mexico and Guatemala. It was a fateful decision taken, perhaps, after centuries of observation that while a corn-heavy diet seemed related to disease, the families of other women, who, for whatever reason, had begun to cook the kernels with lime, grind them into a wet dough on a saddle stone, or *metate*, and pat out little cakes, were less likely to suffer. They could not have known about pellagra, the plague of corn eaters the world over, or that lime-soaking removed the kernels' pericarp, thus increasing the niacin content, which serves to combat the disease. Perhaps the people of ancient Mexico simply liked the particular taste of little corn cakes prepared in that way.

Nor can we know why men, almost exclusively, cultivated the plant in ancient Mexico, whereas only women made tortillas. In the Andes, as we shall see, the division of labor in food production was quite different. But in the hundreds of pre-Columbian Mexican terracotta figurines and in the pre- and postconquest codices, only women are represented bent over the grinding stone. More recently, few travelers in the twentieth century and no important Mexican artist failed to capture in print or paint what the women themselves called their "slavery to the metate." It is safe to say that over the past two thousand years, very few men have touched a metate and we have, to my knowledge, only one male confession (by a non-Mexican) to metate work. The sixteenth-century traveler Girolamo Benzoni tried for a few minutes to prepare his own food. He found "the grinding the hardest work . . . nor did I grind it very much because my arms were undone from hunger and very weak."[20] Here, then, is a cruel paradox: as Mesoamerican people more and more drew their sustenance from the humble tortilla, they came to depend on a plant that is easy to grow but a food item that requires a great investment of time in preparation, nearly all of it the result of female labor. The several hours bent over the metate in the daily grind also defined women's role in food production and put them in the indispensable center of the household. Their importance was enshrined in the symbolic handing of the metate

[20] Quoted in Coe, *First Cuisines*, p. 130; Oscar Lewis, *Tepoztlan: Village in Mexico* (New York: Holt, Rinehart and Winston, 1960), p. 25.

Figure 2.3. Terracotta figure of pre-Hispanic Mexican woman with metate and children. Compare the depictions of food preparation with child care in the previous illustration.

on from mother to daughters (while sons received the *coa*, or digging stick) or in the practice of burying the umbilical cords of newborn baby girls under the metate.[21]

The near total absence of household animals in Mesoamerica further contributed to a strong gender line in agriculture. Unlike in European husbandry where women often tended flocks, fed chickens and pigs, and inevitably milked cows, or even in the Andes, where as we shall see, women were active shepherds of domesticated camelids, the pre-Columbian Mesoamerican regime offered no such opportunities or burden for pastoral work. It seems clear that Mesoamerican women stuck closer to the hearth than did their Andean counterparts, an arrangement that persisted into the twentieth century.

Unlike the Mesoamerican maize tortilla regime, food preparation in the Andes seems somewhat simpler, at least from a distance. Women boiled unpeeled potatoes and prepared maize, either toasted or boiled. Thus the main caloric source was obtained without the laborious procedure of hand shelling, hand grinding, and the use of charcoal-consuming griddles typical of Mexico and Guatemala. Less "enslaved to the metate" than their female counterparts among the seed planters to the north, Andean women participated more in field work. Men normally opened the earth with the chaquitaclla, while women dropped slices of cut potatoes into the furrow. The harvest followed a reverse procedure: men dug up hills of tubers and women gathered them into hampers.

The native chronicler Huamán Poma de Ayala, drawing on observable practice in the early seventeenth century, probably little changed from the pre-European epoch, provides graphic evidence of men and women working in the fields side by side in a gender-integrated agriculture.[22] Spanish chroniclers, who make little or no reference to women in Mesoamerican agriculture, were struck by their activity in the Andes. Cieza de León, writing about the Cañari, remarked that "these women are good for hard work because it is they who open the earth, plant the fields, and gather the harvest while many of their

---

[21] James Lockhart, *The Nahuas after the Conquest* (Stanford, Calif.: Stanford University Press, 1992), p. 92; Arnold J. Bauer, "Millers and Grinders: Technology and Household Economy in Mesoamerica." *Agricultural History* 64, no. 1 (Winter 1990): 1–17.

[22] Felipe Huamán Poma de Ayala, *El primer nueva coronica* [sic] *y buen gobierno*, ed. John V. Murra and Rolena Adorno (Mexico: Siglo XXI, 1980); see, e.g., folios 1033, 1044, 1047, 1050, 1062.

Figure 2.4. "Trabaxos Papa allaimitapi." Man and woman harvesting potatoes. Produced by a native chronicler in the early seventeenth century, writing in a mixture of Spanish and Quechua, this drawing is meant to depict pre-Hispanic Peru. *Source:* Felipe Guaman Poma de Ayala, *El primer nueva coronica* [sic] *y buen gobierno* (Mexico City: Siglo Veintiuno Editores, 1980).

husbands are sitting at home spinning and weaving and fixing their weapons and clothes and taking care of their faces and other effeminate things." Women here also were bearers: "they gave us a large number of women who carried the loads of baggage for us."[23]

Writing later, Garcilaso de la Vega makes a similar point: "Men and women both went to the fields to help each other." Perhaps, in fact, he drew on Cieza for his remark that "in some provinces very distant from Cozco [sic] that were not yet well cultivated by the Inca kings, women went to work in the fields and their husbands stayed home to spin and weave," but that practice, he quickly adds, was both barbarous and unusual "and deserves to be forgotton." Polo de Ondegardo equated wives with wealth and status because the women "made cloth and prepared the fields for the husband."[24] Father Cobo too, in the mid-seventeenth century, was struck by the amount of women's work in Peruvian agriculture. "The women serve their husbands like slaves, carrying the entire weight of work, because apart from raising children, they cook the food, make chicha, make all the clothes they and their husbands and children wear, and work more in the fields than the men do." A century later, Juan and Ulloa repeat the charge of male indolence on haciendas in colonial Ecuador. Nothing can move the men to work; "they leave everything to the care of women. They are the ones who spin, prepare food, make chicha . . . and if the landowner does not force the men to work, they sit squatting down, which is the normal posture of all of them, drinking or cozying up to a little fire, watching the women work." His only task is "to plow the land of the little plot he has to plant; all the rest of the work in the field is the work of women."[25]

The gender line, then, seems to have been much more rigid in Mesoamerican food regimes than in the Andes and, in fact, drawn along very different contours. Why was this so? We can never know

[23] Pedro Cieza de León, La crónica del Perú (Madrid, 1922), p. 156. Cieza mentions that this may be explained in part by the scarcity of men because of the recent civil wars.

[24] Obras completas del Inca Garcilaso, p. 133; Polo is quoted in Karen Spalding, Huarochirí: An Andean Society under Inca and Spanish Rule (Stanford, Calif.: Stanford University Press, 1984), p. 86.

[25] Obras del P. Bernabé Cobo, p. 22; Jorge Juan and Antonio de Ulloa, Relación histórica del viaje a la América meridional, vol. 1, introd. and ed. José P. Merino Navarro and Miguel Rodríguez San Vicente (Madrid: Fundación Universitaria Española, 1978), p. 545.

the original explanation but only observe the scant evidence at hand and speculate. Somehow, for health or taste, once the tortilla with its extraordinarily heavy kitchen labor requirement became established in Mexican and Guatemalan diet, perhaps implicit negotiation over the long term was worked out in which men accepted the responsibility for field work in return for the indispensable tortilla. What began as intermittent and voluntary became customary and obligatory. Perhaps in the Andes, the simpler preparation of boiled tubers and stews left women more time for outdoor tasks. Or perhaps the extreme and brusque climatic changes in the high Andes impelled an urgency in planting and harvest that requires a greater degree of women's work in the fields than in the more moderate elevations of Mesoamerica, and this original necessity hardened into long-term cultural practice.

GOODS AND COMMODITIES IN RITUAL AND POWER

The thick, uneven layer of common goods that we've seen, contained the essential elements of diet, dress, and housing. They formed, in Braudel's term, the "structures of everyday life" for the mass of the population. These items were usually grown or made nearby or in the household for the members' use. They were laid out for barter on a thousand mats in innumerable local market stalls or exchanged among community members in some cases scattered across long reaches of space. They were so common and ordinary that they are barely remarked upon. Nor were these quotidian goods visible in the later European accounts: "Indian housing, clothing, and food, the omnipresent Indian goods, the metates and petates for which Spaniards had small use, the exchange of simple materials in cheap markets, all were features of a native substratum beneath the notice of colonists."[26]

Beyond these common goods, which must have occupied a large part of peoples' time and effort (even though their work must not have been felt or expressed in such terms), there are present even in the earliest archaeological record goods that reveal differences in social and political status. Although it was once possible to think that these goods were a "kind of automatic result of surplus agricultural production," recent research shows their importance in cementing power relations in the

---

[26] Charles Gibson, *The Aztecs under Spanish Rule* (Stanford, Calif.: Stanford University Press, 1964), p. 335.

early indigenous American states and in making and maintaining social relations.[27] People in pre-Columbian America have expressed differences in social and political status for a long time. Moreover, the elite in various city-states had been able to impose its demands on clusters of subordinate people for several centuries. Our focus here is on the decades just preceding the European invasion when societies under both the Mexica-dominated Triple Alliance (which we now call by the misleading but conventional term, Aztec) and the Inca regime were rapidly changing.

The Aztecs began by bringing under control the settlements and towns within the lush, lacustrine valley of Mexico and then by gradually imposing tribute obligations on surrounding regions. Their tribute lists detail the quotas: roof beams, jaguar skins, feathers of all kinds, stones such as the *chalchihuites* treasured by the Mexica, and, above all, a profusion of cloth, came from various outlying peoples. Aztec rulers claimed large surpluses of ordinary foods such as corn, dried chiles and beans, pulque, and fowl for their households. Bernal Diaz and other eyewitnesses provide vivid descriptions of the Aztec elites' Lucullan feasts, where reverential waiters served dozens of exotic dishes of game, fish, vegetables, fruit, and grain.[28] Two goods, cacao (chocolate beans) and cloth, played an especially important role in the definition of social and political power.

From the southeast piedmont of the Soconusco just up the coast from present-day Guatemala, the Aztec state required loads of cacao beans from several peoples, even from those who did not grow the trees. Bales and bales of cotton cloth also found their way on the backs of human carriers up from the lowlands to the lacustrine capital. "The most beautiful materials and the most brilliantly colored embroideries came from the Totonac and Huaxtec countries. The tribute brought thousands of loads of the splendid cloaks, loincloths, and skirts woven in the eastern provinces."[29] Both cacao and cloth, apart from their use or consumability, functioned also as kinds of money goods and in the

---

[27] Craig Morris, "The Wealth of a Native American State: Value, Investment and Mobilization in the Inka Economy," in J. Henderson and Patricia Netherly, eds., *Configurations of Power: Holistic Anthropology in Theory and Practice* (Ithaca, N.Y.: Cornell University Press, 1993), pp. 33–8.

[28] Bernal Diaz del Castillo, *Historia de la conquista de Nueva España*, introd. and ed. Joaquin Ramírez Cabañas (Mexico: Porrua, 1992), pp. 166–8.

[29] Jacques Soustelle, *The Daily Life of the Aztecs* (Stanford, Calif.: Stanford University Press, 1970), p. 132.

absence of small coin. In fact, cacao beans remained in circulation well into the seventeenth century.

Some of these goods, food and cloth alike, ended up in the vast market at Tlatelolco where they were exchanged for exotic items to enrich the diet and dress of the Aztec elite. The merchants responsible for organizing trade and tribute also knew how to display their power in ritual feasting. We are told by Náhuatl-speaking informants still able to remember the years before the conquest that "when some of the merchants or traders believed themselves to be rich, they gave a banquet inviting all other merchants and local notables because they thought it bad form to die without having thrown a splendid party which would reflect well on themselves and give thanks to their gods." Before dawn, the guests began to drink chocolate and nibble on little black mushrooms, "which made them see visions and even provoked lust." When the mushrooms took effect, many began to dance, others sang, some wept. But others sat quietly, overcome by frightening visions of themselves captured in warfare, devoured by beasts, or punished for adultery or theft. Others had happier visions of becoming rich in goods and slaves. As the effect wore off, "they spoke with each other of the visions they had seen." The meal itself might well have included six different kinds of tortilla, several different tamales, turkey stewed with ground pumpkin seeds and several spices (or *pipián* sauce, still popular today), different kinds of wild fowl, a range of squash, tomatoes, and chiles, lake fish, and pulque. The older merchants greeted the guests, giving each a burst of flowers "according to their custom." But the lion's share of tribute was earmarked by the Tlatoani (i.e., in 1519, Moctezuma) for the noble class. The Spaniards were astonished by the huge numbers fed daily. Cortés mentions hundreds of retainers who filled two or three large courtyards, and Bernal Diaz believed Moctezuma's household served more than a thousand meals a day. Ixtlilxóchitl wrote that in the neighboring city of Texcoco the annual consumption of the ruler's palace was 31,600 fanegas (some 50,000 bushels) of maize, 243 loads of cacao, and thousands of cotton mantles.[30]

[30] The merchants' feast is from Bernadino de Sahagún, *Historia general de las cosas de la Nueva España*, also known as the *Florentine Codex*, libro IX, cap. VIII: the description of "las comidas que usaban los señores" is from libro VIII, cap. XIII. Both are quoted in full in Novo, *Historia gastronómica*, pp. 170–3, 167–70. The haluciogenics are called "honguillos negros," or *nanácatl* in Náhuatl. The account of Ixtlilxóchitl is cited in Katz, *Ancient Civilizations*, p. 206.

Apparently, in this nonmonetary economy goods also provided indirect access to labor. Bernal Diaz saw the profusion of Moctezuma's domestic help through European eyes and painfully imagined the salaries: "why, with all his women, servants, bakers and chocolate makers, what huge expenses he must have had!"[31] But legions of retainers and servants were the perquisites of office, paid directly or indirectly by tribute forced from a subject people. Although there is little information on forced workers for public or private works – nothing like the Peruvian *mita* seems to have existed in ancient Mexico – villagers in the valley of Mexico were required to perform labor services. They built the dikes and irrigation works; presumably they or perhaps the semi-slave *mayeques* built the impressive palaces for the nobility in Mexico and Texcoco. Aztec profligacy in human sacrifice, which wasted the potential labor services of thousands of able-bodied men, suggests either the predominance of ideology over economic value or an extraordinary abundance of workers.[32] In any case, Aztec practice contrasts with the much more efficient use of labor by the Incas in the Andes. Because only a minority of ordinary people had sufficient land in the valley of Mexico, numbers of craftsmen, bearers, and construction workers as well as potential military people were maintained out of tribute supplies. Ceremonial feasting, sometimes lasting eight days, helped feed the population and must also have cemented political relations with important members of the bureaucracy.

We know that the nobles' houses were splendid and impressive. The Anonymous Conquistador claimed to have seen "very good houses of the lords, so large with many big and small gardens . . . a marvelous thing to see. More than four times I went into the house of a main lord just to look around but I got so tired that I never got to see it all. It was the custom to have huge salons and large rooms all around the entrance to a grand patio."[33] From this impressive display one stepped down considerably to the dwellings of secondary lords and caciques.

Of all the profusion of goods in pre-Hispanic Mesoamerica, cloth was the single most important marker of social status and power. Lacking horses, or the finely worked manufactures available to contemporary Spaniards as status markers, and of course not having any of the range of prestige goods available today to suggest wealth and power,

---

[31] Diaz, *Historia*, p. 168.   [32] Katz, *Ancient Civilizations*, pp. 170–1.
[33] El Conquistator anónimo, *Rélacion*, p. 46.

fabric provided visible and easily displayed symbolic meaning. It varied in quality from ordinary unbleached bast to the exquisitely worked and multicolored cottons and *plumería* or feather work. None of the European invaders, themselves finely tuned to its importance in their own culture, failed to notice the meaning of dress. When lesser lords talked with Moctezuma "they had to remove their expensive capes and put on others of less value and they had to be cleaned and enter barefoot." "All witnesses," says Jacques Soustelle, noticed the "brilliance and splendor of the blouses and skirts worn by the women of noble families."[34]

On the eve of the Spanish conquest, cloth obtained ever greater importance in use and as a symbol and wealth good. Even from provinces that did not grow cotton, the state often required that subject people scurry about to come up with tribute of *quachtli* (a fine white cotton fabric). Raw cotton and tropical feathers brought up from the hot country were passed on to increasingly specialized women artisans in the capital, who produced the luxuriant dress of native leaders that so bedazzled the first European observers. Bernal Diaz commented on women weavers who made "such a multitude of fine cloth and all of feathers." In the very house of Moctezuma "all the lords' daughters that he had around as friends wove very beautiful things and many other young women who seemed to be something like nuns, also made all sorts of things from feathers."[35]

Tribute goods, requisitioned and produced under state guidance, were used in "state-administered foreign trade" and in market transactions for other luxury raw materials. They may also have been used as gifts to buy support or loyalty among uncertain allies.[36] There are several well-known instances, when in the course of the Spaniards' advance on Tenochtitlan, Moctezuma endeavored through gifts to demonstrate his power and to persuade the invaders to return from whence they came. The Spaniards, of course, interpreted these gestures as weakness. Perhaps the practices of using tribute goods to cement political support were in their infancy among the Mexica, not yet developed to the degree present in the Andes. Certainly, there is some

---

[34] Diaz, *Historia*, p. 166; Soustelle, *Aztecs*, pp. 128–38.

[35] Diaz, *Historia*, p. 170.

[36] Terrance N. D'Altroy and Timothy K. Earle, "Staple Finance, Wealth Finance and Storage in the Inka Political Economy," in Terry Y. LeVine, ed., *Inka Storage Systems* (Norman: University of Oklahoma Press, 1992), pp. 51–2.

Figure 2.5. Starting over. In pre-Hispanic Mexico, at the end of a fifty-two-year cycle, household goods were shattered and discarded. The "devil" indicates that in the eyes of postconquest (and Christian) native informants, this was now seen as a pagan practice. *Source:* Codex Florentino. Courtesy, Biblioteca Medicea Laurenziana, Florence.

evidence that the Aztecs stored goods for ceremonial or practical distribution but they had nothing like the storage network that the Incas had designed, precisely to make wealth goods available for social and political ends.[37]

In Mesoamerica then, we are in the presence of a "tributary despotism," which demanded not labor services directly, as in the case of

[37] Katz, *Ancient Civilizations*, p. 223; LeVine, *Inka Storage Systems*, pp. 50ff.

the Incas, but rather goods themselves – food, cloth, cacao – which, of course, were produced by people compelled to work. These goods were then used to help maintain artisans, construction workers, and the multitude of bearers drawn from the native settlements. Other tribute goods, either through ceremonial display or through direct gifts to the nobility, served to cement political or bureaucratic alliances that gave the Aztecs state access to workers. This process, as we shall see, was a less direct way of acquiring workers than the Incan mita, but it seems to have accomplished comparable ends. The Mexican practice of female workhouses for textile manufacture appears similar to the Peruvian *aklla*. The forced extraction of food, cloth, and building material was designed to obtain luxury and wealth goods for social and political ends. Wealth and status in both ancient Mexico and Peru were consequently created not so much by market exchange as by state-directed compulsion.

A profusion of research on the Inca period, those relatively few decades in the long, rich sweep of Peruvian prehistory, has substantially altered earlier understanding. Underneath the impressive structures of Inca rule lay territorial political units known as *saya*, which included a variable number of communities or *ayllu*. These units, adapting to the extremes of Andean topography, were clusters of households in an endogamous kin group. But their communal territories were spread across a wide range of ecological niches, forming, in John V. Murra's striking term, "archipelagos" or stepping-stone islands of kinfolk, at various elevations throughout the Andes. Thus, a single ayllu might include fishermen on the coast, maize farmers on terraces in the middle elevations, potato growers or quínoa further up, llamas on the high plateaus, and then coca fields in the subtropical valleys on the eastern slope. In Murra's scheme, members strove for self-sufficiency within each ayllu by combining goods and food from the various niches, and consequently they engaged in little trade with other ayllus. An immediate implication is the absence of large markets and consequently of a merchant group.

The first Europeans to see the dramatic topography of the Andean world made no mention of the great markets that had so impressed their companions in Mesoamerica a decade earlier, nor has there been much evidence for an equivalent in the Andes of the Mexican *pochteca*, or long-distance traders. Recent research, however, suggests that the archipelago model was most likely brought into full existence only by the later Incas, when their suppression of ethnic rivalries in the Andes

provided sufficient order to make such far-flung communities feasible.
It is also true that merchant groups or *mindalaes* were present further
to the north, in Quito. In any case, when imagining much of the
Andean world, we should have in our mind's eye a number of adobe-
walled, productive ayllus, scattered like so many brown hankerchiefs
across a dramatically broken landscape. These produced an abundant
yield of the basic elements of Andean diet, clothing, and shelter. A
tendency toward reciprocity among members also seems to have been
a central feature of Andean civilization.

In the decades immediately preceding the European invasion, the
Incas undertook to extract from the Andean peasantry a growing
volume of workers who were then "manipulated by the state to provide
food both to support the labor effort itself and to produce special prestige items that were important to the state as gifts for its subjects." Recognizing not only the Andean tendency toward reciprocity, the Inca
state's exactions were also based on a long-standing "community practice that gave its leaders the right to organize workers." On the eve of
the European invasion, the Inca had mobilized workers in three main
categories: they imposed the mita, a universal labor service; they formed
groups of craft specialists such as the aklla, women devoted to making
chicha and fine cloth; and they forcibly resettled portions of the peasantry in colonies known as *mitmaq*. Administrative cities were then
built "to support a vision of rule based on gift giving and generosity by
the ruler."[38]

Although we can clearly see that the Inca managed to turn an
increasing amount of peoples' work away from personal and local pur-
suits to state projects, the question is *how*, in the absence of strong
coercive force, was this done? One specialist argues that in this
particular "archaic kind of mobilization," that is, where markets and
monetary incentives are weak, the symbolic value of goods drives the
"growth of wealth and power." Goods become signs of prestige, acceptance, and security." According to Morris, "Human labor is not a simple
constant that can be measured by the size, age and health of the
population. People work to gratify needs, some of which are biologi-

---

[38] Morris, "Wealth of a State," pp. 37–8, 45; on the Mandalaes in Quito, see
John V. Murra, "Existieron el tributo y los mercados antes de la invasión
europea," in Oliva Harris, Brooke Larson, and Enrique Tandeter, eds., *La
participación indígena en los mercados surandinos* (La Paz, 1987), pp. 51–64;
Terry LeVine, "The Study of Storage Systems," in LeVine, *Inka Storage Systems*,
p. 17.

cally based, others are learned as part of the cognitive apparatus of culture."[39]

In the Inca world, as in Mesoamerica, cloth was the major carrier of the signs and symbols that guided social relations. Cloth "was given in bride wealth, presented as gifts at weaning, buried in mummy bundles, sacrificed in rituals and used as a status marker." Ceremonies using cloth punctuated life's passage. Both boys' puberty rites as well as marriage required sets of new clothing. Another ritual use of fabric can be seen in the wall hangings in temples and shrines. Cloth was central to Andean creation myths. Huamán Poma describes the three stages of mankind as distinguished by stages of garb. First, people dressed in leaves and straw, then animal skins, and finally in woven cloth. Indeed, one of the civilizing missions cited by the Incas was to clothe the naked savages. "The literature of the Incanato abounds with extensive description of the cameloid herd, their care and culling and even more . . . about the varieties of cloth."[40] The state produced fine fabric through the two basic mechanisms of corvée labor and through the use of the growing number of displaced colonists and specialist female weavers.

Two recent writers believe it reasonable that cloth, especially *qumpi* came to be a kind of special purpose money similar to quachtli in the Aztec world. It now seems clear that the great administrative centers' warehouses were for the storage of food and prestige items, mainly cloth, primarily used during ceremonies as gifts to cement alliances or given in advance for the subjects' anticipated cooperation and only secondary as famine relief. The leader of Chucuito province, near Lake Titicaca, "received 50 to 100 pieces of cloth a year from Inka state warehouses . . . cloth was a perquisite of office." In the excavations of Huánuco Pampa in the central highlands of Peru, there are over 4,000 structures, including 497 storehouses together with cloth and chicha-making facilities, but there is no "positive evidence of a marketplace," nor was Huánuco Pampa a location of permanent family residence. Most of the place "was devoted to public ritual and feasting."[41] Forty

---

[39] Morris, "Wealth of a State," pp. 40–1, 47.

[40] John V. Murra, "Cloth and Its Function in the Inca State," *American Anthro-pologist* 64, no. 4 (Aug. 1962): 712; D'Altroy and Earle, "Staple Finance," p. 56; Louis Segal, "Threads of Two Empires," unpublished essay in my possession. Bruhns, *Ancient South America*, pp. 166–7.

[41] Spalding, *Huarochirí*, p. 84; D'Altroy and Earle, "Staple Finance"; Morris, "Wealth of a State," p. 50.

years after the conquest, Pedro Pizarro, who accompanied his distant relative, Francisco, in the invasion of Peru, spoke in tones still stunned by the enormity of all he saw. "I won't be able to describe all the store-houses I saw filled with clothes and all kinds of cloth and dress that are used in this kingdom. There was not enough time to see and comprehend such a thing."[42] Chicha too, the corn beer of the Andes, lubricated social and political arrangements. It was considered the "essence of hospitality, the common denominator of ritual and ceremonial relationships." It was the drink generous leaders were required to provide as part of their obligations of authority.[43] The terraces and irrigation that brought new warm lands into cultivation in the "sacred" Urubamba Valley and elsewhere in Tawantinsuyu were not to produce ordinary food but for the prestige food and drink that formed part of the substance of sociopolitical relationships.

Finally, the state controlled a large portion of the production and distribution of a specialty crop, coca leaves. The state maintained fields of coca in the deep crevices in the earth that run down to the semi-tropical elevations of the Amazon and along the eastern, warmer slopes of the Andes, which were cultivated by designated laborers, often from colonies established for this purpose. As part of the regular dole to corvée laborers in mines and road work, the state and local elites provided a ration of coca. Coca was one of several (consumable) currencies circulating on the arid central coast and may have been used as a medium of exchange to obtain metals from highland people. Recent research documents the existence of coca leaves as currency in highland Ecuador in the colonial period.

SUMMARY

On the eve of the European invasion, native peoples across the board from present-day Alaska and Canada to Patagonia had devised an array of goods to mediate between themselves and their environment. From

---

[42] Pedro Pizarro, *Descubrimiento y conquista de los reinos del Perú*, Biblioteca de Autores Españoles, vol. 168 (Madrid, 1965), p. 168; see also Terrence N. D'Al-troy and Cristine Hastorf, "The Architecture and Contents of Inka State Store-houses in the Xauxa Region of Peru," in LeVine, *Inka Storage Systems*, pp. 259–86.

[43] Morris, "Wealth of a State," pp. 42–3; John V. Murra, "Rite and Crop in the Inca State," in Stanley Diamond, ed., *Culture in History* (New York, 1960), pp. 393–401.

neighboring or rival groups they rejected some items, accepted others, apropriating and adapting yet others. From an Asian or European perspective, their efforts were as notable for what they had accomplished as for what they had not. Three great food plants – maize, potatoes, and manioc – supplemented by an impressive range of other cereals, vegetables, and fruit had been brought to domestication. Together with an extraordinarily inventive use of the entire biomass, the native people created nutritional regimes that underlay large and complex populations. Without the shear, clothing for the mass of people was plain, shelter generally primitive, and tools rudimentary. Despite the presence of the appropriate ore, native people had not worked out the techniques of iron- or steelmaking, nor had they developed the use of draft animals or the wheel.

In the high civilizations of Mesoamerica and the central Andes, complex states arose to organize production and distribution. There were several similarities in the material culture and state organization of Aztec and Inca societies on the eve of the European conquest and a few striking differences. Eyewitness observers and modern scholars have noticed that the Aztecs extracted tribute in *goods* through political coercion, whereas the Incas tapped into the long-standing Andean practice of demanding *labor* services of their subject peoples, which, it's true, were often used *to produce* goods. Thus, although both regimes got goods from subject people, the means were different. The Andean leaders also directed corvée workers into public projects more effectively than did their Mexican counterparts. The Incas appear more disposed to negotiate with provincial leaders than were the Aztecs, and more inclined to accept reciprocity as principle. The Aztecs pushed surplus food and prestige tribute goods through the market system; the Inca developed more extensive storage systems. Both encouraged textile production using specialized female workers.

As new zones were incorporated into the Mexica tribute empire, particularly as the Aztecs pushed into the lowlands of the southeast, its elite acquired cacao, cotton, or tropical feathers as exotic import items. As the Inca colonized new areas, coca, cotton fabric, and rare sea shells (*spondylus*) conferred status on their possessors. But apart from consuming "exotic imports," the Aztec and Inca elites employed the large surpluses of ordinary goods commanded through tribute or labor services in order to wield social and political influence. The display of abundance represented by Moctezuma's incessant changing into dozens of the same kind of tunic rather than donning a single glittering cloak was his claim to high status. By the same token and for the same ends, the Inca elite amassed thousands of jars of ordinary food such as chicha and bales of cloth – not, as once believed, as stores against famine (although it also served that purpose), but primarily for distribution in order to cement social and political arrangements.

Over the course of several millennia the people of Mesoamerica and the Andes had established their essential elements of diet, clothing, shelter, and tools, some of which would endure through the sixteenth-century invasion and even through the more pervasive intrusions of world markets after the 1870s. Pre-Columbian life was not of course, a "historia casi inmóvil" but rather a world of truck and trade where the most ordinary objects were laid out for display in innumerable village squares, or, in the case of the Andes, exchanged among members of extended communities. Patterns were never immutable. Men and women modified their diet, dress, and shelter to the environment and accepted new materials and techniques.

People across the hemisphere also created a long list of innovations in their material culture. One might begin with the rudimentary hammock or a dugout canoe, or the device used to press out prussic acid in order to make edible the poisonous manioc root, and procede to the sophisticated quipu, or knotted string method of accounting, or the ingenious wind-blown clay furnaces used to smelt silver from ore on the slopes of the great mine of Potosí in Upper Peru. There was, besides the exquisite textiles and elegant pottery, the spectacular work by gold- and silversmiths. To this should be added the development of the remarkably productive agricultural systems that so astonished the invading Europeans. All of these techniques and original products grew out of the elaboration of materials native to aboriginal America.

In the Northern Hemisphere autumn of 1492, the first Europeans appeared from the east, out of the Ocean Sea. They came upon, at first, not the great kingdoms on the high plateaus of Mesoamerica and the Andes, but the simpler island cultures of the Taino and Arawak in the stream of the trade winds. Here they found rudimentary farmers and fishermen able to support a substantial number of people. Into this more or less benign world of polished stone and carved wood, there came, in the words of a Caribbean scholar, "A hurricane of culture from Europe. There arrived together and in mass, iron, gunpowder, the horse, the wheel, sail, the compass, money, wages, writing, the printing-press, books, the master, the King, the Church, the banker . . . at one bound the bridge between the drousing stone ages and the wide-awake Ren-naissance was spanned."[44] The Europeans required three or four decades more to uncover and bring under tentative control the formidable high-land empires of the Aztec and Inca. The conquering Christians intro-duced radically new techniques and tools, new plants and animals, to alter the production of material culture; and they carried new markers of social and political prestige in a world they "turned upside down." The initial assault was quick; its consequences are still with us.

[44] Fernando Ortiz, *Cuban Counterpoint: Tobacco and Sugar*, introd. Bronislaw Mali-nowski, prologue by Herminio Portell Vilá, trans. Harriet de Onís from the Spanish (New York: Alfred A. Knopf, 1947), pp. 99–100.

CHAPTER 3

CONTACT GOODS

Policía was a central concept, a word that summarized the entire project of creating a new society in America. To live in *policía* required the attainment of the European idea of civility including clothing, food hygiene, etc. but above all, to live an urban life.[1]

Ultimately unable to resist invasion from Europe or to negotiate with much success the terms of their own submission, the native peoples of America after 1492 became submerged in patterns of exchange, goods, and values introduced from the outside. Thus the European invasion truncated by force the organic development of material culture in America. We cannot know, of course, what would have happened had this not occurred or had the people of ancient Mexico or Peru been able to incorporate the new goods available from Europe, Asia, and Africa into their value systems on their own terms. But, as it turned out, the introduction of new food, fabric and attire, the organization of public space, architecture, and tools was accompanied by political and religious compulsion, so as we observe the interplay of adoption, rejection, or appropriation of new goods, we must remember that we are always in the presence of a *conquest* and, later, a *colonial* culture. Furthermore, in the sixteenth-century Iberian world, the spread of Christianity was inseparable from the expansion of Spanish imperialism: the two were mutually reinforcing. As we shall see, hand

---

[1] Alan Durston, "Un régimen urbanístico en la América hispana colonial: el trazado en damero durante los siglos xvi y xvii," *Historia* (Santiago, Chile) 28 (1994): 88.

in hand with both went a new ceremonial calendar of consumption, new rituals, and new regimes of goods and commodities.

In the midst of the scrabble for goods and wealth no one doubts that from the very first the Europeans were committed to the spread of Christianity. The task of evangelization was made explicit in the crown's instructions and in papal confirmation of the crown's mission. Columbus was puzzled at first that the Taino seemed to have no proper faith but, ever optimistic, he imagined that their spiritual tabula rasa would make the implantation of Christianity easier. He carried no priest, however, on the first voyage; but he did find room for a notary, a surgeon, and a translator who knew some Arabic, which the crew presumably hoped would be useful on the East Asian coast. Christopher Columbus had a mystical sense that he, like the saint for whom he was named, would bear Christ across the waters.[2] Evangelization of the island people actually began with the humble work of the Catalán friar, Ramón Pané, one of six clerics from the second voyage who landed on Hispaniola in late 1493.[3]

At almost exactly the same time, other friars were undertaking a parallel mission among the newly conquered Moors of Granada, the culmination of the seven-centuries-long Reconquista of Spain. The contemporary evangelization of Granada provides a useful background to Iberian attitudes and policy in the Indies as well as perspective on the spread of material culture. During the first decade following the Spanish conquest of Granada in 1492, the Christians displayed a surprising tolerance toward the newly conquered Muslims. Moors were permitted to practice their own rituals, "the muezzin still made the call to prayer" from the city's minarets, and Muslim leaders sat on the city council of Granada. Unfortunately, the tolerant policy in Granada yielded few converts and because of that, a hard line was imposed in the first years of the sixteenth century. Near the center of the city, the Muslim population of a new district, the Albaicín, which had been established as a refuge for people fleeing the Christian advance, had only slowly begun to accept the conquerors' religion. Impatient with

---

[2] William D. Phillips Jr. and Carla Rahn Phillips, *The Worlds of Christopher Columbus* (Cambridge: Cambridge University Press, 1992), pp. 158, 214, 173.

[3] Pané was the first evangelizer in the new world. He preached first in the district of Macorix, near today's Santo Domingo, lived among the Taino, and learned their language. "A simple and well-intentioned man," in the words of Las Casas. *Cronistas de las culturas precolumbinas* (Mexico City: Fondo de Cultura Económica, 1963), pp. 47–8.

the pace of conversion, the Catholic monarchs in 1499 called upon Francisco Jiménez de Cisneros, primate of Spain, reformer of the Franciscan Order, the queen's confessor, future inquisitor general and cardinal, to insist that the archbishop of Granada, Fray Hernando de Talavera, take a harder line. The violation and destruction of mosques, forced conversions, and deportations soon followed.[4]

The new militant and uncompromising policy in Granada formed the immediate background for Hernando Cortés's entry into the Aztec kingdom a few years later as "the coercive methods of Cisneros were practiced in lock-step with the military conquest of Mexico." Indeed, Cortés's entry into Mexico was the first major conquest of a non-Christian people since Granada, a fact very much in the mind of the conqueror who was naturally drawn to compare the lucustrine capital of México-Tenochtitlan with the population and economic character-istics of Granada. Moreover, he "used the only vocabulary he had to describe the abominable elements of a heretical faith," calling Aztec temples *mezquitas* and their priests *alfaquí*. And as Cisneros "occupied mosques and burned Korans, so Cortés destroyed idols, while the Fran-ciscans, including two of the famous first Twelve who had previously served in Granada, threw Aztec and Maya codexes on the pyre. Pizarro's entry into the Tahuantinsuyo was no less destructive of Inca temples and idols.[5]

Now there were, of course, from the Spaniards' point of view, fun-damental differences between Islamic Granada and the "idolatrous" realms of the Aztecs and Inca: the difference between an infidel but still familiar enclave within Spain itself and an unknown new world; between a people "of the Book," often more sophisticated than the con-

---

[4] Ryan D. Crewe, "Unam Fides et una Baptisma: Theological Imperialism in Granada and Mexico, 1492–1570" (Honors thesis, University of California, Davis, 1999), pp. 1–89.

[5] Ibid., pp. 23–5. Martín de Valencia and Andrés de Córdoba, were the two Fran-ciscans with prior experience in Granada. The Spanish usage of *principales* (as in "Indios principales") was also drawn from Moorish precedent. Notice that native people resorted to various linguistic devices to name things they were unfamil-iar with, calling Spanish horses, *macatl* or "deer" and iron and steel, *tepoztli*, meaning "copper." See the fascinating article, James Lockhart, "Sightings: Initial Nahua Reactions to Spanish Culture," in Stuart B. Schwartz, ed., *Implicit Under-standings* (Cambridge: Cambridge University Press, 1994), pp. 218–48; and Miguel Angel Ladero Quesada, "Spain, circa 1492: Social Values and Structures," in ibid., pp. 96–133. Ladero acutely points out differences between Granada and the New World in the conquistadors' minds.

querors themselves, and the American natives, often described as barbaric. Nevertheless, by the early sixteenth century in both cases, the church insisted on forced conversion and the state on political subjugation. A fundamental issue in both church and crown policy was whether changes in conversion and subjection should be accompanied by changes in food, dress, and housing? Did these necessarily go together?

To demonstrate the close association in the minds of sixteenth-century Spaniards between imperial evangelization and the spread of a new regime of goods and commodities, we begin with a fascinating document, written, it seems, in 1501 or 1502, just as the expansionist Castilian state, arm in arm with the church militant, pressed forward on two fronts: the last ancient Moorish corner of the Iberian Peninsula and the rapidly opening stretches of pagan America. The "Memorial, al parecer, de Fray Hernando de Talavera para los moradores del Albaicín" begins by laying out the conventional behavior that the people of the Albaicín should practice. "You should forget all ceremonies and prayers having to do with fasts, festivals regarding birth, weddings or burials or having to do with baths and all other things Moorish. Everyone should know, and you should instruct your women and children, large and small, about the way to make the sign of the Cross, use holy water, how to say the Our Fathers and Ave Maria, how to adore the Holy Cross and to pay the appropriate reverence to images."

The document goes on to tell of the sacraments and the ways of "los cristianos de nación." But then comes the material core of the argument: "So that your behavior will not be scandalous to proper Christians, so that they will not think that you still have the sect of Mohoma in your heart, it is important that you conform in every way to the good and honest behavior of the good and honest Christians in the way you dress and shave, the footwear you use, in what you eat, that you sit at table, that you eat cooked food the way it is normally cooked; be careful in the way you walk [vuestro andar] and in your give and take [vuestro dar y tomar] and above all to forget as soon as you can the Arabic tongue and never speak it in your houses."[6]

---

[6] "Memorial, al parecer, de Fray Hernando de Talavera para los moradores del Albaicín," in Antonio Garrido Aranda, ed., Organización de la iglesia en el reino de Granada y su proyección en Indias (Córdoba: University of Córdoba, 1979), pp. 307–9.

The Catholic monarchs' objective, unevenly applied to be sure, in both Granada and America, was to spread the true faith, a campaign, as we see in the memorial to the settlers of Albaicín, that was inextricably tied to Hispanization. Had the word been in their vocabulary, sixteenth-century Spanish officials might have talked of a "civilizing" mission or even the need to accompany Christianity with "civilizing goods" or "civilizing order." But lacking that term, they drew on the Greek *polis* instead of the Latin *civitas* to set out their urban project. Their subject people were to live in *buena policía*. *Policía* meant laws, order, behavior, customs, respect; indeed, very much what "civilized" would come to mean in subsequent centuries.[7]

Power, energy, and conviction, of course, are what tempted sixteenth-century Spanish imperialists to accompany their evangelizing mission with a deliberate program of buena policía. Shortly after the reconquest of Granada and the intrusion into America, other religious – Franciscans, Dominicans, and Jesuits – fanned out across the Asian littoral, endeavoring to carry their faith to China and Japan. But, unaccompanied by colonial power, they harbored no illusions about reordering the landscape or changing the dress, food, drink, clothing, or language of the people they worked to convert. Indeed, they sought to fit in, unobtrusively; the clerics even adopted native Chinese and Japanese dress. In the Indies, the Spanish regime in its efforts to shape American material culture, wielded its clerical and civil power directly, and often quixotically, by decree. More importantly, the colonial regime, by its very nature, set up layered standards of consumption or "consumption reference groups," that encouraged emulation by those people wanting to ascend the social scale. Let us turn now to the interplay of statecraft and commodities as the varied class and ethnic inhabitants of the emerging colonial world contemplate each other, in order to explore the links between colonial power and consumption. We begin with the early decades when Europeans and native Ameri-

---

[7] The verb "to civilize" and the noun "civilization" came into common usage only fairly recently. Lucien Febvre finds no mention of "civilization" in French until the last half of the eighteenth century. The adjective "civilized" appears earlier, in the later sixteenth century; the verb in the mid-seventeenth. *Police* or the adjective *policées*, in the sense of laws and order, appears much earlier in Latinate languages. As the great French historian says, "it is never a waste of time to study the history of a word." Lucien Febvre, *A New Kind of History*, ed. Peter Burke, trans. K. Folca from the French (New York: Harper and Row, 1973), pp. 219–29.

cans were busily engaged in sizing each other up, in a kind of experimental free-for-all.

During the very first days of his contact with the people of the Caribbean, Columbus had in mind the model of Portuguese expansion on the African Gold Coast, which he knew from previous experience. He imagined a series of fortified posts to acquire whatever commodities might be present in exchange for European goods. The Catholic monarchs, Isabel and Ferdinand, he proclaimed, will have as much cotton and spices "as they shall command"; as much mastic and aloe wood "as they shall order to be shipped." Presented with the green and red bulbs of a plant called *ají* by the Caribbean natives, Columbus took a bite, found it hot and spicy and persuaded himself, against all contrary evidence, that he had found *pimiento*, or pepper, the coveted spice from the East, the search for which had largely propelled his journey in the first place. But his "pimiento" was actually a *capsicum*, a plant utterly unrelated to the Asian pepper (*piper nigrum*). A bit later, other Spaniards found the same plant on the Mexican mainland where it was known in Náhuatl language as "chilli." Brought back to Spain and thence around the globe – it's hard to imagine India without curries or Hungary without paprika – Columbus's "pimiento" confused English-speakers. Unable to decide, we hedge our bets and call the plant a "chili pepper." On his second voyage, Columbus brought along a botanical expert. Dr. Diego Chanca was nearly overwhelmed by the new varieties of plants and especially by one exotic species which combined all in one the aromas of clove, cinnamon, and nutmeg. Today, we call that "allspice," and its only source is still the Caribbean.[8]

Soon, faced with the reality of only scant and primitive goods and only a small market for European produce, Columbus's thoughts turned to colonization as a way to make the islands profitable. By the Northern Hemisphere spring of 1496, however, under pressure from his rapacious companions who formed the colony, he decided on direct exploitation of the people he had misnamed. The Great Navigator, a genius at sea but a disaster on land, imposed a tribute of "a Flemish hawk's bell . . . full of gold . . . or an arroba of cotton," to be paid every

---

[8] Novo, *Historia gastronómica*, pp. 51–7; Jean Andrews, "The Peripatetic Chili Pepper," in Nelson Foster and Linda S. Cordell, eds., *Chilies to Chocolate: Food the Americas Gave the World* (Tucson: University of Arizona Press, 1992), pp. 81–93. Allspice comes from Jamaica.

three months by the people on the island of Hispaniola, who, he claimed, "love their neighbors as themselves, have the sweetest speech, are gentle and always laughing." In the following decade, as the native inhabitants of the entire Caribbean rapidly melted away under the assault of European depredations and pathogens, the Castilians engaged in deadly brawls among themselves.[9]

Apart from "serving God and the king," the invading Spaniards obviously wanted to better their lot. So here, in these early years, we must have in our mind's eye, several hundreds of unruly men, now and then accompanied by African slaves and occasionally by women, from all walks of life, with varied skills and various motivations, fanning out from the islands along the Caribbean littoral, across Panama, down the long Pacific coast, not yet in these early years to farm or mine but, rather, to find any commodity that might be traded for European products, or at least goods that might be pillaged to serve the Spaniards' subsistence needs. They were less fortunate than the Portuguese, who were by now paying with bullion for loads of spice, silks, and exotic manufactures from Malacca, India, and the south China coast. The native people of the Antilles and the circum-Caribbean did not grow the pepper, clove, and cinnamon so coveted by Europeans, and they were disinclined to part with their scant amount of gold except under compulsion. In fact, the Portuguese and the Spaniards in these early years had opposite commercial problems. The former had no trade goods to carry from Europe sufficiently acceptable to the sophisticated societies of the East and consequently had to pay for Asian spices with precious metals; the Spaniards were prepared to supply a range of ordinary European products but found no market even for these among the less economically advanced inhabitants of the Caribbean. Thus they turned to force and direct exploitation.

From the beginning of the colony in the Caribbean, Columbus installed the *encomienda*, an arrangement that gave the right to tribute, in principle a tax collected by royal officials, to the conquerors and their descendants as a reward for service to the crown. It was the Europeans' initial, formal exploitative institution, organized with the complicity of local Indian leaders. In the absence of coin, individual native households were required to come up with the most basic food, cloth, and building materials, but finding these barely acceptable, the holders of

---

[9] Phillips and Phillips, *Worlds*, p. 185. The tribute, or head tax, was normally levied on adult males; on the mainland, on the heads of households.

encomienda insisted on personal labor services in place of tribute. After contributing to the devastation of the islands, the encomienda was extended to the continental mainlands. In Mexico, the first conquerors took over the Aztecs' *own* tribute system by capturing its command center at Tenochtitlan, and then assigning the tribute of the numerous Indian communities to individual conquerors who in this way gained the rights to goods and labor.

Even in rich Mexico, the encomiendas at first yielded little more than a range of exotic *animalitos*, such as salamanders, grubs, and eels "that failed to appeal to Spanish palates." But chickens, carried on the earliest voyages, quickly reproduced, and soon more appealing local foods became available. Tribute through encomienda also yielded loads of cotton cloth (the preconquest quachtli), and cacao, which could be exchanged for items such as gold pebbles or fodder for horses, both prized in the European value system. But here, too, tribute was quickly commuted to labor services. In Peru, an encomienda might embrace several islands in the "archipelago" of people scattered through the Andean landscape. Everyone of the first 169 conquistadors present at the capture of the Inca Atahualpa in Cajamarca, for example, received grants of native workers and the subsequent invaders bent every effort – and battled to the death – to acquire more. These encomiendas commonly produced personal servants along with loads of maize, potatoes, and building materials. In Peru as in Mexico, cloth was a tribute item highly prized by the Spaniards either for their own use or for exchange for other goods.[10]

In these first decades of the sixteenth century, as the complexity of the advanced societies of Mexico and Peru became clear and after much debate and experiment among jurists and administrators, the Spaniards tried to establish a pattern of settlement in which the numerous "Republics of Indians," while remaining under the crown politically autonomous and socially segregated, would supply the small "Republic of Spaniards" with rudimentary goods and labor services. The early friars, however, could not accept that the native population remain in spiritual darkness and accordingly established their missions or, to use the contemporary term, their *doctrinas* within the native communities.

---

[10] Gibson, *Aztecs*, p. 341; James Lockhart, *Spanish Peru* (Madison: University of Wisconsin Press, 1968), p. 13; Efraín Trelles Aréstegui, *Lucas Martínez Vegazo: funcionamiento de una encomienda peruana inicial* (Lima: Catholic University Press, 1982).

With colonial order established, both church and state directly and formally tried, with uneven success, to influence the consumption habits of their own countrymen in the Indies through such measures as urging the construction of stone houses and wheat-flour mills or insisting on a strict arrangement of public space in the new towns and cities. At the same time both institutions encouraged the native people to embrace Christianity, learn Spanish, and adopt elements of European diet, dress, and urban order. Other royal decrees forbade certain goods, such as alcohol or horses and steel weapons, to ordinary native people in order to discourage resistance. At the same time, these very goods were permitted to the Indian elite – the caciques and kurakas – as part of the policy of co-optation. Thus, early on, one might see a native leader wrapped in an old-fashioned cape, advancing on horseback, "wearing armor and bearing dagger, sword and lance, at the head of his retinue and porters." Chairs with arms, plush rugs, and cushions "began adorning the homes of rich caciques." The Catholic friars from the very beginning organized new rituals centered on churches and chapels that required the purchase of clerical accouterments and new vestments and candles. During feast day celebrations, "silver vessels and Murano glassware in red, green and gold were used alongside Mexican terra-cotta receptacles . . . rural parishes began to look like exotic bazaars with fabrics and chasubles from Rouen, Castile and Holland, chalices and candelabra forged in local silver . . . Michoacán flutes, Italian trumpets."[11] Outside the parish doors, in the name of decency, the friars encouraged women in the tropics to cover their nakedness and native men to wear trousers.

Clerical penetration, in more ways than one, provided not only an immediate channel for the flow of a new religious culture but also of Iberian material culture into the native communities. Towns were staked out in what came to be the familiar checkerboard pattern around a central plaza. Set squares, levels, saws, planes, chisels, and other tools for carpentry and masonry were essential for building the first churches,

---

[11] Such, for example, in the Royal Decrees of May 4, 1534, "Para que los que tuvieren indios encomendados hagan casas de piedra," or June 7, 1550, "Que se les enseñe a los indios la lengua castellana" (Those who hold Indians in encomiendas should build houses of stone; Indians should be taught the Castilian language.) Richard Konetzke, *Colección de documentos para la formación social de Hispanoamerica, 1493–1810*, 3 vols. in 5 ps. (Madrid, 1953–62), no. 86; For caciques' goods, see Serge Gruzinski, *Painting the Conquest: The Mexican Indians and the European Renaissance* (Paris: UNESCO, Flammarion, 1992), pp. 148–50.

which in turn required the paraphernalia of Christian ritual.[12] Longing for familiar food, the Mendicant clergy introduced chickens and European seed for plants. Franciscans and Dominicans brought the medieval system of ritual kinship or *compadrazco* in which the sponsor and candidate in the sacraments of Baptism and Confirmation familiarly bonded, creating additional practices of celebration and gift giving. In time, these four – religion, town planning and Iberian town government, compadrazco, and, much more haltingly, language – were to become the fundamental Iberian cultural contributions to America.

As the colonial centuries wore on, the imposition and intermingling of new elements of material culture in Latin America were ultimately impressive. The demand was driven by monetarized, economic growth and an accelerating racial mixture that, within the hierarchy of colonial power, encouraged people across the class and ethnic spectra to construct new identities by entering the European world of goods. Obviously this was less true as one moved out from cities and towns into the countryside where the lack of purchasing power alone, not to mention the adherence to custom or cultural resistance, slowed the pace of occidentalization. European clergy and laymen alike imagined that in time the native population under their direction would be persuaded to accept the elements of European material life believed essential for civilized people. But in the beginning, in the early sixteenth century, apart from a handful of precious metals or pearls, all, in European terms, of high value in relation to weight or bulk and thus exportable in the tiny ships of the day, there was as yet no large volume of New World commodities that might be exchanged for European goods.

So at this point, say, by the 1540s, before the great silver strikes or the growth of Spanish agriculture, which was called into existence to supply the growing population of new Spanish towns and cities, there was still not much exchange with the native people. Rudimentary goods – building beams and stone, fodder, common cotton – were extracted from the native people by force. Fabrics, iron, tools, a hundred items running from needles to bridles, were brought from Europe until local textile workshops and an artisan class gradually arose to supply many of these goods. Fifteen years after settlement,

---

[12] George Kubler, *Mexican Architecture in the Sixteenth Century* (New Haven, Conn.: Yale University Press, 1948), 1:4.

a merchant in Panama in 1526, for example, still had to ask his coun-terpart in Spain to send common thread, linen cloth, some "fine serge" from Carmona and nails to shoe his string of mules. In these early decades there were, in effect, "two different populations with different patterns of consumption: a Spanish world wishing to eat wheaten bread, oil, meat and wine, to dress in European clothing made of wool and silk and to live with European furniture in houses built according to European standards as against Indian worlds living . . . on maize and in South America manioc, potatoes, etc., wearing native American clothing of cotton, agave and in South America wool from camelids, and living in native-style huts or houses, furnished in native fashion."[13] Even in the short run, however, adaptation was necessary, and con-querors and conquered alike soon began the complex intermingling of material culture.

Central to control of the Indies and fundamental to the interplay of material culture was the crown's urban policy in the Indies. Through-out early America, the Spaniards, following royal directives, established their own towns and cities, often de novo, sometimes, as in the cases of Tenochtitlan-Mexico or Cuzco, on the ruins of native structures. Cities for European settlement, such as the original Veracruz, Panama, or Quito, were the first to be laid out in the now familiar gridiron or checkerboard pattern. Charles V's 1523 Ordenanza instructed the embryonic colonial state: "When the plan is made, lay out the plaza, streets and town lots with a cord and rule. Begin with the plaza mayor, tracing out the main roads and city gates in such a way that although the population may strongly increase, it will always spread out in the same form." Dozens of cities – to name a few, Santiago de Chile and Mexico's Puebla and Valladolid in the early 1540s, and Córdoba and Salta in present-day Argentina in 1573 and 1582, respectively – fol-lowed later in the century. Moreover, the model was extended to native resettlements.[14]

As the indigenous population dried up, the Spanish clergy urged closer supervision of the survivors while, at the same time, Spanish miners and landowners clamored for a more organized work force.

---

[13] Lockhart and Otte, *Letters*, p. 23; Woodrow W. Borah, *Price Trends of Royal Tribute in Nueva Galicia, 1557–1598*, Ibero-American Series, vol. 55 (Berkeley: University of California Press, 1991), p. 5.

[14] *La ciudad hispanoamericana: el sueño de un orden* (Madrid: Secretaría de Obras Públicas, 1991), p. 15.

Figure 3.1. City plan of Charcas, 1750, now Sucre, Bolivia. Notice how the grid plan is laid over mountains and rivers. *Source:* Archivo general de Indias (Seville), reproduced in *La Ciudad Hispanoamericana: el sueño de un orden* (Madrid: Ministerio de Obras Publicas y Urbanismo, 1994).

The crown consequently undertook to concentrate Indians into Mediterranean-type villages with contiguous houses together with the corresponding Spanish-style town governments. Between the first, La Navidad in Santo Domingo in 1492, and the last, Quenac in southern Chile in 1809, the Spanish colonial administration established over nine hundred stable urban settlements across America, "the greatest city-building enterprise ever carried out by any people, nation or empire in all history."[15] Planners of the new cities rearranged public and private space to provide a stage for new rituals, ceremonies, and spectacles. From the urban foundations occupied by the invading Spaniards, political control, religious values, economic culture, and goods were diffused into the hinterland. The new cities also served as centers of collection, which sucked up colonial taxes, tithes, and tribute and private wealth.

Native resettlement had a different purpose and in some cases created a drastic impact. This was truer in the Andes than elsewhere. Where before the native people had organized their ayllus or communities, particularly in the central and south highlands of Peru, to gain access to an "archipelago" of different ecological niches at varied elevations, the resettlements promoted by Viceroy Francisco de Toledo in the 1570s compressed the disperate components of a single ayllu into new Indian towns where householders were to live in side-by-side dwellings. Indeed, the people who directed the resettlement at times had the previous hamlets burned to discourage a return to previous patterns.

The checkerboard pattern marked off with "compass, cord, and rule" around a central plaza was influenced in some cases – such as Tenochtitlan-Mexico or Cuzco – by the pre-Hispanic antecedent. It also, no doubt, drew from the cultural baggage of Spaniards who were familiar with similiar layouts in Spain; for that matter, the rectangular pattern can be seen in ancient Greece and Rome. But town planning in the New World in the course of the sixteenth and seventeenth centuries developed independently from Iberian antecedent and came to represent the imposition of a new idea in new circumstances, "with specific goals in mind."[16] It is a particularly good illustration of a directed, formal effort by the state to bring "order," and what later Europeans

[15] Ibid., p. 13.

[16] George Foster, *Culture and Conquest: America's Spanish Heritage* (New York: Wenner Gren Foundation for Anthropology, 1960), p. 49.

Figure 3.2. Urubamba, Peru, part of a vast resettlement plan in the 1570s. Viceroy Francisco de Toledo gathered dispersed native households into new towns such as Urubamba in the south highlands. *Source:* Private collection. Courtesy, Ward Stavig.

would call "civilized" ways of living, to the native people of America. The new urban planning was much more than a convenient layout for the European settlements or a practical solution to problems of clerical efficiency and labor supply; it carried a heavy symbolic weight as well.[17]

Once the Spanish settlers staked off the central plaza of their new towns, the first essential act was the establishment of the pillory to represent the imposition of order and civil authority. Next came the lots either for the town council or the church. Straight streets set at right angles, the principal ones "oriented" – in the strict sense of that word – on an east-west axis, were explicitly designed by the Spaniards to symbolize a bow toward Jerusalem and the presence of *buena policía* or *buenas costumbres* in the hierarchy of the colonial regime. We might notice, however, that the European tendency to orient the altar of cathedrals toward the east was less commonly observed in America. The houses of the rich and powerful were aligned closest to the church and government buildings; smaller urban lots and houses stretched out away from the plaza, eventually tailing off into the native districts that soon surrounded European towns.

The congregation of native people into the new *pueblos de indios* followed the same procedure: caciques and Indian leaders clustered near the plaza, ordinary people in descending rank further away. The friars themselves who "stretched out the cord, measured the streets, assigned places for houses and the church," frequently carried out the organization of native towns. In these Indian towns a large cross and later a fountain were often put up in place of the pillory.

We have a rare picture of such a place in the 1740s, after two centuries of colonial rule. The Indian town of Amozoc, just east of the large city of Puebla in central Mexico, was the site of dense native population at the time of the conquest. Reorganized into a "pueblo de indios" in the course of the sixteenth century, it too had been laid out with *cordel y regla*, and the Franciscans had supervised the construction of a large church on the central square. Although founded as an Indian town, by 1742 Amozoc had some three thousand inhabitants, of whom 15 percent were considered by the authorities to be Spaniards, mestizos, or mulattoes, who had managed to infiltrate into the village and occupy the better houses. The rest were "Indians," a classification in

---

[17] Durston, "Un régimen urbanístico." Much of the discussion follows Durston's original article.

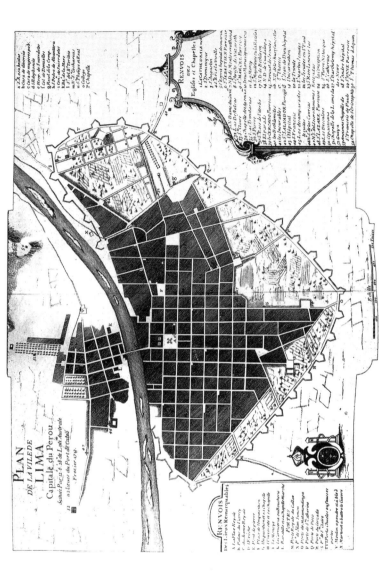

Figure 3.3. European-style cities such as Lima (founded 1535) were laid out from scratch. The wall was meant to protect the city not from internal but external, European, enemies. *Source*: Amedée Frezier, *Relation du voyage de la mer du Sud aux cotes de Chily et du Perou fait pendant des annés 1712, 1713, & 1714* (Paris: Chez Jean Geoffroy Nyon et al., 1716). Courtesy, Special Collection, University Library, University of California, Davis.

part determined by their knowledge of Náhuatl, the local native language, although many undoubtedly would have spoken Spanish as well.
Spaniards, mestizos, and mulattoes along with a small number of village
elite – the *caciques* and *principales* – were also set off from those considered to be ordinary Indians by their right to dress in the Spanish
manner, bear arms, or ride horseback rather than walk.

Indians from Amozoc produced their own crops, owned a few
animals, and supplemented their income through day labor on nearby
haciendas. Ironwork was introduced by the Spaniards and in time the
village artisans came to be famed for their production of spurs; in fact,
even a century and a half later, the revolutionary leader Emiliano
Zapata "cherished the Amozoc spurs he won in a contest."[18] The
archival record also describes two rather better-off houses in the village.
One, which seems little changed from pre-Hispanic days, was actually
a compound of small unconnected adobe huts roofed with sticks or thin
slabs of wood. Two detached rudimentary kitchens were close by.
Another dwelling consisted of one, two-room adobe hut, a detached
kitchen and stable, a *temescal* or Aztec-style sweat bath, an enclosed
white-washed patio, and a private shallow well. A long table and three
small boxes, but no chairs or bed, made up the furnishings. Such a
dwelling cost between 300 and 350 pesos in the mid-seventeenth
century.

Innumerable comments by crown and clerical officials in the decades
following the conquest associate the order of straight streets lined with
proper, solid houses with "buena policía" or refinement, urbanity, order.
So intent were the early Spaniards on the creation of symbolic order
that they laid the checkerboard plan right over the most broken and
steep terrain. In La Paz (Bolivia) the grid ran right up a sharp hillside;
in Quito and Caracas over deep ravines. Once in place, town governments insisted with a "virtual fanaticism" that the the straight lines be
kept in place, even ordering that protruding houses be demolished.
Policía "was a central concept, a term that summarized the entire
project of creating a new society in America. Life in policía implied a
series of customs related to European concepts of civility including
clothing, food, and hygiene; above all, "to live in policía meant urban

---

[18] Edith Couturier, "Micaela Angela Carrillo: Widow and Pulque Dealer," in David
Sweet and Gary Nash, eds., *Struggle and Survival in Colonial America* (Berkeley:
University of California Press, 1981), p. 364. The description of Amozoc is based
on her article, pp. 362–75.

life." The jumble of streets and ricketey native dwellings stood in sharp contrast to the ideal of "policía" and "orden," and a challenge to Spanish town planners. Viceroy Toledo's Jesuit confessor, one of the main promoters of the native resettlement project in the Andes, pointed out in a 1572 letter that the Indians lived in pinched little rancherías in dirty and dark huts. In order for them to live in policía they would have to be organized into proper towns with straight streets and proper houses.[19]

Beyond its apparent practicality and efficiency, the checkerboard plan with central plaza, pillory, church, government buildings, straight streets in geometric design, and arrangement of housing demonstrated a new ordering of public space suitable for the hierarchy of the colonial regime. The new urban design's stone houses, plazas, fountains, gardens, and crosses were elements in a transplanted material culture, yet more examples of "goods" designed to "civilize" the native inhabitants and their descendants. Construction materials helped define social hierarchy. The degree of a peoples' civility could be determined by a "hierarchy of elements": stone was more "noble" than wood; "people who built with wood were less civil than those who built in stone."[20] In the new European settlements the "proper" householders with families, dependents, and servants – *vecinos con casa poblada* in the language of the day – had Indian and black masons and carpenters put up their dwellings.

Almost everyone is conservative about diet, and the sixteenth-century Spaniards were no exception. Although the early chroniclers wrote ecstatic descriptions of new products, "some as sweet as if they had been dipped in syrup . . . others so fragrant they perfumed entire houses," the settlers themselves soon bent every effort to bring from Europe the "civilized" food they longed for. Although the Spaniards did not turn up their nose at cassava bread, tortillas, or the humble spud while on the march to Tenochtitlan or Cuzco, perhaps more than other conquering Christians in the sixteenth century they quickly insisted upon their notion of proper food – beginning with the conventional trinity of wheat bread, olive oil, and wine – once they were settled. Columbus's son, Ferdinand, adds three other items – garlic, vinegar, and

---

[19] Durston, "Regimen urbanístico," pp. 78, 88.
[20] Ibid., pp. 87–8; see also Marcelin Defourneaux, *Daily Life in Spain in the Golden Age* (Stanford, Calif.: Stanford University Press, 1979), pp. 61, 96, 103.

cheese – to what he considers the "the necessities of life"[21] The early efforts to form a Mediterranean food regime in the Indies was made difficult by the absence of Spanish women.

It would be fascinating for us now had someone recorded an early postconquest dialogue between the first Spanish immigrants, say, one Isabel Rodríguez, who, Bernal Diaz tells us, "was at that time the woman of some guy (fulano) from Guadalupe," and the Náhuatl-speaking women in the household she was just setting up in Mexico City.[22] Who was expected to put food on the table? We know that wheat flour, spices, imported animals, and even saffron, were already available. Did "Isabel" insist, across the language and cultural barrier, on the familiar preparation of a Castilian dish? Were she and her "fulano" prepared to eat, and even sit on the ground, like the Nahuas? Who in the world were the cultural or even the linguistic interpreters in these early years?

During the subsequent two decades (from 1521 to 1539), a recent study shows that 845 Spanish women entered Mexico. A similar number, about a 1,000, came to settle during the two decades following the conquest of Peru, a ratio of one female to every seven or eight Spanish men. All across the Indies, the negotiation of food regimes must have occurred in the households that other Spanish men formed with native women and, in fewer cases, in the unions formed between Spanish women and native men. Three Castilian women, for example, married three (baptized, of course) descendants of the cazonci (cacique) of Michoacán: don Pablo Huitzimengari, don Constantino Huitzimengari, and don Francisco Tariacuri.[23] Surely these women, Castilian and native, were responsible – and surely they enlisted the kitchen help of native women – for the daily meals as well as for the much more elaborate banquets that were common in colonial capitals.

How one would love to have a peek at their houses! It's easy to imagine a few shouts and frustration across the rude kitchens. They were undoubtedly the site of conflict, experiment, and negotiation

---

[21] Coe, First Cuisines, p. 228; Ferdinand is cited in J. H. Parry and Robert Keith, eds., New Iberian World (New York: Times Books and Hector and Rose, 1982), 1:131.

[22] Diaz, Historia, p. 371.

[23] Lockhart, Spanish Peru, pp. 151–2; Pedro Carrasco, "Matrimonios hispano-indios en el primer siglo de la colonia," in Alicia Hernández and Manuel Miño, eds., Cincuenta años de historia en México (Mexico City: Colegio de Mexico, 1991), 1:103–18.

among cooks. We know that iron pots, hooks, steel knives, and fry pans were high on the list of those things brought to the Indies, and just as they shared space with clay dishes and grinding stones in the kitchens of the first settlers, so novel ingredients blended into new dishes. Inevitably this interaction at the level of the household contributed to the perpetuation of Iberian practice but it also eventually led to the emergence of hybrid culinary regimes.

The transfer of Old World plants and animals to the New, one-half of what Alfred Crosby called the "Columbian Exchange," derived originally from diet or more particularly, from the inclination of colonizers to insist on familiar food in their colonies. As sixteenth-century Europeans pushed out into unfamiliar latitudes and the often exotic agricultures of the non-Christian world, they had either to come to terms with strange foods or produce locally what they considered to be the essential elements of a civilized diet. The Portuguese came to accept manioc flour on the Brazilian littoral; the Spaniards reluctantly did without wheat in the Philippines. The English settlers in what became New England appear somewhat more inclined to accept items of the Indian diet, out of necessity at first and later by taste, an adaptation present today in the menu of the North American "Thanksgiving Day": another invented tradition, to be sure, but still symbolic of a certain early culinary syncretism.[24]

Many of the animals and plants of the Mediterranean world crossed the Atlantic on Columbus's second voyage in 1493. His caravels served as a veritable Ark and down the gangplank (or, most likely, swimming) to innumerable American beaches came species of livestock to multiply amid the luxuriant vegetation of the tropics in the unfenced fields of native farmers. Perhaps the most useful of all were common chickens, carried, legs tied and squawking, in the ships' boats eventually to thrive in households across the hemisphere. The first inconspicuous cuttings of sugarcane came on this voyage, a fateful plant whose spread everywhere across tropical America would eventually lead to the forced importation of several millions of enslaved Africans to satisfy a Western taste for sweetness. Wheat, barley, broad beans, lettuce, radishes, and European fruit trees quickly followed. Before all these became abundant,

[24] Alfred Crosby Jr., *The Columbian Exchange: Biological and Cultural Consequences of 1492* (Westport, Conn.: Greenwood Press, 1972); Arnold J. Bauer, "La cultura mediterránea en condiciones del nuevo mundo: elementos en la transferencia del trigo a las Indias," *Historia* (Santiago, Chile) 21 (1986): 31–53.

Figure 3.4. Spaniards land with livestock near present-day Veracruz, 1519. *Source*: Codex Florentino. Courtesy, Biblioteca Medicea Laurenziana, Florence.

the Europeans either brought their own supplies or tried, reluctantly, to make do with local fare. Faced with unfamiliar and even suspect food regimes in the Caribbean, Columbus was inclined to provision the island of Española as if it were a Spanish caravel. To one of the most abundant fishing grounds in the world, he brought dried cod; rejecting tropical fruits, he insisted on stale buns and imported raisins; understandably unable to foresee that he was bound for what would become the richest sugar colony in the world, he carried four arrobas of white sugar. A full pound of saffron, almonds, honey, and three arrobas of pig's lard were other items the admiral "greatly needed."[25]

[25] Parry and Keith, *New Iberian World*, 2:185–8.

With remarkable speed, European foul multiplied and soon eggs and chickens became standard tribute goods. Cattle were already thick on the ground by the early sixteenth century so that Europeans accustomed to beef were able to "stuff themselves with it unrestrainedly in the New World." Pigs, that "mainstay of Spanish cuisine," became even more rapidly abundant. They enthusiastically occupied the America tropics and multiplied so quickly that even the early Spanish expeditions were accompanied by herds of porkers. A decade after the first entry into Peru, Gonzalo Pizarro, on his unfortunate search for the land of cinnamon, "went escorted by swine." Even so, one Spanish immigrant, yearning for a particular taste or flavor, beseeched her brother still in Spain to go to the trouble of finding "four cured hams from Ronda" and bring them over on the perilous crossing of a six-teenth-century caravel.[26]

The practice of importing European food continued into the fourth decade of the European occupation, a remarkable fact, considering the danger and high cost of maritime transport. Enterprising Iberian merchants had stocks of olive oil, honey, vinegar, wine, and flour in Panama in 1526; one man, writing from Cuba, complained that he had much imported wheat flour on hand but "the country is [already] full of it." The early adventurers, unwilling to live off the land, melted down the scarce pebbles of gold and divided it among themselves to pay the merchants.[27]

The most spectacular early demonstration of the transfer of a Spanish culinary regime to the new world can be seen in two extraordinary banquets offered on successive nights by Viceroy Mendoza and Hernando Cortés in the very heartland of Indian Mexico, the awed description of which fills several pages in Bernal Diaz's chronicle.

---

[26] Braudel, *The Structures of Everyday Life*, p. 105; Coe, *First Cuisines*, p. 230; Herman Viola and Carolyn Margolis, eds., *Seeds of Change: A Quincentennial Celebration* (Washington, D.C.: Smithsonian Institution 1991), pp. 101–3; J. Benedict Warren, *La administración de los negocios de un encomendero en Michoacán* (Morelia, Michoacán: Secretaría de Educación Pública, 1984); Lockhart and Otte, *Letters*, pp. 135–6. On meat consumption, see John C. Super, "The Formation of Nutritional Regimes in Colonial Latin America," in John C. Super and Thomas C. Wright, eds., *Food, Politics and Society in Latin America* (Lincoln: University of Nebraska Press, 1985), pp. 1–23, and for a more comprehensive treatment, *Food, Conquest and Colonization in Sixteenth-Century Spanish America* (Albuquerque: University of New Mexico Press, 1988).

[27] Lockhart and Otte, *Letters*, pp. 27–38.

In 1538, only sixteen years after the conquest in the central plaza of
México-Tenochtitlan, hundreds of the first Spanish settlers together
with their wives dressed in silk and damasks, dripping with gold and
silver, sat from sundown to 2:00 A.M. to feast on salads, roast kid and
hams, quail pies, stuffed chicken, *manjar blanco*, then *torta real* and more
chicken and partridge.

This gave way to a serious second course of boiled mutton, beef,
pork, turnips, cabbages, and chick-peas, accompanied by casks of red
and white Spanish wine. The exotic *guajolote*, which the Spaniards,
groping for names, called *gallos de papada*, or "double-chinned roosters,"
although not yet cooked up in the exquisite seventeenth-century invention of *mole* sauce, was on the menu. The equally exotic chocolate,
served up in frothy cupfuls, also made its way to the Europeans' table.
We are told that many dishes were for display, not consumption. Live
rabbits, quail, and doves encased in pastry shells, provided a whimsical
touch. When cracked opened simultaneously, the rabbits "went fleeing
over the table tops," while the birds fluttered about. Bernal Diaz almost
forgot to mention the roasted whole steers stuffed with chickens, par-
tridges, and ham, served in the lower patio to the "mounted servants,
mulattos and Indians."[28]

The late Sofie Coe contrasts the Spanish banquet and its egregious
display of culinary abundance with the "gravity, economy and
decorum" of Moctezuma's feasts on the eve of the conquest. We also
notice the presence, a scant few years after the conquest, of a wide
range of food almost entirely of European provenance. Local fruit was
on the table, but good Bernal does not bother to name it. Along the
dark streets beyond the pine-resin torches that lit the banquet halls
in México-Tenochtitlan, we may imagine a thousand households of
Náhuatl-speaking villagers settling down to the local fare, overawed by
the conquerors' unrestrained gluttony for meat and repelled no
doubt by the stench of animal fat from the nearby banquet. "The dis-
taste of the Indians for the fat of European animals is recorded over
and over." In fact, in one case they listed "basting with lard" along
with prisons and beatings as the major horrors of the conquest.[29] It
is hard to imagine, by the way, a more revealing metaphor for the
differences between Iberian and English invaders than this exuberant Spanish banquet in contrast to the austere, plain, and largely

---

[28] Diaz, *Historia*, pp. 545–8; Coe, *First Cuisines*, pp. 243–6.
[29] Coe, *First Cuisines*, p. 234.

native fare the gloomy Puritans put on their plates a century later in Massachusetts.

Clothing, both the lack of it entirely or the specific use of cloth – or for that matter, if we consider clothing in the broadest sense to include footwear, makeup, hairstyle, adornment, even mutilation or defor-mations of the body, tattoos and scarification – was always the fundamental marker of identity and status. In a world of very few com-modities compared with the obscene abundance of our own time, cloth represented the major household investment. Or the major prize of thieves and brigands. Both the English word *robe* and the Spanish *ropa* ultimately derive from robbery and booty.

Among the essential items of material culture, food regimes and housing tend to change slowly, whereas clothing is the most vola-tile, more susceptible to the vagaries of fashion. The kinds of dress, the fabrics and quality of weave, and the colors and adornments were all keenly noticed by the Europeans from their first moment of contact with America "at the same time that the Indians were themselves taking in the strange floating houses, alarmingly fast animals, strange men with rare and excessive clothing." At first the complete lack of dress drew attention but for the sixteenth-century Spaniards nakedness was for some less a source of scandal than a cause for commiseration. Nakedness was naturally associated with poverty, rarely if ever seen as repellent or astonishing, but more commonly as merely curious; in fact, inadequate or ragged clothes provoked more negative reaction than no clothes at all. The church, it seems, had not yet adopted the attitude of shame toward the naked body as it came to centuries later.[30]

We can see that both Spaniards and Indians shared the under-standing that clothing represented something beyond mere protec-tion from the environment in two events that took place as the Cortés expedition in 1519 moved along the Yucatan littoral toward conquest. From his probes along the coast, Cortés heard that a fellow Spaniard, shipwrecked several years before, was still alive, living among the Maya. Sent for, he appeared on deck carrying one sandal and wearing the other, dressed "in an old cloak and a loin cloth even worse."

---

[30] Pilar Gonzalbo Aizpuru, "Vestir al desnudo: un acercamiento a la ética y la estética del vestido en el siglo xvi novohispana," in Rafael Diego Fernández, ed., *Herencia española en la cultural material de las regiones de México* (Zamora, Mexico: El Colegio de Michoacán, 1993), pp. 329, 333ff.

Scandalized by the scruffy dress, Cortés immediately ordered that he be given a shirt, jerkin, trousers, and slippers and even took off his own "long yellow, crimson-lined cape" and gave it to Aguilar as an external sign of the change of life he was about to undergo. A few days later, Melchorejo, an Indian captured on the previous Grijalva expedition and brought along now by Cortés as translator, decided to abandon the Spaniards and return to his people. Leaving behind the mark of submission to a foreign power, "he hung the Castilian clothes he had on a hook and left by night in a canoe."[31]

The pattern of Aztec dominance in central Mexico influenced the nature of dress. The Aztecs' tribute system, for example, supplied the high lacustrine capital of Tenochtitlan with loads of cotton cloth from the hot country to the southeast. At the same time their harassment of the rival Tlaxcalans cut off the access of that kingdom to hot-country cotton, as Xicoténcatl pointed out to the invading Spaniards in explaining why his people wore henequén instead of cotton. Among the Aztecs, cotton fabric was the privilege of lords and priests. In contrast, "Poor people dressed in 'nequen' (that is, henequen) which is the coarse cloth made from the maguey while the rich dress in cotton fringed with feathers and rabbit fur." In fact, before the conquest, the pre-Columbian elites endeavored to exercise their own power to control directly just who should wear what. In Mexico fine cotton cloth was strictly forbidden to ordinary people and even the sons of nobles were in for serious punishment if, "before the appropriate time they dress vainly." But common people might earn the right to better dress through heroic exploits or escaping capture by their enemies. In such a case, the subsequent change from henequen to cotton was cause for public celebration during which other cotton garments were distributed to the participants.

After the conquest, Vasco de Quiroga's utopian project in Michoacan tried (not wholly successfully) to continue pre-Hispanic practice by specifying that common Indians in Michoacan dress in a standard cloth, style, and quality in order "to diminish envy, and not sow discord and dissension." In the Andes as well, on the eve of the conquest, sumptuary laws governed what kind of cloth a person might wear. The Incas basically had two types, "domestic plain weave and warp patterned fabric intended for ordinary people and kombi (cumbi), a finely woven multicolored cotton which was restricted to use by the nobility." People of the high Andes had llama and alpaca wool for capes and caps, no

---

[31] Diaz, *Historia*, pp. 47, 52; Gonzalbo, "Vestir al desnudo," pp. 339–40.

doubt a blessing in a cold climate. With the conquest came new styles and changes in material.[32]

Once the Aztec capital fell in 1521 and the process of establishing the colony begun, "one of the first preoccupations of the friars was to modify the dress of the Indians." Let us remember that without steel shears it was difficult to shape the ordinary rectangular fabrics produced on native looms into anything other than straight-sided tunics or skirts. The Aymara of Upper Peru knitted wool for hats (as they still do today), but trousers or sleeves were exceedingly rare. After the conquest, wide trousers, the puffy *zaragüelles*, actually of Flemish origin and just recently popular in Spain, were widely promoted under clerical pressure and, together with the Castilian shirt and jerkin, came to form the standard male Indian dress. By the 1570s, the information compiled in the *Relaciones geográficas* shows its diffusion throughout the Americas. The friars expected men to wear trousers in the Andes as well, which they customarily did under the pre-Hispanic tunic or *unku*. The unku then became known by the Spanish term *camiseta*. On the other hand, "shirt" (*camisa*), was one of the very first Castilian words that found its way into written Náhuatl, the lingua franca of central Mexico. As early as 1550 the European fitted and buttoned shirt "had become so popular that whole trade groups were devoted to making shirts and collars." Women's dress, closer to European style before the conquest, was less altered in either Mexico or Peru. In Michoacán, skirts became longer but the only new article of clothing added there was the Spanish *toca*, or wimple, for head covering.[33]

Baptism of the native population also brought a forced change in hairstyle and adornment from Mexico throughout the Andes. In the lowland tropics of the Spanish Main and the Amazon headwaters, priests looked askance at unusual ornaments and body paint in place of clothes. Hairstyles then as now attracted attention. As a royal decree directed to the archbishop of New Granada (present-day Colombia) put it, "We have been informed that from ancient custom the Indians of that province wear their hair to the shoulders and even to the waist.

[32] Torquemada, cited in Gonzalbo, "Vestir al desnuda," p. 335; Bruhns, *Ancient South America*, p. 167.

[33] Gonzalbo, "Vestir al desnudo," p. 340; James Lockhart, *The Nahuas after the Conquest* (Stanford, Calif.: Stanford University Press, 1992), pp. 198–9. Virginia Armella de Aspe, "Vestido y evolución de la moda en Michoacán," in Fernández, ed., *Herencia española*, pp. 291–324. Gruzinski, citing the Florentine Codex, in *Painting the Conquest*, p. 127.

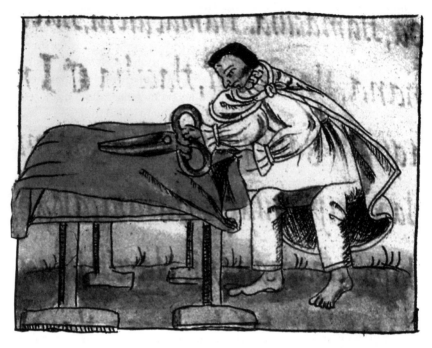

Figure 3.5. Native tailor with shears. Shears unknown in pre-Hispanic times are shown here exaggeratedly large. Notice that the tailor is dressed in post-conquest trousers. *Source:* Codex Florentino. Courtesy, Biblioteca Medicea Laurenziana, Florence.

They consider long hair their principle and most treasured ornament and feel most affronted, if for some crime or excess, the cacique or Spanish official cuts it." Because their hair is also cut at baptism, "many flee from being Christians" for fear of being taken as criminals by those who have not yet accepted the faith. The crown's policy in this case is to order that *all* male Indians' hair be cut leaving only a small tuft. On the other hand, the wide variety of women's hairstyles continued since the "feminine world tended to preserve ancient customs." In ancient Mexico women were "in the habit of wearing their hair down to the waist," while others "had the skull completely shaved with locks on each side of the temples and ears."[34]

---

[34] Royal Decree, March 5, 1581. "Sobre que se ha entendido que por cortar el cabello a los indios que bautizan dejan muchos de ser cristianos." Konetzke, *Documentos*, no. 398.

Figure 3.6. Women's hairstyles. Although Spanish priests insisted that native men's hair be clipped, women retained more variety even after the conquest. Notice again, in this late-sixteenth-century drawing, that native (noble) women are shown in sleeves and short trousers, both rare or nonexistent before the European invasion. *Source*: Codex Florentino. Courtesy, Biblioteca Medicea Laurenziana, Florence.

For the early Spanish migrants to the Indies, cloth and clothing were, apart from precious metals, overwhelmingly the most important commodities, the most obvious markers of status, and the most revealing element in European self-identity. Pedro Arias de Avila's entourage of Castilian noblemen and noblewomen landed on the sweltering Panama coast in 1514 dressed up to the nines in ruffled shirts, fine woolen and velvet cloaks, diamonds, and gold chain. Antonio de Mendoza, New Spain's first viceroy, came accompanied in 1535 by seven tailors and chest after chest of clothing, including three dozen shirts and a dozen exquisite silk capes. Spanish women were the carriers of cloth across the Ocean Sea, a central element in their efforts to establish un hogar or home, sometimes una casa, or a house, as opposed to the terms such as choza, bohio, jacal, or ruca used by many Spaniards to describe a native dwelling, often of adobe and thatch, which didn't measure up to their idea of a proper house. Letter after letter records that Spanish men implored their wives to fill their trunks with all manner of European cloth while the wives themselves, packing up in Seville to join their husbands in the Indies, filled their inventories with silk and lace fringe, fine woolens, thread, and buttons. One woman carried dozens of silk hose and silk capes for her husband and several wimples for herself.[35]

Mourning clothes were de rigueur; indeed, mourning seems such an intense occupation that there are royal decrees against excessive spending on mourning clothes and even against the mourning of inappropriate people. A brother in Cartagena (present-day Colombia) advises his sister in Spain to "bring all your clothes, don't throw anything away." When one doña Antonio Briceño died in Panamá in 1594, she left an enormous wardrobe of every imaginable cloth, colored and white, silk, linen, finest wool. She listed four other possessions as well: four piezas de Indias – four "pieces" of enslaved humanity – namely Esperanza from Biafra, Catalina from Angola, and Rafaela and Baltasara, both Mandingas. Men, too, aimed to be all decked out for the New World. One Juan de Espinoza de Santa Maria la Mayor explained in a 1607 letter how he bought for two young men about to embark "six silk capes, a great quantity of fine wool, which alone cost 500 ducats," more than the price that a respectable house in Mexico City sold for at that time. But Juan de Espinoza knew that "for an honor-

[35] See Lockhart and Otte, Letters, and Gonzalbo, "Vestir al desnuda," p. 347. For recent discussion, see María del Carmen Pareja Ortiz, Presencia de la mujer sevillana en Indias: vida cotidiana (Seville: Excma. Diputación Provincial de Sevilla, 1994).

able man and good sons of parents in the Indies that one always gives them gala clothing, fancy food and money to spend." Clothing also figures widely as gifts spelled out in last wills and testaments.[36]

There are few references to "bedrooms" – or for that matter to the bed itself – perhaps because sleeping space in houses had not yet been commonly "named" as the intimate quarters we've come to be familiar with. But inventories show long lists of bed *clothes*, sometimes staggering in their abundance. Even at the end of the sixteenth century in Peru, when local textile mills were producing good quality woolens, the trunks of Spanish women landing at Callao were typically packed with several sets of sheets, gold-edged pillows, linen towels, woolen blankets, wall hangings, and in one case a "small carpet for the head of the bed." Guests were commonly received, entertained, and served chocolate and sweets in a large room that also served as sleeping quarters. Clearly the major display of textile opulence took place in this space; furnishings for other rooms – the occasional buffet, a cedar chair – are sparse by comparison.[37]

Inevitably, the Spaniards' insistence on certain garments for the native people, a loosening of pre-Hispanic controls, and the sudden introduction of a whole range of new cloth and clothing from Europe began to jumble the social order. The surviving native elites complained about the changes in dress codes and petitioned for special privileges. This was not so much an attempt to regain their former position at the top of the social scale, which was now out of reach in the new order, but at least to find a privileged space in the new regime. The viceroys, in response, conceded to caciques and *indios principales* access to Spanish clothes and the right to ride and to bear arms. Ordinary people, often forced into the Spanish mining sector or agriculture through encomienda or other coercive devices, also found their material world rearranged. But surely the most important impulse for change in consumption patterns came from biology. To a degree unparalleled in any other colonial relationship, whites, blacks, Asians, and native Americans came together to create a baroque proliferation of ethnic types, each seeking the most advantageous identity within a hierarchy of power and status imposed by the colonial system itself. Food, clothing, adornment, and dwelling, along with language, were the most obvious elements in the fluid construction of identity.

[36] Pareja Ortiz, *Presencia*, pp. 154–5, 278.
[37] Ibid., pp. 163–4.

The simple matter, for example, of the distance above the ground (or floor) that one slept or ate was laden with meaning. In the tropics, many native Americans slept in a hammock, the ingenious device invented and named by the Taino in the Caribbean. But in both the core areas of Mesoamerica and the Andes, Indians slept on reed mats and ate without chairs or tables, a practice remarked upon by several Spaniards. In their eyes, "sleeping on the ground like a Turk," or "like beasts," was a sure mark of indecent behavior. Captain Monségur noticed that Indians in Mexico City had "such an aversion" to cots and mattresses, which they believed caused illness, that it was necessary to remove them from the hospitals." A poor Spaniard in Oaxaca is described in a lawsuit in 1543 "as so despicable that he eats with Indians on the ground like an Indian." In time, as we go through the subsequent centuries, "getting off the ground," away from the earth, was to move to non-Indian status. This might be done by sleeping in raised beds rather than on mats strewn on the dirt floor; by using metal rather than earthen, clay pots; or by wearing shoes rather than sandals in order to distance one's self from the ground, inevitably associated with the lowly natives.[38]

Ethnic and class divisions are present in many countries but they are particularly marked in colonial and postcolonial societies. Among these, Latin America contains a number of peculiarities. A moment's reflection suggests the broad differences. In some parts of the globe European clerics and traders were not accompanied by political control; in the case, for example, of sixteenth- or seventeenth-century Japan and China, they understandably made barely a dent on local culture. In fact, far from imagining that the people of China might adopt European styles of clothing, sixteenth-century Jesuits sought "to fit in" by shaving their heads and wearing Buddist robes – in short, to "become Chinese in order to win China for Christ."[39] In the full-fledged later colonial regimes of the British in Burma or the Indian subcontinent,

---

[38] Gibson, Aztecs, p. 336; Las nuevas memorias del Capitán Jean de Monségur, ed. and introd. Jean Pierre Berthe (Mexico: UNAM, 1994), pp. 39–40; Carrasco, "Matrimonios hispano-indios," p. 113. For a recent analysis, see Benjamín Orlove, "Down to Earth: Race and Substance in the Andes," Bulletin of Latin American Research 17, no. 2 (1998): 207–22.

[39] Willard J. Peterson, "What to Wear? Observation and Participation by Jesuit Missionaries in Late Ming Society," in Stuart B. Schwartz, ed., Implicit Understandings (Cambridge: Cambridge University Press, 1994), pp. 403–21, esp. 408–9.

or of the French in Indochina, the invading culture did not reach so deeply into the mass of people as in the Spanish colonies in the Americas. This in part is because neither the British nor the French had such a devastating demographic impact in Asia as the Spaniards had in America. The inhabitants of India or Southeast Asia remained largely intact; consequently, the numbers of English and Frenchmen in relation to the local mass remained relatively small. There was also less "mestizaje" so the line between European occupiers and the native mass was more clearly marked and presented less ambiguity than in Spanish America. Although both British and French established schools, and both were determined to spread European scientific and literary culture, in the end, after decolonizing during the post–World War II years, the mass of people continued, and continue, to speak local languages and pray to non-Christian gods. In contrast today, the mass of people in Latin America, across the class and ethnic spectra, speak Spanish or Portuguese and practice Christianity.

Nor was the material culture of ordinary people altered very much by the European presence in Asia and Africa. Indeed, Indian curries and Indochinese dishes had more impact on food in England and France than did European food or styles of cooking in their colonies. But whereas British, French, and German colonial regimes left the large local populations of China, India, East Asia, and Africa largely intact, the Spanish and Portuguese intrusion into America led to massive demographic change, and that made all the difference.

The figures for the native population of America at contact will forever be disputed but whether we begin with 35 or 100 million everyone agrees that the European advance brought high mortality. As much as 70 percent of the native population perished in the core Mesoamerican and Andean zones, and more in the tropical lowlands, during the first colonial century. Had demographic collapse of the native population not followed European contact, the large mass of native people would undoubtedly have been more likely to preserve intact their language, faith, food, and dress. Under these circumstances, one can still imagine European control in America: a thin, insulated, layer of European officials and entrepreneurs ruling a non-Christian, Quechua- or Náhuatl-speaking mass with the assistance of co-opted, native elites. But as it worked out, after the striking decline of native populations, there emerged between the small groups that thought of themselves as white and the reduced but still substantial Indian population an expanding stratum of mixed bloods and ambivalent cultures.

Moving out from the initial points of contact at a much faster pace than we see in other zones of European expansion, Spaniards of all classes and occupations fanned out from the Caribbean across North and South America to reach into present-day Kansas and southern Chile as early as the 1540s. Beginning in 1492, some 150,000 Spanish immigrants in the first century and 450,000 in the next mixed culturally and ethnically with a variety of native peoples and enslaved Africans to set in motion the eventual formation of the mestizo society we see today.[40] What might have been a typical picture of a late sixteenth-century Spanish immigrant? The composite male would be "a poverty-stricken Andalusian male aged 27, unmarried, unskilled, semi-literate, driven by hunger to make his way to Peru in the employ of any who would pay his passage and had secured the necessary permit"; the composite female, "an Andalusian woman, already in her early 30s, traveling to Peru with her 36 year-old husband, two young children, a manservant and a maid."[41] The actual number or percentage of female migrants to the New World is hard to determine. One migratory sample of the years 1595–98 found that about two-thirds of the total were male; another informed opinion for the first three decades of settlement in Peru suggests that one in ten there were women. Therefore, "in view of the old tradition among historians of ignoring them, the cultural and biological contribution of Spanish women to the building of a European society in Peru requires emphasis." Nevertheless, of the 600,000 to 700,000 Spanish immigrants to the Indies in the sixteenth and seventh centuries, the large majority, perhaps 70 to 90 percent, were men – again, an unusually high disproportion in the history of European colonialism.[42]

Mestizaje in the Hispanic world began in Spain long before the 1492 encounter as we can see in the fact that some 10 percent of women migrants to early Peru were moriscas and mulattas. Indeed, if we take Jared Diamond's long view beginning with the flow of migrants out of Africa 500,000 years ago, we are all biological mestizos. But in the

---

[40] Woodrow Borah has a higher estimate of 750,000 Spanish immigrants during the sixteenth and seventeenth centuries. See Woodrow W. Borah, "The Mixing of Populations," in Fredi Chiapelli, ed., First Images of America (Berkeley: University of California Press, 1976) 2:708.

[41] Peter Boyd-Bowman, "Spanish Emigrants to the Indies, 1595–98: A Profile," in Chiapelli, First Images, 2:723–36.

[42] Lockhart, Spanish Peru, pp. 150–1. The sex ratio in Portuguese Brazil was similar to that of Spanish America.

present, culturally constructed sense of the word, mestizaje in America began immediately, most likely on October 13, 1492, and the number of mixed bloods grew steadily at first and then explosively from about the mid-eighteenth century on. By the end of the colonial period, all mixed groups – the *castas* in colonial parlance – were rapidly increasing. In all of New Spain (the colonial term for central Mexico), for example, the Indian population increased from its low point of some 1,270,000 in 1650 to about 5,200,000 in 1800, but the castas grew four times faster, from some 130,000 to over 2,2700,000, and, of course, that growth has accelerated down to the present.

In the Andean highlands, from Ecuador to northern Chile and Argentina, native mortality rates were somewhat less steep in the early years of the European contact and then later, in the seventeenth century, fell in a pattern different from that of New Spain. Moreover, because the Spaniards chose to found their capital on the Peruvian coast rather than in the very center of the Indian world as in the case of Mexico-Tenochtitlan, because of a more difficult topography and a more hesitant evangelizing effort on the part of the early friars in Peru than in Mexico, and because of greater native resistance, a greater separation between the European and native culture occurred in the Andes, and consequently there was less mestizaje than in Mexico. In the early nineteenth century, while the Pacific littoral of Peru was largely white, black, and mixed, at least 80 percent of the people in the high Andes continued to think of themselves as Indian.[43]

In regions peripheral to the Mesoamerican and Andean cores, such as Chile, the Argentine Pampa, Colombia, Costa Rica, and Nicaragua, a less deeply rooted native population was unable to withstand the European advance and either perished or became incorporated into the European economy and society. Here, by the end of the eighteenth century we are already in the presence of essentially a mestizo culture shading into a thin layer of whiter elements at the top with the relatively small Indian groups pushed into "zones of refuge," not yet attractive to European colonizers. In the tropical lowlands of the Caribbean and circum-Caribbean and Brazilian littoral, the native population was nearly obliterated and, in the course of the eighteenth and nineteenth

---

[43] For demographic impact, see David Noble Cook, *Born to Die: Disease and New World Conquest, 1492–1650* (Cambridge: Cambridge University Press, 1998); for a comprehensive survey of population, see Nicolás Sánchez Albornoz, *The Population of Latin America* (Berkeley: University of California Press, 1974).

centuries, repopulated by the forced immigration of Africans. Nearly 80 percent of the ten million Africans brought in bondage ended up in the Caribbean and Brazil creating a largely Iberian-African regime of material culture in those areas.

As colonial society evolved from its sixteenth-century beginnings, the rewards and penalties of colonial classification led all ethnic groups to develop strategies for their advantage. Spaniards, and those who might plausibly pass as Spaniards, were permitted – and, where possible, eager – to dress in silk, to carry and use arms, to ride, to travel and trade, to be appointed to clerical and governmental posts, and "to pursue their fortunes as freely as was legally and morally possible." Light-skinned or not overly dark-skinned castas (called variously *castizo, mestizo, morisco,* and so on) consequently "had a strong interest in being identified, or trying to self-identify as Spaniards." Meanwhile, Indians seeking to escape tribute payment or labor obligations "often found themselves trying to convince skeptical officials, local priests or other power holders that they were mestizos, castizos or whatever other name was popular at the time."[44]

A telling example of the high stakes involved in ethnic classification may be seen in Viceroy Marqués de Castelfuerte's effort to add several hundred "so-called mestizos" to the tribute rolls in Cochabamba (in present-day Bolivia). Crown officials believed they "were simply Indians" who had exchanged their indigenous cultural garb for Western clothing and identity. The proposed reclassification would have put these questionable mestizos into the category of Indian tributary, which made them liable for the head tax as well as forced mine labor. Understandably, the mestizos opposed the move and in their uprising killed the crown official and fifteen creoles. Their leader, Alejo Calatayud and his followers, were subsequently strangled in the central plaza, "their dismembered bodies strewn along the road as a gruesome warning to the restless plebe."[45] Runaway slaves and lighter-skinned Africans who had any hope of social and economic success sought to be identified as mulattoes or any other dark-skinned

---

[44] Jorge Klor de Alva, "*Mestizaje* from New Spain to Aztlán," in *New World Orders: Casta Painting and Colonial Latin America* (New York: Americas Society Art Gallery, 1996), pp. 64–6.

[45] Archivo General de Indias, Charcas, leg. 344, Expediente sobre el levantamiento de los mestizos en la villa de Cochabamba." For acute treatment of the incident, see Brooke Larson, *Colonialism and Agrarian Transformation in Bolivia* (Princeton, N.J.: Princeton University Press, 1988), pp. 110–15.

casta in order to escape their servitude or the legal restrictions that limited their life chances.

Emerging between the European and native societies, the mixed population was understandably ambivalent in its cultural identity. But except for the rare cases where mestizos might plead to be recognized as tribal members in order to have access to Indian land or gain a position in native government, they more generally have gone to great lengths to avoid the consequences of being taken for "indios."[46] The most obvious and effective way of changing identity was to change one's material culture: what and the way one ate, one's fabric and dress, the very rituals of consumption, the nature of houses and furniture.

Not just the mixed races, but the settler elite itself, having mingled sexually and socially with local ethnic groups, had cultural anxieties and conflicted political loyalties. From the first American-born generation in the sixteenth century onward, one can discern an elite – later to be called "creole" – torn between European cultural models and the familiar practice of its American homeland. Members of this elite sought in the food, drink, clothing, and architectural style imported from Europe the cultural markers and symbols that would set them off from what they considered to be their social inferiors in the colonies. At the same time, perhaps more than their later British or French colonizing counterparts, the Spanish American elite settlers also *identified with* their New World homeland, and in time managed to lead successfully their often darker-skinned compatriots to independence from Spain. Again, for a broad comparison, one might notice that in the 1960s, the French colonial leaders in Algeria and the white Rhodesians tried to set themselves up, in effect, as "creoles" aiming to lead their newly founded countries to separate politically from France or Britain while maintaining themselves in command of local politics and economy. But the wide cultural, linguistic, or religious differences between the white elite and the mass of Islamic Algerians or black Rhodesians condemned such movements to failure.

Although the nomenclature of caste or race that came into common use in Latin America after the first few generations was believed, by those who used the terms, to reflect a genetic or biological reality, it is easier to see now that ethnicity is either in the eye of the beholder or a self-designation – in both cases a social-cultural construction. Of course, the terms themselves were invented, imposed from the outside.

[46] Klor de Alva, "*Mestizaje*," p. 68.

Figure 3.7

Figures 3.7. and 3.8. "Español and Yndia Beget Mestizo," "Español and Mestiza Beget Castiza," and so on. These curious "castas" paintings, which depict ethnicity in biological terms but with cultural attributes, show the diversity of people in eighteenth-century Mexico and Peru. This selection shows four panels; usually there are sixteen. *Source:* Private collection.

There were no "Indians" in America until the Great Navigator named them. But whether invented or constructed, ethnic designations came to be accepted as important and, of course, had powerful social and legal effect. Labels such as mestizo, indio, or español conferred privilege or disadvantage. "Mulatto," "coyote," and "cholo," and many others inscribed in baptism and census records and used daily in the street reveal the insecurity, contempt, or resentment of people in rival groups.

The Spanish invasion into indigenous society and the nearly simultaneous introduction of Africans and their cultures muddled the American world, suddenly introducing new categories of race and class. Any discussion then, of material culture must thread its way through a scramble for identity in a maze of conflicting values, where the consumption of wheat bread or tortillas, wine or pulque, silk or hemp was determined not just by supply and demand but by the symbolic meaning of these commodities in colonial society and politics.

The Europeans' invasion laid on America a new hierarchy of status and power that included new ethnic categories. If the aboriginal world itself had been divided between civilized and barbarous, empire and subject, noble and commoner, the Europeans complicated matters with an array of unusual food, dress, tools, and shelter, new tastes and styles. The emerging regime of material culture might be imposed by clerical or state decree or through the forced sale of cloth and iron practiced by trade-driving magistrates, the new values communicated by the merest glance of disdain. Consequently, the kind, quantity, and the way food was placed on the table, the quality of cloth and the design of shoes were all finely tuned instruments of social and political standing, quickly grasped by all those jostling for position.

We turn now to the contested project of "civilizing goods," tracking the hesitant changes we saw in the early years into an ever evolving material culture. This was driven by the intermingling of new plants and animals, the use of new tools and techniques, the organization of public and private space, along with the emergence of new values and fashion within the regime of colonial power.

CHAPTER 4

CIVILIZING GOODS

Y mirad que es la voluntad de Dios que andéis vestidos y cobijadas vuestras carnes.[1]

More important than the formal and direct efforts by church and state to modify by decree the nature and rituals of consumption in colonial Latin America were the thousands of daily, informal, and mainly voluntary decisions made by all members of colonial society from the grandest archbishop to a llama herder. Like people today, they made their decisions on the basis of style and taste and their economic capacity to buy. Men, women, and children acquired goods, taking into account the constraints and encouragement offered by hierarchies of power and status, in this case the Spanish colonial regime. By the 1570s the main force of conquest had run its course, and Spanish and Portuguese civil and ecclesiastical administration settled into place. European pathogens continued on their deadly course as new epidemics worked their way through the native population. At the same time, additional Europeans crossed the Ocean Sea to the Indies, a still relatively small number of Africans were forced across the South Atlantic (at this point mainly to sugar plantations on the Brazilian coast), and generations of mixed offspring began to emerge everywhere. The settlers' demand for workers, and their power to acquire them, channeled men and women into such colonial enterprises as silver mines and rural estates.

---

[1] "Pay attention to the will of God that you go about dressed with your flesh covered." Pedro de Córdoba, O.P., *Doctrina Christiana*, cited in Gonzalbo, "Vestir al desnuda," p. 319.

After initial sparring in the realm of goods, at times characterized by mutual repugnance at each other's food, clothing, and lifeways, the halting beginnings of a mestizo material culture were underway. At least two of the indispensable Mediterranean trinity, wheat and wine, began to be produced locally; olive oil remained an import. European livestock and fowl multiplied. People drank chocolate almost everywhere, but particularly in the Mexican viceroyalty and on the Spanish Main (the north coast of South America); mule trains carried yerba mate throughout much of the land south of the equator; and a profusion of tomatoes, potatoes, and local fruit found its way onto tables. Imported fine cloth was still the most important article on merchants' inventories but local wool textile workshops, the infamous *obrajes* and *chorrillos*, sprung up wherever sheep were available. Master artisans with mestizo, Indian, or black apprentices turned out shoes, iron goods, weapons, silver candelabra, hats, horseshoes, and cooking utensils, while native craftsmen and women created for themselves and the market an impressive array of pottery, woodwork, musical instruments, furniture, and rudimentary clothing.

Let us not forget, however, that in the midst of all this truck and trade, a great many people, if not untouched, remained on the margin of the colonial economy. When once told by an elderly Mexican campesina that she lived four hours (by mule back, it turned out) from a rustic hamlet in the state of Jalisco, I idly asked what it was she "did" there. She looked at me with some compassion: "pues, vivir no más." To "just live," which by no means suggests an empty or unworthwhile existence, describes the activity of a great many common people on the planet, then and now.

Private houses, ecclesiastical and civil buildings, often of stone, sometimes with the Roman arch, grew up along the carefully aligned streets in the centers of new towns and cities, while a few blocks away people built with adobe, previously known in Spain and fundamental in the Indies. Temporal rhythms moved in accordance with the Christian seven-day calendar, introduced deliberately and not without opposition, while a new schedule of saints' days and festivals punctuated daily life. New converts were given saints' names and had their original last names (or newly adopted one) confirmed in the baptismal records. Metallic coins rattled in the purses and trousers of European and Indians alike, although a great deal of exchange was still governed by barter or by money of account, that is, with sales, purchases, and wages merely recorded in the account books of mining and hacienda administrators or local stores. Spanish measures – the league, almud, fanega – many in fact of Moorish origin, began to infiltrate the marketplaces. Along with introducing measures and money, by naming people, developing tribute lists, and carrying out early population counts, the colonial state and church were precocious in their efforts to make society "legible."[2] Now, in this maturing colonial world, let us slightly reform our original question: Why do people acquire the *specific* goods they do?

Food, Drink, and Cooking

First of all goods have to be available. To begin this section, let us turn from the previous emphasis on socially and culturally derived demand to production and its consequences. We begin with food. Underneath changes in diet lay ever changing and evolving patterns of production. An illustrative example of the way a conventional food at home becomes fraught with social meaning in a colonial regime, along with its impact on the development of new agricultural systems, can be seen in wheat bread, the most basic element in European diet. Spaniards in Spain at all social levels yearned for wheat bread; indeed, Sancho Panza liked to chide his Quixotic master for wanting *pan de trastrigo*, or a "better bread than is made from wheat." In America, Spaniards no doubt longed for its familiar taste not only in loaves but also in pastries and empanadas. Moreover, their consumption of wheat served to set themselves off from the maize- and potato-eating natives.

The introduction of European cereals – wheat and barley – provided an arena for the entire range of native reaction from resistance, halting and at times enthusiastic acceptance, to negotiation. The Spaniards initially tried to get the indigenous people to grow wheat by making it part of the tribute requirement. This had scant success any place in Spanish America, but Indians seem to have resisted the plant more in Mesoamerica than in the Andes. Central Chile, where the Mapuche were either pressed into the southern forests or incorporated into the new European estancias, was an exception and quickly became a wheat area, as did, much later, the Argentine pampa. From the Indian point of view in Mexico and the Andes, the European cereals seemed inferior to maize, which yielded up to ten times more than wheat measured in proportion to seed and perhaps one and a half times as much in terms

[2] James Scott, *Seeing Like the State*, particularly ch. 3.

of area sown or labor time. Moreover, because the plants and animals liable for the ecclesiastical tithe in America were originally based on the list of agricultural products in the diocese of Seville, wheat paid the 10 percent tithe whereas maize, if produced by natives, was often exempt. Finally, wheat in volume greater than a garden plot required the plow, European draft animals, and the sickle or scythe – all of which were absent in aboriginal America and costly to acquire in the colonies. But, perhaps most significantly of all, after harvest wheat and barley kernels were threshed out by treading – that is, by running animals over the sheaves – a practice unknown in the New World, and one that further increased the entry costs for a native producer. Moreover, the small European cereals were ground into flour by an entirely different and more efficient milling technique than those the native people employed for maize.

By the mid-sixteenth century in Mexico, wheat was almost entirely produced on *labores*, or fairly small wheat farms, with Indian labor under European guidance.[3] In Peru, perhaps because people here were familiar with quínoa, another small cereal, but also because wheat fit into a rotation with potatoes and did not directly compete with maize for land or labor as it did in Mesoamerica, the European cereals seem to have been somewhat more accepted by native Andean people. Small fields of wheat and especially barley – better suited to cold, high elevations – emerged in various native communities all along the Andean spine and constituted an important crop under Spanish control in Cochabamba (present-day Bolivia), near Bogotá and the high plain of Quito.

European cereals, then, were haltingly introduced into the Indies in the sixteenth century, received skeptically by native peoples, and consequently produced only in small batches near the clusters of European settlement. As we go through the subsequent centuries, however, the number of immigrants from Europe grew steadily. More important, the hybrid offspring of Europeans, Indians, and Africans came to choose wheaten bread over maize, certainly not because of relative price – wheat was from two to ten times more expensive than maize – but for reasons of taste and status. Spaniards and their descendants in the New World, promoted wheat as the "civilized" cereal from the eighteenth century, and even into the 1920s and 1930s.

Having withdrawn from the attempt to force the introduction of wheat upon the native population of Mexico, Spanish settlers took steps to insure their domination of its production. Spanish wheat farms

[3] Gibson, *Aztecs*, pp. 322–6.

Figure 4.1. "Yndios segando en minga" (wheat harvest in Trujillo, Peru). This lyrical rural scene depicts a form of "festive labor" common in the Andes. *Source:* Martínez Compañón, *Trujillo del Perú.* Courtesy, The Bancroft Library, University of California, Berkeley.

were conspicuous in the Atlixco valley of Puebla and the Bajío. By the eighteenth century the Hispanized segment of the population grew and wheat bread became both a prestige and dietarily satisfying food. In Guadalajara, the urban population – mostly mestizo – increased sixfold and the demand for wheat and wheat flour consequently "reached far down into the lower strata of the population."[4] The mixed populations of eighteenth-century Mexico City and Lima and such European settlements as Arequipa or Santiago were essentially wheat eaters. The change in diet had social implications in the countryside. Spaniards and their descendants grew wheat on their home farm, irrigated, desmense land using directly supervised workers drawn from the service tenantry and the surrounding villages. The low cost of land, the provision of cheap labor by the dispossessed native population, and the availability of threshing mares at little or no cost led to substantial economies. The Spaniards' familiarity with Mediterranean techniques, extended and enlarged in the New World, together with the need for heavy investment in storage and transport, also served to give European producers a decided advantage in the control of production and the market.

After wrestling with the unfamiliar biota of the humid tropics and the unanticipated plants and animals of the Mesoamerican and Andean high plateaus where wheat really must be forced into barely appropriate niches, the Spaniards were delighted to find a Mediterranean climate in central Chile at southern latitudes roughly equivalent to Andalusia. Here, more than in any other niche in the Americas, the Europeans were able to replicate an essentially Andalusian agricultural regime of wheat, cattle and horses (the two animals the Spaniards called "major livestock"), pigs, grapes, and olives. A native population, less deeply rooted in central Chile than in central Mexico or the high Andes, was either obliterated or pushed into the rainy south. One way or another, in the beginning with coerced Indian workers in Mesoamerica or the Andes, or through settler agriculture in Chile and Argentina, the Spaniards were successful in establishing agricultural systems that enabled them to reproduce the essential elements of their Mediterranean nutritional regime, and to supply those areas inappropriate for vineyards or wheat fields, such as the Caribbean or the tropical littorals, with imports either from Europe or North America. Wheat or wheat flour, for example, was brought to Cuba from Mexico and Louisiana; Chileans exported grain to Lima. Alas, Spaniards and their descendants had to get by mainly with rice in their Philippine colony.

[4] Eric Van Young, *Hacienda and Market in Eighteenth-Century Mexico* (Berkeley: University of California Press, 1981), p. 62; Bauer, "La cultura mediterránea en condiciones del nuevo mundo," pp. 31–53.

Indigenous farmers and herders, themselves possessors of an aston-
ishingly productive agriculture, reacted to the arrival of European agriculture, its techniques and tools, in varying ways. Native people
immediately saw the benefit of some imported food items and happily
incorporated them into their diet. European chickens and eggs were
quickly found outside every peasant hut. Sheep, a natural addition to
the llamas and alpacas in Andean pastoral economy, were also accepted
by native Mexicans who ran flocks of several thousand head. These
creatures then spread northward into the arid lands of the present-day
southwestern United States, where without sheep the Navajo would
have been hard-pressed to create their famous blankets.

At the same time, such native fruits as avocados, pineapples, tomatoes, and guavas found their way to European tables. Each, of course,
has its story but there is room for only a few here. In the early sixteenth
century the "Chronicler of the Indies," Gonzalo Fernández de Oviedo,
trying to make sense out of things he had not seen before, wrote, "On
the mainland there are some trees called pear trees but they aren't pears
like those in Spain, they are different but no less valuable . . . they
weigh over a pound each and have seeds like a chestnut." Náhuatl
speakers were perhaps closer to the mark, calling the plant *ahuácatl* or
"testicle tree." Oviedo, of course, was looking for the first time at the
avocado tree and his original mistake carried over into the English
"avocado pear" or, more alarmingly, "alligator pear." Two seventeenth-
century travelers were as enthusiastic as present-day consumers.
Thomas Gage, the renegade English Dominican, thought the fruit "fed
and fortified the body, enlivened the spirit and excessively promoted
lubricity." Gemelli Carreri believed it was "better than any European
fruit." The young George Washington found avocados had spread to
Barbados where, traveling with his half brother in 1751, he noticed
they were abundant and popular. Not until 1911 however, did
an American horticulturist, Carl Schmidt, find a variety in Atlixco
(near Puebla, Mexico) that acclimated well to California's climate. In
1938 the California Avocado Association placed a metal plaque
in the central square of Atlixco to commemorate Schmidt's success.[5]

---

[5] Novo, *Historia gastronómica*, pp. 38–42. Avocado derives from Spanish *aguacate*,
in turn from Náhuatl, *auácatl* from *ahuácatl* (testicle) and *cuáhuitl* (tree). Luis
Cabrera, *Diccionario de aztequismos* (Mexico City: Oasis, 1980), p. 28. Gage was
not alone. Men are forever hoping that the consumption of some exotic, previously unknown, plant will boost their potency.

Tomatoes (Náhuatl *tómatl*), quickly carried across the Atlantic, were incorporated into Spanish sauces and renamed "golden apples" (*pomodoro*) by the Italians as early as 1544. But in the United States, where one cannot imagine life without ketchup, there is no evidence of tomato cultivation until the later eighteenth century and only occasional consumption before 1900.[6]

In the beginning Spaniards looked askance at the innumerable tubers native to the Andes. One of these, the potato, was taken to Spain in 1570 and slowly diffused across the planet. Always a main food source in the Andes, not until the later eighteenth century did the common spud begin to provide a major source of carbohydrates – or a base for vodka and other firewaters – in Europe. Today, people in Poland, Germany, and Belgium eat more potatoes per capita than do the original domesticators in Peru. And, of course, how might we exist without French fries? All this glory is due to the assiduous experimentation over seven thousand years ago, by the first Andean farmers, speaking a language long forgotten, grubbing in the earth, selecting the varieties most adaptable to the cold, harsh landscape of high Peru.

Spaniards had little taste for the flesh of American mammals. They disdained the Andean household staple of guinea pigs and were repelled by the hairless dog. They were impressed by the great variety of water fowl and what they called a "double-chinned rooster." Almost immediately taken back to Europe, this bird diffused across the Mediterranean so quickly that when the earnest Puritans came ashore at Plymouth Rock in 1620, they – somehow – associated the gobbler with Turkey. Native people everywhere, on the other hand, immediately saw the benefit of what the Spaniards called "minor livestock," that is, sheep and goats, and also mules and burros for carriage. Mesoamerican natives, whose unfenced maize fields were quickly trampled by the invaders, were understandably hesitant when faced with cattle; the people of the high Andes, long accustomed to llamas and alpacas, were more accommodating.

Talk of food leads to cooking and the various kitchen pots and vessels required to produce meals. Native people across the board in the Americas, but particularly in Mesoamerica and the Andes, had developed a rich variety of pottery shapes and forms. Although many native Americans saw the attraction of the Europeans' iron tools, some animals and many new plants, the superiority of their pottery was not

[6] Novo, *Historia gastronómica*, pp. 42–3.

immediately apparent. Consequently the long tradition of native crafts continued as men and women created an extraordinary array of plates, bowls, flowerpots, cups, and vessels of all kinds. Native potters saw the benefit of the simple Spanish kiln, whose higher temperature permitted glazing, but were less attracted to the potter's wheel. In fact, the very absence of the wheel in pre-Hispanic America may account for a less standardized, more varied pottery.[7] In any case, the persistence of native pottery (and basket ware) in the face of metal pots and kettles was still the rule at the end of the colonial epoch.

When we come to the stories of stimulants or, in the German word, *Genussmittel*, those "articles of pleasure" that are eaten, drunk, or inhaled for pleasure rather than caloric necessity, the trajectories of two great indigenous American beverages offer contrasting stories of material culture. *Cacao* – the word refers to the tree and pods, whose product is *chocolate* – is native to the lowland tropics of Central America and the Orinoco and Amazon headwaters. A prestige drink long before the arrival of the Spaniards, chocolate was a coveted drink in Moctezuma's Tenochtitlan, where the Europeans were impressed by the elaborate rituals of its consumption. Loads of cacao beans figured in the lists of tribute due the Aztecs from the lands to the southeast. The Aztecs traded them throughout the empire, and later the beans themselves served as low-value "coins," beans being worth about 100 one Spanish real in the sixteenth century.

Carried across the Ocean Sea to Spain by Cortés in 1528, the Spaniards, ever on the lookout for commodities of sufficient value in relation to weight to bear the cost of Atlantic freight, gained control of the cacao trade. Chocolate, catnip for the Spaniards, became a popular drink throughout the lands of Mediterranean Catholicism, in part because it has high food value; moreover, because of the church's "principle that liquids do not break fasts" (*Liquidum non frangit jejunum*), it conveniently served as a nutritional substitute during fasting periods, a feature not present, and less required, in the teas and coffees that later swept into the Protestant North. From Spain, chocolate migrated to Italy and France and became fashionable among the courts of Europe. As Wolfgang Schivelbusch puts it, "breakfast chocolate had little in common with the bourgeoisie's coffee. . . . whereas the middle-class family sat erect at the breakfast table with a sense of disciplined propriety, the essence of the chocolate ritual was fluid, lazy,

---

[7] Foster, *Culture and Conquest*, pp. 101–2.

languid, motion." Not a few contemporary paintings show chocolate served in elegant silver vessels to the languorous consumers of the day, enclosed in elegant sheets and bedcovers, surrounded by pillows. While coffee was meant to jar its drinkers to action; chocolate marked the start of a "day's carefully cultivated idleness."[8]

Chocolate spread east, from Mexico into the Pacific as well. One Pedro de Leguna carried cacao seedlings to the Philippines in 1663 where chocolate has been a traditional drink ever since. In the land of its origin, chocolate, mixed with sugar and "other spices," less expensive than in Europe, quickly diffused outward through much of the European and mestizo population to become a common drink even among the urban poor of Mexico City. In 1800 "there were many chocolate shops. . . . it was drunk at breakfast, at the siesta hour and at bedtime."[9]

The second hot drink, practically indispensable to the inhabitants of much of South America in the colonial era and a key marker of *Argentinidad* today, did not stray from its American homeland. *Yerba mate*, also known as Paraguayan tea is native to the fluvial reaches of the Rio de la Plata. Central to ceremonial practice of the pre-Hispanic Guaraní people, its use spread after the conquest through the mestizo and white population, fanning outward to Brazil, the Andean region, Chile, and Argentina. Promoted in the seventeenth century by the Jesuits, ever eager for revenue to support their educational and missionary enterprise, merchants carried tons of mate upriver to the mining center of Potosí and on mule back across the Uspallata Pass to Chile, where it had previously been unknown. Although now and then taken as a cold *refresco* or drunk in cups (the so-called Jesuit tea), mate is characteristically prepared hot, just below boiling temperature, in the

---

[8] Antonio de León Pinelo, *Question moral si el chocolate quebranta el ayuno eclesiástico*, prologue by Sonia Concuera de Mancera (1636; reprint, Mexico City: Condumex, 1994). León Pinelo, born in Peru but resident in Madrid, searched in vain for the famous papal bull that everyone at the time agreed exempted chocolate from the fast. It turns out the bull never existed. Wolfgang Schivelbusch, *Tastes of Paradise: A Social History of Spices, Stimulants and Intoxicants*, trans. David Jacobson from the German (New York: Vintage Books, 1993), pp. 85–92.

[9] Foster and Cordell, *Chiles to Chocolate*, pp. 111, 115; Sonia Concuera de Mancera, *Entre gula y templanza* (Mexico City: Fondo de Cultura Económica, 1990), pp. 84–8. Luis González Obregón, *La vida en México en 1810* (1911; reprint, Mexico, 1979), p. 20.

honda de la calabaza or gourd, and then sipped through the *bombilla*, usually a reed straw or silver tubes.[10]

Mate might be drunk several times during the day but especially with breakfast and again in the late afternoon. From its distant, indigenous beginnings, mate remained an intensely convivial or communitarian drink but was rarely consumed in public places – there were no "mate cafés" or "mate-houses." Small groups of people passed the gourd among themselves and took sips from the same bombilla, perhaps much like friendly people in the distant 1960s passed around a joint of marihuana. Everyone who writes about mate consumption underlines this feature. "It is difficult to transmit, to those who do not enjoy mate, the deep feeling shared in passing the bowl from hand to hand, a feeling accentuated by using always a common straw." This practice commonly cut across class lines and had the rare effect of subverting the barriers of colonial society, "of uniting people beyond their differences." In Chile as in the Rio de la Plata, it became, in effect, the national hot drink at the end of the colonial regime with the wealthy using elegant objects made of silver, the poor more ordinary ones of plant material.[11] Ordinary teas from Asia or coffee was unknown in Latin America until nearly the end of the colonial period.

All kinds of alcoholic drinks flowed in colonial societies, some imported, others local in origin. Many were the offspring of imported plants such as sugarcane or the result of distilling, a technique also imported from Europe in the seventeenth century. Alcoholic drinks marked fairly clear divisions between native and European sectors; however, many people, particularly the *castas*, but also the category of "poor Spaniards," partook of the entire range of choices – no small task, since an eighteenth-century document lists seventy-eight different alcohol drinks in Mexico beginning with *aguardiente*, ending with *zambumbia*.[12]

The mass of common people preferred pulque in Mexico and chicha in the Andes. Pulque, the fermented sap of the agave, was a venerated drink before the conquest, shown by the importance of Mayahuel, the

[10] Juan Carlos Garavaglia, *Mercado interno y economía colonial* (Mexico City: Grijalbo, 1983), pp. 42–7.

[11] Ibid., p. 47. See also Benjamin Orlove and Arnold J. Bauer, "Chile in the Belle Epoque: Primitive Producers; Civilized Consumers," in Orlove, *The Allure of the Foreign*, p. 135.

[12] Janet Long, *La cocina mexicana a través de los siglos* (Mexico City: Clio, 1996), 4:19.

goddess of pulque who in one case is represented as earth mother with four hundred breasts. "The association with divine femininity is repeated in the colonial period with the Virgin of Guadalupe, who was acclaimed as the mother of maguey." In pre-Hispanic times the Aztecs made some effort to limit excessive consumption, yet pulque was widely drunk throughout the tableland as an integral element on festival days, a practice continued after the conquest as the Christian calendar provided additional opportunities for celebration. It is easy to exaggerate the ability of the Aztecs to limit alcohol; in fact, the nature of their incipient state gave them only limited control over the social life of central Mexico. In the early years of the colony, pulque was a household product usually under native and frequently female control but by the eighteenth century, huge pulque haciendas just north of Mexico City and especially in the present-day state of Hidalgo were the main producers. In 1784 adult per-capita consumption of pulque reached 187 gallons a year. Such a figure, even allowing for a fairly wide margin of error, had to include people across the ethnic spectrum. No doubt the low price of pulque was hard to resist, even by those who liked to think of themselves as Spaniards, and even as they condemned pulque for its disgusting and low-life qualities.[13]

Differences between native and European alcoholic consumption were reinforced by ritual and religion. In pre-Hispanic feasts, pulque, "heaven's water," was offered to the gods and after the conquest pulque remained closely associated with "planting and harvest ceremonies, marriage, birth, death and healing." Native people before and after the conquest apparently often drank to unconsciousness; indeed, devotion was "measured by the degree of intoxication." Spaniards, in Spain at least in the opinion of foreign observers, had a certain fame for abstention, "One could not enrage them more than to accuse them of being drunk." Such an opinion is not precisely compatible with the accounts we have of gross behavior in the early days in the Indies, but it does seem that they were inclined to see the moderate consumption of grape wine a "symbol of civilization and Catholic heritage" as well as "an essential part of the diet." After all, wine was honored by Christ himself as a noble drink and He "chose to transform it into His most precious blood." Pulque on the contrary was considered by the Spaniards (who nevertheless drank it) a vulgar and unrefined drink that dulled the nerves and led to stupor. Spaniards also generally valued a Mediter-

---

[13] Taylor, *Drinking, Homicide and Rebellion*, pp. 31–67.

ranean ideal of drinking mostly at mealtimes and being able to "hold" their liquor without losing control. From that point of view, the consumption of pulque to the point of stupor "was considered barbarous, disgusting, ridiculous and a blot on a man's honor." The rare Indian, such as a rich cacique of Querétaro, who sat at a table and drank wine, was more acceptable.[14]

Chicha, a Taino word, appropriated by Spaniards to describe alcoholic drink everywhere in the Indies but here meaning *chicha de jora*, the Peruvian maize beer, occupied a similar position in the Andes. Widespread in the pre-Hispanic era, chicha remained integrated into postconquest ritual and religious ceremony and continued in the colony and even today to be a principal popular drink. Here, too, what began as a household product, mainly produced by women, had become by the eighteenth century, an industrial product in such places as Cochabamba, processed by European milling techniques. We may notice in passing that the two great native American popular drinks never merged and still do not, even though the ingredients to make them were present in both Mesoamerica and the Andes. Chicha did not move above Panama nor did pulque go south.

Spaniards, like other Mediterranean people drank wine. Imagining the techniques of European and colonial wine making before the later eighteenth century sends shivers down the spine of present-day consumers. Crushed in open vats, fermented in grungy wooden barrels or stone troughs, stored and transported in leaky barrels or pitch-lined clay jars, and often carried in goat skins, wine in the colonial years must almost always have been an oxidized, vinegary, ill-smelling brew. Yet, it was an essential item on the tables of Spaniards and those who aspired to Spanish tastes. Incredibly, in the very first feast to celebrate the conquest of Mexico, just weeks after the fall of Tenochtitlan, Cortés somehow managed to have a barrel or two of wine brought up – One wonders how? In a litter? On the backs of Indians? – over the escarpment from Veracruz "off a vessel that had come from Castile." Equally astonishing, at least a dozen Spanish women were also present at the fiesta. Bernal Diaz, writing thirty years after the fact, names them all. They sallied forth to dance on the tabletops with the young men.[15] Imported wine during the colonial years was generally too expensive for ordinary consumption but it was certainly available among

[14] Ibid., pp. 38–9; Defourneaux, *Golden Age*, p. 153.
[15] Diaz, *Historia*, p. 371.

high-living miners at Potosí and Zacatecas and in the houses of the colonial elite, particularly in Lima and Mexico. The cheapest European wines even filtered down to the native and mestizo mass.

Unfortunately, there were few places in America where the wine grape (*vitis vinifera*) flourished. Both the tropics and the high plateaus were inappropriate. The early friars were intent on wine making to reduce the need and bother of imports for the Mass as well as for their own consumption. They introduced an ancient, common black grape in the sixteenth century, known as *mónica* in Sicily and Spain. In the subsequent centuries this vine became practically extinct in the lands of its origin, but carried across the Atlantic, it took on new life wherever viticultural conditions were even barely appropriate. The grape came to be called *misión* in Mexico, *chica criolla* in Argentina, and *uva del país* in Chile. The Jesuits spread this grape into Baja California in the seventeenth century; here the best wine in Mexico is still made but now from different varietals.

Central Chile's Mediterranean climate within a latitude equivalent to the great grape-growing regions of Europe was ideal, and the settlers there produced a barely drinkable wine from the uvas del país. In 1578, during their circumnavigation of the globe, Francis Drake's coarse-palated crew managed to liberate a few casks at Valparaíso. They found it perfectly acceptable. The Ica and Pisco Valleys on the Peruvian coast and Arequipa a bit further up as well as the present-day Argentine piedmont province of Mendoza yielded a few thousand jars of wine of indifferent, if not dreadful, quality. In all of the Western Hemisphere, only in Chile and present-day Argentina have ordinary people become wine drinkers, no doubt because of the higher quality of the local product but also because of their identification with Hispanic culture. In modern Argentina, of course, immigrants from Italy and Spain brought their wine-loving culture with them.[16]

The Europeans also introduced distilling techniques and soon began to provide coarse "firewater," at first in fairly small volume from sugar-cane, later from grapes on the Peruvian coast. The 1613 will of one Pedro Manuel, who left his slave vats of aguardiente and a large copper cauldron where she might make more, provides the first reference to what became known as pisco. At about the same time rude distilleries came into existence all through tropical America, including those making the first rum in Barbados in the 1620s.[17] In the Mexico high-

---

[16] José del Pozo, *Historia del vino chileno* (Santiago: Editorial Universitaria, 1998).
[17] Ibid., p. 24.

lands distillations from the cooked cores of various species of the maguey yielded all kinds and mixes of firewater, the most enduring being mescal, particularly the mescal tequila, this latter named for the small town near Guadalajara. These cheap and powerful intoxicants appealed especially to uprooted people who found refuge in the popular quarters of the new cities, or to peddlers, mule drivers, and local peasants drawn into towns precisely for the opportunities they provided to escape the humdrum of everyday life. In practice familiar to anyone today, the Spanish state inveighed against drunkenness while finding the tax on alcohol an irresistible source of revenue.

Many Spaniards in sixteenth-century Spain had acquired a taste for cold drinks. Nicolás Monardes's curious work, *Libro que se trata de la nieve y de sus provechos*, first published in 1571, shows that packed snow was commonly used to cool wine and water throughout Europe, sold in Constantinople all year round, used by important people such as "businessmen, those who have much to do, and those who walk a lot." He thought it a remedy for bad nerves, stomach problems, liver sickness – in short, good for what ails you. Following the practice of Moorish kings, snow, packed in straw, was brought down some six leagues from the Sierra Nevada to the city of Granada. Monardes, a Sevillano, complains that his own city has no snow so people suffer through the hot summer without cool drinks. In Madrid too, in the years of Felipe II, ice and snow came from forty miles away, stored in "snowpits" in the city and sold during the summer "when cool drinks and sherbets were much in vogue."[18]

I have seen no indication that pre-Hispanic people in either Mesoamerica or the Andes were interested in cool drinks. But once firmly settled in the Indies, the Spaniards turned their attention to the problem of ice in the tropics. Happily for them in both Peru and Mexico high peaks with eternal snow thrust up from the hot country. Taking advantage of an already thriving private practice, the colonial state made snow a state monopoly in Lima in 1634 and in Mexico in 1719, which yielded the crown a modest annual revenue of 25,000 to 30,000 pesos a year. Ice in Mexico cooled the drinks of the wealthy and was packed into ice boxes to preserve food for those who could afford it, such as the Jesuits in their magnificent convent at Tepozotlán some thirty miles north of Mexico City.

---

[18] *Libro que trata de la nieve y de sus provechos*, Biblioteca Monardes (Seville: Padilla Libros, 1988), pp. 188–206; Defourneaux, *Golden Age*, p. 65.

The rights to provide glacial ice for elaborate banquets or to cool "ante con ante," the flavored wines indispensable for the pleasure of Limeña ladies, were farmed out to contractors. They, in turn appealed to the state for workers. In the province of Huarochirí, just inland from Lima, Indians were provided through the forced labor system of mita. Assigned to the contractor but under the supervision of black overseers, they found their way to the snowy realms, cut the ice and packed it in straw (as in Granada), and hurried down the rocky escarpment to Lima before the fruit of their labor melted on their backs. The ice mita "was more widely hated than any other form of forced labor." The crown monopoly of ice and snow lasted through the entire colonial period, even until 1815, five years into the independence struggle in Mexico.[19]

Separation from Spain did not diminish the taste of ice for those who could afford it. In the first half of the nineteenth century, an enterprising entrepreneur, Frederick Tudor, organized a flourishing trade that carried lake ice from New England in the holds of sailing vessels to Calcutta, Ceylon, and Hong Kong and into the Caribbean and to Rio de Janeiro. Mme Calderón de la Barca seems to have considered the easy availability of ice in the "suffocating" heat of Havana in 1839 completely natural. The ice trade continued until the last third of the nineteenth century when mechanical refrigeration and ice making gradually became available. Still, ice in the tropics remained rare. The opening line in Gabriel García Márquez's *Cien años de soledad* has colonel Aureliano Buendía remembering "that remote afternoon" on the hot Colombian coast, "when his father first took him to touch the ice."[20]

A great many observers, even European travelers accustomed to the excesses of the ancien regime, noticed the enormous difference

[19] C. H. Haring, *The Spanish Empire in America* (Oxford: Oxford University Press, 1947), p. 293; Jean Descola, *Daily Life in Colonial Peru* (London: George Allen and Unwin, 1968), p. 130; Karen Spalding, *Huarochirí: An Andean Society under Inca and Spanish Rule* (Stanford, Calif.: Stanford University Press, 1984), pp. 165, 185); John J. Tepaske, *La real hacienda de Nueva España: la real caja de Mexico, 1576–1816* (Mexico City: INAH, 1976).

[20] *Life in Mexico: The Letters of Fanny Calderón de la Barca*, ed. Howard T. Fisher and Marion Hall Fisher (New York: Doubleday, 1966), p. 24. Gabriel García Márquez, *Cien años de soledad*, 9th ed. (Buenos Aires: Editorial Sudamericana, 1968), p. 9; for the story of Frederick Tudor, see Elizabeth David, *Harvest of the Cold Months: The Social History of Ice and Ices* (London: Michael Joseph, 1994).

between the daily austere diet of the mass of people and the spectacular banquets of Spaniards and creoles in the colonial capitals of Quito,
Lima, Potosí, and Mexico, and the displays of generosity that not infrequently spilled over into sheer gluttony. In fact, simple and austere food
and drink was the rule of daily life even for the colonial elite except
for the (not infrequent) Christian feast days and civil ceremonies.
Perhaps the tradition began in the immediate aftermath of the fall of
Tenochititlan. We have already seen, that from the very first days of
the European occupation, that huge feasts were put together, so coarse
and unrestrained that they scandalized some of the participants themselves. Cortés disorderly feast in 1521 seems to have consisted mainly
of roast pig and barrels of wine. It's hard to imagine that the Tlaxcalan
allies, present for the occasion but standing at some distance from the
main affair, did not provide at least stacks of hot tortillas. But there is
no mention of them or of any other native food.

As we go through the colonial centuries, Iberian cooking filtered
outward from the main cities through mining camps and Spanish outposts in the countryside. Cooks worked local ingredients into familiar
recipes; a hodgepodge stew, the *cocido*, for example, a staple of Spanish
cooking everywhere, incorporated Andean potatoes and maize to create
the *sancochados* and *cazuelas*. Even the quintessentially Peruvian and
seemingly indigenous raw fish, *cebiche*, is inconceivable without the
juice of imported lemons or bitter orange. Indeed, the very word may
derive from the Arabic *sebech*, meaning "acidic food." The Orders of
nuns and the young women they were charged with bringing up
also enriched the culinary life of the American colonies. Famous for
their exquisite pastries and sweets they were also known, in the midst
of vowed austerity, for their elaborate banquets served to important
visitors or colonial officials. The friars as well put out the red carpet.
The gluttonous and dyspeptic Thomas Gage, for example, spent five
months in the Carmelite convent of San Jacinto near Mexico City.
He reports that his stomach begged ceaselessly for food despite the
daily intake of all kinds of fish and meat. Every Monday, dozens of boxes
of *dulce de membrillo* or quince jelly, marmalade, fruit, and pastry arrived
at the door. None of this, however, satisfied his hunger. Orders of
nuns in the new convents established throughout the colonies beginning in the mid-sixteenth century, not only instructed the *niñas
bien* – that is, the creole and at times, mestiza, daughters of the colonial elite in the culinary arts – but also invented dishes of mixed European and native ingredients such as *chiles en salsa nogada* or *mole*

poblano, both to become the quintessential mestizo dishes of present-day Mexican cuisine.[21]

Amid the baroque splendor of seventeenth-century Lima and Mexico and systems of forced labor that helped create it, the creole elite gained a legendary reputation for excess and display so egregious that the crown even issued a series of royal decrees (impossible to enforce) against the "superfluous expense" that creoles lavished on fiestas for their own officials. The viceroys of Lima and Mexico, the king's direct representatives, carried the ancien regime practice of ceremony and feasts across the Atlantic to the New World, providing irresistible models for all who aspired "to live like kings." Around their courts and rituals turned the new gastronomical fashions and routines of display.[22] Gaudy welcoming feasts began with the arrival of a new viceroy in the ports of Veracruz or Callao and continued until his triumphal entry into the capital. Anyone knowledgeable about monarchical progressions through the provinces of England, France, or Spain in the same centuries will readily recognize a familiar practice. In 1696 the count of Moctezuma and Tula passed through the city of Puebla on the road to Mexico accompanied by 199 relatives, a hoard of assistants and servants including sixteen cooks and a dozen pastry chefs. The guests stayed for thirty-six days. The awed and close-counting reporter of this progression recorded that the party was able to ingest 306 sheep, 100 goats, 18 calves, 2 deer, 40 suckling pigs, 12 pairs of pigeons, 80 bulls' tongues, 23 hams, 600 chickens, 100 capons, 48 local turkeys along with fish, 1 barrel of red and 26 barrels of white wine. This rather meat-heavy diet was accompanied by sweets, chocolate, and pastries.[23]

Such a picture of spectacular feasting, on a somewhat lowered scale, can be duplicated many times over in the banquets given by the thin layer of well-off creole landowners, mine operators, and merchants, most of whom built their urban residences hard by the plaza mayor, where they might rub shoulders with the Iberian and creole wealthy. Their display and lavishness were not limited to fellow magnates; their open-handedness occasionally extended to their own workers, retainers, and hangers-on. All was part of the ethos of the "gran señor de

---

[21] *Cocina mexicana*, 4:59; Kathyrn Burns, *Colonial Habits: Convents and the Spiritual Economy of Cuzco, Peru* (Durham, N.C.: Duke University Press, 1999), p. 106.

[22] *Cocina mexicana*, 4:54.

[23] Ibid., 4:54.

tierras e indios," even if, as was often the case, such generosity on Sunday, so to speak, required skimping the rest of the week.

It is one of the apparent ironies that, despite the large variety of new plants and animals introduced from Europe, Africa, and Asia, colonial rule led to a compression of the dietary regime for the shrinking numbers of men and women who continued to think of themselves as, or were considered to be, Indians. Many native American settlements lay off the main road of European intrusion, and consequently their residents were not caught up in the regimes of forced labor or drawn into the urban orbits of the new towns and cities. Those on the outskirts included the still mainly nomadic people on the northern Mexican frontier, residents of the Zapotec villages in Oaxaca, Maya farmers of present-day Chiapas or highland Guatemala, Andean people marginal to the mining economies of Peru, and those such as the Chiriguano of present-day Bolivia or the indomitable "Araucanians" of southern Chile. None of these was entirely untouched by the European advance but most were either unable or unwilling to alter very much their food regimes. The original indigenous staples of potatoes and maize, for example, probably provided a greater proportion of caloric intake at the end of the colonial period and even into the early twentieth century than they had in early years following the European contact.

Creoles – those who either thought of themselves as white, or were white, or wanted to be thought of as white – strained, through the things they bought, to associate with the Spaniards they often resented, and to separate themselves from the mixed races they later aspired to lead. The emerging mixed populations across the board from northern Mexico to Chile accepted more readily the ingredients of the new alimentary universe, such as occasional stews of beef or pork, the truly ubiquitous chicken and broad beans, into the main elements of their ancestral diet. They combined these imports with maize tortillas, beans, chile, pulque, potatoes, ají, chicha, and coca to produce a hybrid food regime. Even such an apparently quintessential dish as Mexico's mole poblano has more ingredients of European and Asian provenance than Mexican.

Between the inevitably blurred and overlapping boundaries that separated European and native strata emerged the mixed populations that would come to constitute the new republics in the nineteenth and twentieth centuries. They were the fundamental carriers of a hybrid material culture. In the beginning, understandably ambivalent about their identities, they, as well as those above and below, sought in part, through what and how they ate, to find their way through a labyrinth of cultural meaning. Food, meals, and ways of eating and drinking provided one arena of contested identity; cloth and clothing, another.

CLOTH AND CLOTHING

Of our three fundamental categories of material culture, dwellings were the slowest to change. Whether because of scant income or taste, people also tend to be conservative about diet. But clothing was another matter. No doubt the pace of change in dress was slower in colonial Latin America than in our fashion-crazed world, but people nearly everywhere were influenced by their neighbor's new weave; they noticed the dress of people at Mass, and picked through new ribbons or adornments laid out in innumerable market stalls. Fernand Braudel's lofty judgment that "to be ignorant of fashion was the lot of the poor the world over . . . their costumes, whether beautiful or homespun, remained the same," seems very much a view from a distance.[24] Close up, there is evidence of constant innovation and adaptation as new techniques, new fabrics, new dyes, or new decorative details appear. These changes may be as subtle as the expansion or contraction of mens' hat brims or the use of tiny silver earrings or shell necklaces, or as obvious as the sixteenth-century helmets adopted by Tarabuqueño men in present-day Bolivia or a wholesale change from wool to cotton by many ordinary people in the eighteenth century.

George Foster, whose *Culture and Conquest* is one of the very few systematic studies of material culture in colonial Latin America, insists that the conventional opinion of many people that folk and peasant culture is strongly conservative and changes little from century to century gives "an utterly false picture of traditional, rural ways of life." Rather, people are "strongly motivated to change by influences that emanate from the city . . . that is, the modes and customs . . . filter down . . . to the level of the proletariat and the countrymen . . . in spite of being reworked to conform to local patterns." The motivation "is prestige; the process of imitation." He continues to say that "clothing – as a visible symbol – is one of the most important cultural categories in which this process works."[25]

[24] Braudel, *Structures*, p. 313.
[25] Foster, *Culture and Conquest*, p. 96.

Change in material culture in colonial Latin America had economic and social ramifications. Apart from food and drink and their impact on agricultural change, this can perhaps be seen best in clothing and textile production and in the Spanish crown's determination to reorder urban and village space.

New clothing fashion called into existence imports from abroad and new modes of production at home, which in turn had far reaching effects on colonial life. In a famous passage, Adam Smith followed out the consequences of the demand for a common woolen coat. It is, he points out, "the joint labor of a great multitude of workmen. The shepherd, the sorter of the wool, the wool-comber or carder, the dyer, the scribbler, the spinner, the weaver, the fuller, the dresser, and many others, must all join their different arts in order to complete even this homely product."[26] So too, in the Indies. The output of colonial textiles created a rippling demand for specialized workers that affected villagers throughout the core areas of the Indies.

To indigenous societies justly famed for their abundant and often exquisite textiles, the invading Europeans introduced not only new tools and equipment but also wool-bearing animals where none was present; in the case of the Andes, they supplemented the camelids, long a source of wool for the inhabitants of high plateaus and valleys. One item alone, the steel shear, must have revolutionized life for Andean herders, whose pre-Columbian techniques for separating the fleece from the alpaca must have been painful to shearer and sheared alike. New varieties and ways of working cotton fiber and cloth accompanied the Europeans to extend the range of possibilities for the comfort and decoration of people throughout America.

Nearly everywhere the Europeans came into contact with native people they found men and women spinning thread and weaving cloth. In the absence of the wheel they used the drop spindle and, from Mexico to Peru, the rudimentary backstrap loom. With this simple equipment the ancient Andean weaver produced some of the most complex and sumptuous textiles the world has ever seen. It is also true that the backstrap loom limited cloth width to about thirty-two inches and production rates were low. In the absence of data from pre-Columbian or colonial times, calculations have been made from

---

[26] Adam Smith, *An Inquiry into the Nature and Causes of the Wealth of Nations*, ed. Edwin Cannan, introd. Max Lerner (New York: Modern Library, 1937), p. 11; Richard J. Salvucci, *Textiles and Capitalism in Mexico: An Economic History of the Obrajes, 1539–1840* (Princeton, N.J.: Princeton University Press, 1987), p. 170.

Figure 4.2. Backstrap loom, Guatemala, 1940s. This is the typical household loom from pre-Hispanic times to the present. *Source*: Courtesy, Latin American Library, Tulane University, New Orleans.

present-day practice. A recent study estimates that with pre-European technology a weaver required some seven to nine days to produce a little more than a square yard of plain cotton cloth. When all members of a household contributed to the various preweaving operations – cotton was cleaned, beaten, combed, and spun, all by hand, of course – they produced some four to five square yards a week. Small wonder it was highly valued. Even in the relatively more abundant material world of eighteenth-century Pennsylvania, cloth and clothing represented the single largest item of household expense for most families.[27] In both ancient Mexico and Peru, specialized groups of women wove distinctive kinds of cloth, thus perhaps achieving some economies of scale.

Within two decades of first contact, the Europeans transferred to America treadle looms, carding boards, spinning wheels, rotary wheels,

[27] Laurel Thatcher Ulrich, "Cloth, Clothing and Early American Social History," *William and Mary Quarterly*, 3rd ser., 53, no. 1 (Jan. 1996): 18, 39–48.

Figure 4.3. *Exvoto de San Miguel en un Obraje Textil 1740*. Spaniards established wool and cotton textile mills throughout Spanish America beginning
in the sixteenth century. *Source*: Painting by Carlos López. Photograph by
Rafael Doniz, Fomento Cultural Bamamex, A.C. Courtesy, Colección Museo
Soumaya.

and other devices for the manufacture of woolen cloth. These encouraged division of labor and "permitted large increases in output" once workers were organized into fairly large workshops, which came to be known as *obrajes*. They were present throughout the viceroyalties of Mexico and Peru wherever a market justified the investment, where sheep were close by, and where workers might be attracted or coerced. The more effective obrajes required running water to drive the fulling mills, a feature that had a major influence on location. Obrajes were consequently concentrated in the Valley of Mexico, the Bajío, and Puebla-Tlaxcala; in the Ecuadorian highlands; and near Cuzco. They were owned by private investors, the religious Orders, and, in Ecuador at least, by Indian communities.

The demand for cotton and wool led to increased plantings in zones of warmer climate and the spread of sheep across the face of the viceroyalty of New Spain and onto the highland or temperate regions of South America. When they made their appearance, Castilian sheep moved easily among Peruvians accustomed to a pastoral economy. Sheep were fairly quickly accepted in Mesoamerica as well, spreading northward into the Bajío and, ultimately, in the eighteenth century to present-day Arizona and New Mexico. With the establishment of textile workshops, wool was incorporated into Mesoamerican dress as alpaca wool had been centuries before in the Andes. If consumers gradually adopted new designs and colors of cotton and woolen fabrics, the technology of obraje production was frozen in the original sixteenth-century mode. Amid the revolutionary changes in textile production that took place in northwest Europe and even in Cataluña, there is no evidence that American obrajes, even such an establishment as the great Jesuit-owned San Ildefonso mill near Ambato (Ecuador) that employed over four hundred workers, introduced anything but the slightest technological change over the three centuries of colonial rule. Nor did the colonial obraje ever eliminate the parallel household and small workshop looms where tens of thousands of native producers adopted some features of imported techniques but also continued to employ the drop spindle and backstrap loom of their ancestors. Obrajes often interacted with peasant production by acquiring yarn from innumerable household spinners in a "putting out" system that seems similar to the proto-industrialization of the Low Countries in the seventeenth century. For that matter, obraje work was often seasonal as villagers tended their crops during the growing and harvest season and then, reluctantly and often coerced, entered the obraje sweatshops, one of the more degraded and oppressed working sites in the colonies, during the rest of the year.[28]

Because of the high price of maritime passage, either from Seville to Veracruz, or higher still to Peru (which required the terrestrial crossing at Panama), only finer cloth with high value relative to weight or bulk was able to bear transportation costs. Freight costs consequently offered protection to colonial entrepreneurs. But, as a rule, obraje owners generally sold their coarser woolens within the small radius of a regional market. In turn, smaller, less efficient chorrillos, deeper in the hinterland, were able to supply a more isolated, smaller market. Locally made cloth circulated in close-by markets, keeping local spinners and weavers – who often combined textile work with agriculture – in business.

The sleepy little district of Belém, twelve days by muleback from Salta, five from Cajamarca, deep in the interior of what is now Argentina, provides a nice picture of such a provincial and modestly successful life. Founded in 1678 by a handful of enterprising artisans and rustic encomenderos (one encomienda had but a single tributary Indian) and isolated by the contraction of colonial trade circuits, the people of Belém, protected by the high freight costs borne by imported cloth, began to make textiles for themselves and the local market from the wool of sheep and the native vicuña and llamas. These were Quechua-speaking settlers; in fact, in 1691 the local priest was transferred out because, not knowing the language and "with great scandal and in prejudice to the people," he heard confessions through a translator. Women spun and wove while men made hats and shoes, carried in the firewood, and drove mules. By the 1770s this artisanal industry supported a modest settlement with a few well-off vecinos. In the house of one of them, a Juan de Castro, lived his wife and son together with nineteen dependents and sixteen hangers-on. Another had a wife and son, "his slave," a dependent and wife, his mother-in-law, and, "among nephews and grandchildren, twelve more." By the later eighteenth century with the development of the port of Buenos Aires and the subsequent reordering of trade routes (before this, Belém had faced northeast, toward Potosí and Lima), imported cloth began to enter the settlement from Spain and even from Italy and Holland, part of a large

[28] Salvucci, *Textiles*, pp. 47–52, 20–31. Manuel Miño Grijalva, *La protoindustria colonial hispanoamerican* (Mexico City: Fondo de Cultura Económica, 1993), especially p. 12. The nature and destruction of the San Ildefonso mill is discussed in Archivo general de Indias, Quito, leg. 403, various folia.

industrial process that swamped Andean textile producers with less expensive, high-quality cloth.[29]

The colonial textile trade flowed into segmented markets: there was a small but lucrative market for luxury cloth from Europe, household production satisfied a large part of the local needs as we have seen in Belém, and obraje output supplied the rest. In the case of New Spain, obrajes accounted for about 40 percent of the total textile market. In rare cases, the very best obraje cloth was competitive with imports in the interregional market. For a time, in the sixteenth century, before the crown banned the trade, woolens from Puebla (Mexico) reached Peruvian markets. The fine woolens of Quito were also traded, throughout the "Andean space," drawn particularly by the wealth of Potosí, but sold as far distant as central Chile. But by the mid-eighteenth century, as larger ships took the Cape Horn passage and thus avoided transshipment across Panama, the now antiquated obrajes, especially those producing woolens, were unable to withstand competition from either the rising tide of European imports or the thousands of cottage industries, revitalized by merchant capital. Obrajes lingered on into the early nineteenth century, never making the transition to industrial textiles.[30] In part, too, the obrajes' decline followed a broad, nearly global shift from consumers' preference for cheaper, more comfortable, and easier to wash cotton in place of wool.

Almost from the beginning of the Spanish regime in Latin America, and certainly by the time the various ethnic strata began to settle out, cloth and clothing became a contested cultural terrain. In 1593 in Quito, one of the major colonial textile centers, an unnamed informant reported to the crown that "the caciques and Indians of this province want to imitate the 'Spanish nation.'" As best they can, they enjoy Spanish usage and form, "dress up, particularly on feast days, in fancy shirts and silk scarves." But since, "as often happens to subordinate people, the local authorities strip them naked, take their clothes and tell them they should wear only cotton."[31] Over a century later as the varieties of cloth became ever more subtle markers, the social meaning of dress is nicely captured by Jorge Juan and Antonio Ulloa in their

---

[29] Esther Hermitte and Herbert Klein, "Crecimiento y estructura de una comunidad provinciana de tejedores de ponchos: Belém, Argentina, 1678–1869," in *Documento de trabajo, no. 78* (Buenos Aires: Centro de Investigaciones Sociales, Instituto Torcuato di Tella, 1972), pp. 1–4, 8ff.

[30] Salvucci, *Textiles*, pp. 135–69.

[31] Archivo General de Indias, Quito, leg. 211, fol. 73.

remarks based on several years residence in Ecuador in the late 1730s. White cotton trousers, promoted by the church in the sixteenth century in the name of decency, were now common. They hung loose at the calf of the leg and accompanied a kind of sacklike shirt and a coarse woolen *capisayo*, or poncho. Together with local hats and sandals, they were universally worn by the common Indians. For everyone else, especially in the mixed race and shifting class categories, changes in fashion were acutely important. The inhabitants of colonial Quito, as elsewhere, seem engaged in a finely tuned struggle for status and identity through subtle but distinctive differences in dress. This began with "the more suitable Indians, particularly the Barbers and Bloodletters who are somewhat set off from the others as they make their breeches out of a fine cotton, wear a shirt bordered by lace four fingers wide, and wear shoes with a silver or gold buckle." For the Andean Indian, hairstyle seemed as important as dress: "for men and women alike, cutting their hair is the greatest offense that can be done to them. They take it as the gravest affront and insult so that, even though they may not complain about corporeal punishment dished out by their masters, they will never forgive them for that."[32]

On the other hand, "all Mestizos cut their hair in order to set themselves apart from Indians." Mestizos in general were marked by cloth cheaper than that worn by creoles or Spaniards, undoubtedly the product of local obrajes. Juan and Ulloa noticed that "the dress of Mestizos is all of local, blue cloth." This is the same indigo-dyed blue wool available, it seems, across the board from northern Mexico to the Andes. As far as economically possible, however, the mestizos strove through lace and silver and gold adornment, to approach Spanish styles. Mestizo women endeavored to dress in the same manner as the Spanish, although they could not equal them in the richness of the material. Shoes, as opposed to sandals, also enabled the caciques to establish difference between themselves and common Indians. Ecuadorian caciques wore essentially the same style of cloak and hat as did the more wealthy mestizos, but they never appeared in public without shoes, "since this made all the differences between themselves and vulgar Indians."[33]

---

[32] Juan and Ulloa, *Relación histórica*, 1:366–70.
[33] Ibid., 1:369; Van Young, "Material Life," pp. 63–5, for remarks about indigo-dyed cloth.

The political and social rivalries between European and American-born Spaniards were expressed in the most subtle detail in dress and adornment. "People of fortune [in Quito] affect great magnificence in their dress, wearing very commonly the finest gold and silver tissues," undoubtedly imported. In the stylized differences in clothing and demeanor represented in the various paintings of the "castas" that appeared in the eighteenth century, hardly any distinction is made between American and Peninsular Spaniards. Yet, more than one Bourbon official complained about creole vanity and display, and several note that the local elite had already in mid-eighteenth century begun to adopt Parisian style. Everyone agrees on the opulence and ostentation of the dress of the colonial elite; even observers such as Amédée Frezier or Alexander von Humboldt, closely familiar with the styles of European capitals, were astonished by the richness of clothing and especially by women's dress in the viceregal capitals.[34]

The crown and the church tried, with predictable failure, to persuade their colonial subjects to attend to "decency" and to wear clothes appropriate to their station. In April 1678, for example, the bishop of Michoacán wrestled with the fact that not only is dress in his diocese "of scant honesty," he is also scandalized that ordinary people and nobles alike dress in silk and other expensive cloth, and both "wear jewelry of gold, silver, and pearls." This "disorder" is even worse among women. And especially among black and mulatto women. A measure of crown frustration may be seen in a 1725 royal decree to the viceroy of Peru pointing out that two years before, an order published and posted under the arcade of the Audiencia or high court of Lima designed "to moderate the scandalous excess of the clothes that Negroes, mulattos, indios, and mestizos of both sexes wear" had little effect. Worse, two female slaves owned by the count of Torres, a judge of the very same court, had torn the order off the wall. The royal decree demands that the order be repeated and if ignored again the law should proceed – against the tailors who made the clothes! Captain Jean de Monségur, a keen observer of commerce and society in early-eighteenth-century Mexico, believed that Creole women there too were enormously given to "an excess of show and ostentation" in their

---

[34] Juan and Ulloa, *Relación histórica*, 2:71; see also the fine pictorial material in J. Vicens-Vives, dir., *Historia de España y América* (Barcelona: Editorial Vincens-Vives, 1961), 5 vols. See especially vol. 4: *Burguesía, industrialización, obrerismo: Los Borbones. El siglo xviii en America.*

dress; but in fact, the "mestizos, indios mulattos, and negras" were even "more addicted to all these kinds of passions."[35]

In the minds of crown officials and clerics an orderly world required hierarchy. Not only should specific ethnic groups have specific obligations and privileges, so too should goods and commodities in America reflect and help maintain the divisions in colonial society. Sumptuary regulations, however, like so much colonial legislation, were inevitably statements of principle, goals to be attained, rather than enforceable laws. We can infer from the documents very little about colonial *practice*, but they do suggest the presence of common anxieties about tensions and conflicts among different social groups. Food, dress, adornment, and dwellings are everywhere markers of status and power, and violations of their use cause disquiet among the forces of order. We need only think of the decrees in our own society against, say, body piercings, or the rules against facial hair on certain baseball teams. But our "sumptuary laws" do not *limit* consumption; they require us to dress "up": "No shirt, no service."

In their efforts to maintain social divisions by decree or to regulate consumption, the Spanish administration was fighting an outgoing tide. By the late colonial era the rosy dawn – or the gathering storm – of capitalist production (depending on whether one was a beneficiary or victim of the system) and the "consumer revolution" in northwest Europe was already on the horizon. In Latin America itself, demographic recovery – a late-flourishing Silver Age in Mexico and the quickening of trade along the peripheries of the old viceregal cores, in Chile, Argentina, western Colombia, and the Mexican northwest – led to greater purchasing power, particularly in the narrow stratum of the slowly growing urban population. Lower maritime freight rates, rising levels of contraband goods, and the British and French insistence that Latin American ports be opened to their trade led to an ever more irresistible array of goods that any legislation would have been impotent to control. Moreover, the very logic of colonial society with its high-stakes scramble for position and survival led people all along the class and ethnic spectra to pick through the material world for those goods deemed necessary and capable of letting them reinvent their ever shifting identities.

---

[35] Cedulario de Ayala, "Real Decreto aprobando un bando del virrey del perú para moderar el exceso en los trajes que vistian los negros, mulatos, indios y mestizos," in Konetzke, *Documentos*, no. 114; Monségur, *Nuevas memorias*, p. 43.

If colonial officials in the later eighteenth century threw up their hands at the impossibility of getting their subjects to dress, drink, eat, and build in accord with their appropriate station in life, they were successful to the point of provoking armed resistance when it came to forcing unwanted goods into the households of unwilling consumers. The forced sale of merchandise, for the simple goal of making money, was practiced in much of Latin America. It has been especially noticed in the viceroyalty of Peru in the eighteenth century. There, Lima merchants, in league with colonial agents in the Andean central highlands, worked out a coercive commercial system that ultimately forced the Indian communities to buy such things as cloth, iron goods, and mules. The colonial officials or *corregidors* had originally, in the sixteenth century, been appointed by the crown to bring royal justice and administration to the colonial provinces. A century later, driven by the ever present need for revenue, however, the state offered administrative positions for sale. By the eighteenth century the practice of buying one's office had become common.

Corregidors bid for, and if successful paid for, their position by borrowing money, often from merchants, sometimes from the church. If, say, the position cost ten thousand pesos at 5 percent for a five-year term, the corregidor hoped to recover his investment and earn a profit through fees charged on judicial or administrative services. Soon, however, it became apparent that trade offered additional possibilities. Merchants, often from the viceregal capital of Lima, advanced on credit bales of cloth or boxes of shears, metal plow points or hoes, carried up on mule trains to the highlands. Other commercial agents arranged for the sale of coca leaves or droves of mules, newly bred in the lush pastures of present-day Argentina, also to be delivered to the corregidor. Taking advantage of his position of authority over the kurakas – the native or mestizo leaders in Indian communities – the corregidor forced the sale of these goods through the kuraka to the villagers at excessive prices, frequently paid for in the form of labor services.[36]

"Forced purchases" or, to use the colonial term, the "distribution of merchandise" has a strange ring to our ears because the goods *we* buy are foisted upon us by more subtle means. And we are wonderfully pliant consumers. For the native people of eighteenth-century Peru, the

---

[36] Among a large literature, see Jurgen Golte, *Repartos y rebeliones* (Lima: Instituto de Estudios Peruaros, 1980); Scarlett O'Phelan-Godoy, *Rebellions and Revolts in Eighteenth-Century Peru and Upper Peru* (Cologne: Bohlau Verlag, 1985).

practice of being made to buy on a schedule not one's own, at unimaginably excessive prices, constituted one of the major abuses of the colonial regime and an important feature in the massive Tupac Amaru rebellion that swept through the Andes in late 1780. Forced consumption also nicely demonstrates the wide industrial and cultural breech between the burgeoning centers of Atlantic capitalism and the scant acquisitive means and peasant values of a distant, different world. While a "consumer revolution" made up of tens of thousands of eager customers in Britain inspired ever greater investment in Lancastershire mills at home, their product had to be driven down the throats of resistant consumers in highland Peru.[37]

Towns and Houses

Had a native American Rip Van Winkle, having dozed off in the early sixteenth century, sprung to life in the later eighteenth and been able to travel across the vast expanse of the Iberian empires in America, which in the later eighteenth century stretched from Upper California to Patagonia, and reflect on the changes that the physical landscape had undergone, some enduring features would have gone unnoticed but he surely would have been full of stories about others. Everywhere the rhythm of daily life remained slow. Seasons and weather with their consequent cycles of abundance and want shaped the lives of nearly everyone. No one anywhere moved about faster than the pace of a horse and the large majority no faster than an ordinary walk. Goods still moved on the backs of long strings of plodding mules along narrow trails; the more important travelers rode on canvas litters whose side poles were attached to the mules' harness. Occasionally, human carriers lugged their individual passengers over mountain paths. Roads suitable for carriage and coach were only found in the environs of the larger towns and cities.

After nightfall, utter darkness still enveloped town and countryside in a blackness nearly unimaginable to our electrified world. Tallow candles provided the cheapest source of light, and their use condemned to death thousands of cattle. No doubt, the candles would be snuffed early in the evening because of their smoke and smell. In some places people lit resinous pinewood torches. Expensive beeswax candles were

[37] Ward Stavig, *The World of Túpac Amaru: Conflict, Community, and Identity in Colonial Peru* (Lincoln: University of Nebraska Press, 1999), pp. 215–20.

only for the better off and whale-oil lamps were still in the future. Our traveler might have remarked on the naked landscape around the great mining centers where trees had been cut to fuel smelting furnaces. The great tropical forests, however, were still virtually untouched, the luminous air above the barely stirring cities still taken for granted.

The changed patterns of settlement, however, along with different construction would no doubt have attracted attention. The towns of Spaniards and Indians alike were now usually aligned on rectangular streets around a central plaza. The large churches or convents built throughout the empire in a time of dense population must have seemed strangely disproportionate, towering over villages just now beginning their demographic recovery. Indeed, the rearrangement of public space and the appearance of monumental constructions far from the indigenous capitals of Cuzco and Tenochtitlan where they were previously concentrated no doubt would have called attention to anyone able to remember the pre-Hispanic years. Within the new towns and cities, some houses and furnishings were clearly more sumptuous than their blocky and crude sixteenth-century antecedents.

The introduction of European tools for carpentry and masonry, such as saws, chisels, hammers, nails, planes, and levels, and the use of the arch created the houses of the better-off residents and transformed the nature of native civil and ecclesiastical buildings. On Inca stone foundations in Cusco, native workers under Spanish direction raised new beamed and tiled houses. Almost always of one low story and built along Mediterranean and Moorish lines, with interior patios and fountains toward off the summer heat, the best Spanish-style houses were decorated with the brilliant flowering of local plants. The exterior walls presented a plain exterior to the street. In Lima, elaborate iron grillwork "clearly separated the aristocracy whose family lived in the interior rooms from the rabble that invaded the streets and public plazas of the city."[38]

This building and decorative tradition, whose elements brought by the Muslim conquests along the desert side of the Mediterranean into Andalusia to merge with Roman patterns, fit nicely with the essentially dry landscape of highland Mexico and Peru. This adaptation contrasts with the Anglo-American insistence on transplanting the lawns and gardens of rainy England even into the arid climates of California and the U.S. Southwest. Had the Spanish conquest originated not from the

---

[38] Alberto Flores Galindo, *Aristocracia y plebe: Lima 1760–1830* (Lima: Mosca Azul, 1984), pp. 78–9.

Figure 4.4. "Mestiza de Riobamba trabajando en su herrería." Woman blacksmith. *Source:* Martínez Compañón, *Trujillo del Perú.* Courtesy, The Bancroft Library, University of California, Berkeley.

hot southern provinces of Andalusia but the rainy and green estuaries of Galicia or the Basque provinces in the north, or had the first Pilgrims come to New England from an arid land, it would perhaps have been a different story. If the Spaniards, however, were sparing with water, they were profligate with firewood. As we have seen, their stoves required ten times the fuel of native kitchens.

By the eighteenth century, the burgeoning silver-mining economies in Mexico and Peru together with richer trade provided income for the construction of many impressive town houses, some occupied today by banks or museums, in Mexico City, Guanajuato, Lima, and Sucre. In eighteenth-century Lima a wealthy merchant built a lookout into the house in order to observe the arrival of ships in the nearby harbor of Callao. Another worked into the facade of his house the prow of a ship. In Peru as in Mexico a well-founded concern for seismic disaster discouraged the construction of buildings over one story. Consequently large rooms with high ceilings were arranged around a central, rectangular patio. In Lima, these were upwind from the slave quarters in the second patio in the back.[39] In provincial capitals, such as Aguascalientes where, for example, the Rincón Gallardo family built, an occasional mansion dominated the main plaza. In the countryside large clusters of sometimes imposing but usually rustic hacienda buildings created focal points for rural sociability. Although discussion of powerful landowners often dominates the history of Latin America, the splendor of their rural estates should not be exaggerated. Their houses did not in any way rival the great manors that dominated the countryside of contemporary England, France, or Spain.

Spaniards of the sixteenth and seventeenth centuries, the Golden Age of Spanish power and culture, transferred to the New World their attachment to fancy carriages, perhaps a more obvious and certainly a more public display, than houses. Carriages were much more than a way to get from one place to another, particularly because roads, rarely adequate even for oxcarts, were remarkably unsuitable for more delicate wheeled vehicles. In Spain, like the Knight of the Sad Countenance and his rustic sidekick, many people traveled by horse or muleback; most walked.[40] Carriages were primarily for show and consequently their owners paid close attention to detail. Craftsmen shaped and polished the fine wood of the frame and box, and fancy fringes of gold- or silver-threaded cloth hung above the doors. The owners emphasized their own aristocratic restraint by outfitting the *lacayos y mozos de silla* – liverymen and driver – in gorgeous costume, the mules brightly caparisoned.

[39] Ibid., p. 79.
[40] Defourneaux, *Golden Age*, pp. 110–11.

The grandest carriages, not a mere *coche* but a galleon-like *carroza* or *estufa*, attracted more attention in a promenade than a Lambourguini might today. Indeed, in one of her wildest reveries, Sancho Panza's equally rustic wife Teresa imagined life at court carried along in a grand carriage, "dazzling the eyes of a thousand envious people" who will wonder, "who *are* those ladies in the coach?"[41] In the cities of America, equally elaborate carriages were thick on the ground. Captain Jean de Monségur, looking out on Mexico City in 1708, saw "many magnificent carriages run through the streets, proportionately in as great a number as in Madrid." Toward the end of the eighteenth century the city had a "thousand coachmen, hundreds of grooms." In Lima, carriages were also of special importance. "The aristocrats showed themselves off in them on Sundays cruising the Alameda that Viceroy Amat had built." The author goes on to say, however, that in the particular case of the coastal landowners, "more than anything else, high status was conferred by the possession of other men: by the number of slaves."[42]

Despite their formidable ability to raise revenue in America, neither the Hapsburg nor Bourbon colonial administrations invested much in public buildings or, for that matter, in roads, ports, or urban improvement. The laborious construction of the great drainage canal at Huehuetoca aimed at preventing floods in the lacustrine basin of Mexico City was a singular and failed effort. The only substantial public construction money was put into the defensive walls protecting Lima from maritime attack or the great fortresses at Cartagena de Indias, at Havana, San Juan, and Veracruz. The Roman arch and techniques of European masonry and carpentry led to improvements over native temples and palaces in interior space if not in sheer size. In several provincial cities a number of solid aqueducts, which still stand, for example, in Morelia and Querétaro, remind one of Spain's Roman heritage. Still, the colonial elite was not distinguished by its architecture, nor did the public buildings of the civil administration impress; in fact,

---

[41] Miguel de Cervantes y Saavedra, *Don Quijote de la Mancha*, ed. Martín de Riquer (Barcelona: Editorial Juventud, 1958), 2:919.

[42] Monségur, *Nuevas memorias*, p. 30; John Kizca, *Colonial Entrepreneurs: Families and Business in Bourbon Mexico City* (Albuquerque: University of New Mexico Press, 1983); Flores Galindo, *Aristocracy*, p. 80. The crown issued a "Pragmática contra el abuso de trajes y otros gastos superfluos" in 1684, and again in 1691 and 1716. This last was designed for the Indies and aimed at curbing the excess in carriages, among other things.

Figure 4.5. "Visita de un Virrey a la Catedral de Méxicol" (Viceregal visit to the Cathedral of Mexico City). Notice the fancy carriages, the opulent dress of Mexico's elite, the bustling stalls of the Parián market on the main plaza. *Source*: Anonymous early-eighteenth-century painting courtesy, Instituto Nacional de Historia e Antropología, Mexico City.

nothing built by the colonial administration was able to overawe its American subjects the way the great houses of Moctezuma or the Incan Coricancha in Cuzco apparently did.

For architecture designed to impress we must look to the church with its hundreds of parishes, labyrinthine convents, massive cathedrals, and wonderful baroque constructions such as the Jesuit churches in Lima, Quito, or Tepozotlan, each costing in the eighteenth century more than a million silver pesos. Whereas the Spanish state strained to extract revenue from its colonies to wage war and pursue European policies, its church plowed back a great lot of its wealth into the American economy. Because today even its most impressive temples are dwarfed by the glass and steel monsters in every city, we can only imagine how impressive the church's towers and bulk must have seemed to people in the seventeenth century.[43]

By the end of the Spanish regime in America we are in the presence not only of a *colonial* material culture, which had introduced a whole range of foreign goods, but also a *Catholic* material culture. The latter required, among other things, that the Christian seven-day calendar, an interval of time not marked by any celestial motion, be imposed on people regulated by different temporal rhythms. This change meant, for instance, a shift from Aztec and Maya decimal periodization, which included a twenty-day month, eighteen-month year. Market days, for example, were now wrenched into a seven-day cycle and fell on the same day of the week all year long. Adjustment took place gradually in the early and mid-sixteenth century. Huitzilpochco, in central Mexico, shifted from the twenty-day to a weekly schedule in 1563; however, Tulanzingo held to twenty-day intervals until the seventeenth century.[44]

With the new calendar came the schedule of church holidays, festivals, fasts, and ceremonies. The basic observances of the ritual calendar – Christmas, Epiphany, Candlemas, Lent, Holy Week, Corpus Christi, All Saints, and All Souls – are the same in America as in Spain but the popular fetes of Spanish folk Christianity did not cross the Atlantic. At times, the celebration of Christian and "heathen"

[43] Adriaan C. Van Oss, *Inventory of 861 Monuments of Mexican Colonial Architecture* (Amsterdam, 1978); Kubler, *Mexican Architecture*; Valerie Fraser, *The Architecture of Conquest: Building in the Viceroyalty of Peru, 1535–1635* (Cambridge: Cambridge University Press, 1990).

[44] Gibson, *Aztecs*, pp. 353–7.

festivals, unwittingly or by design, seemed to overlap. It is not always clear who was subverting whose party. In any case, in requiring that the faithful purchase a range of spiritual goods, that is, to pay for the sacraments associated with masses, weddings, baptisms, and burials that punctuated daily life, the church promoted new rituals of consumption that helped make and maintain social relationships. There is widespread evidence of its success. Juan and Ulloa, for instance, no admirers of the church to be sure, reported that eighteenth-century families in Quito engaged in enormous display at funerals so that "pomp and vanity reached such heights that families were ruined and many fortunes destroyed, all this stimulated by a desire not to be seen as less than the next person. . . . On such occasions one can reasonably say that people work and earn while they live in order to have enough for their funerals." Referring to the use of tithe revenue and other church income, a modern sober assessment is that "the agricultural production of an entire region (the Diocese of Michoacan) went to support the daily liturgical celebration. . . . some 3,250 pesos alone were spent on candles each year."[45]

Local people "from the poorest villagers to members of the local elites took much pride . . . in the construction and decoration of their churches, in much the same way that we are told, medieval Europeans did," and, like them, came to feel a sense of possession. We are less informed on what ancient Andean or Mexican workers may have felt about their work on say, Paramonga or the great temples at Teotihuacan. Ecclesiastical construction also led to a demand for vast quantities of cut stone, bricks, timber, and windows, and for glassmakers, carpenters, and day workers. Petitions for new buildings often made it clear that construction would create new jobs in the community. When agents for the Condesa de la Selva Nevada, for example, urged the crown to permit construction of a Carmelite convent in Querétaro in the eighteenth century, they pointed out not only the undoubted benefits that would derive from the daily prayers of twenty-one young women, but also the salaries that would accrue to "the artisans and workers who build it."[46]

[45] Juan and Ulloa, *Relación histórica*, 1:378; David Brading, "El clero mexicano y el movimiento insurgente de 1810," in Arnold J. Bauer, ed., *La iglesia en la economía de América Latina, siglos xvi al xix*, trans. Paloma Bonfil from the English (Mexico City: INAH, 1986), p. 136.

[46] Van Young, "Material Life," p. 53; the Carmelite foundation is in Archivo general de la Nación Conventos, vol. 18, fol. 160.

Church ceremony and ritual also altered native dietary and dress regimes. Bread and wine were, of course, essential to the Mass and required local production or imports. Franciscans and Dominicans in colonial Guatemala demanded daily *servicio* from native parishioners in the form of European chickens, eggs, and wheat bread. Certain church festivals required the preparation and consumption of special dishes, while the practice of resting on Sunday and the innumerable feast days on the church calendar drew the country people into the head towns where a peasant community's entire yearly savings might be displayed in one glorious burst of fireworks in celebration of the local saint. Moreover, the clergy itself presented a significant demand for specialized forms of clerical dress, some elaborate and imported, that clothed the high clergy, as well as the coarser cloth for the "spreading clerical proletariat" of the eighteenth century.[47]

In many other ways, members of the clergy contributed to the diffusion of new goods. For the inhabitants of tropical America, perhaps no single element in the array of goods made available by the Europeans seemed as valuable as the iron ax. The endless task of beating back the forest with dull, heavy, and easily broken stone axes, tied imperfectly to crude handles, is unimaginable today. With the introduction of the iron ax, it was no small wonder that "the fame of this fabulous metal spread rapidly throughout the forests of tropical America long before the white man penetrated them." The Jesuits in the seventeenth and eighteenth centuries, in effect, traded iron axes in return for converts. Or at least the early success of the Jesuit missionaries "must be attributed to the Indians' fascination with the iron ax." The Black Robes, "were the bearers of this metal as well as the revolution to which it gave rise." From its first introduction, the iron ax not only "transformed the entire rhythm of agricultural work" in the tropics but also became the prize of most subsequent warfare. The colonial Jesuits also were instrumental in commercializing chinchona bark (the source of quinine) as well as yerba mate, the "Jesuit tea."[48]

Into a world of drums, reed flutes, pan pipes, and conch shells producing music that must have sounded dissonant and cacophonic to European ears, the sixteenth-century invaders introduced new

---

[47] Adriaan C. Van Oss, *Catholic Colonialism: A Parish History of Guatemala, 1524–1821* (Cambridge: Cambridge University Press, 1986), pp. 87–8.

[48] Alfred Metraux, "The Revolution of the Ax," *Diogenes*, no. 25 (Spring 1959): 28–40.

instruments and aesthetics. This began at the very beginning. A decree directed to Columbus as he set out for his third voyage to the Indies ordered that he "should carry musical instruments for the enjoyment of the people who are going to be there." From all accounts, native people looked for ways to incorporate new instruments and musical ideas into their culture. For the subsequent five hundred years the negotiation we have seen in other realms of material culture took place in music as well. Indeed, as the post 1960s revival of Andean instruments in the Nueva Canción shows, the process continues today. "Music occupied a central place in pre-Columbian ceremonial life and musicians enjoyed considerable status and prestige."

As time went on, European stringed instruments, which had not existed in pre-Columbian America, together with the range of wind instruments available in early modern Europe, were accepted and became part of the melodic heritage. Small "trumpet and cornet orchestras" performed at civic ceremonies, and the colonial aristocracy undoubtedly enjoyed the occasional sounds of woodwind and strings. Nevertheless, church sponsorship of music remained preeminent. An inventory of the pueblo de la Purísima Concepción, deep in the tropical Moxos province of present-day Bolivia, enables us to visualize the spread of European instruments, often made by local artisans, into the most remote church and *doctrina*. In 1787 Purísima Concepción's storehouse held thirteen violines, four violones, one arpa, three monacordios, two oboes, two clarines, and an organ. Only twelve instruments of pre-Hispanic origin, all of them *chirimias*, a kind of wooden clarinet, remained in the native repertoire.[49]

Finally, it seems likely that the church helped mediate between individuals and the community "in ways now lost to our contemporary sensibilities." In both native American and Mediterranean culture much of "nonwork" life was lived outside the house, in public spaces where people tended to identify more strongly with local communities than we do, sealed in our houses with television and the Internet. Thus, "amongst the most highly valued material things" in colonial Spanish

---

[49] Pareja Ortiz, *Presencia de la mujer sevillana*, p. 164; Guy P. C. Thompson, "The Ceremonial and Political Roles of Village Bands, 1846–1974," in William Beezley, Cheryl Smith, and William French, eds., *Rituals of Rule, Rituals of Resistance* (Wilmington, Del., 1994), pp. 309–10; Lourdes Turrent, *La conquista musical de México* (Mexico: Fondo de Cultura Económica, 1993), pp. 115–75; Mason, *Ancient Civilizations*, p. 234; Archivo general de Indicas, Charcas, leg. 623.

America, were the village plazas and "the objects which filled them," especially the churches and sacred and ritual artifacts. In a hundred ways, Catholic Christianity provided an important organizing whole for the new values of consumption and material culture, present in colonial society.[50]

Let us try to imagine, among the dozens of crown inspectors and curious travelers who came out to the Indies in the later eighteenth century, at the end of the colonial regime, four or five keen-eyed observers as they wait at dockside for the ships that will carry them to Europe.[51] Summing up their experience in a particular region of Latin America, each will return with informed but, inevitably, conflicting reports. Any traveler would surely have been impressed not only by the enormous volume of stone and artwork in the cathedrals, the hundreds of parish churches, the uncounted convents and monasteries, the great baroque jewels of Jesuit churches, but also by the grand opulence of dress and adornment of the high clergy. This same person would have noticed the stolid mansions of the rich, particularly in the mining centers and colonial capitals. He would have noticed the thriving international circuits of trade, the imported goods laid out at the great commercial fairs by wholesale merchants and distributed by retailers throughout the empire. Just as the French captain Jean de Monségur had noticed some years earlier, he would have seen dozens and dozens of fabrics, ribbon and lace, Dutch cheese, Asian silks and decorative panels, elegant stockings, steel, spices, and fancy furniture displayed for sale. Had he gone on to visit the newly independent United States, as Alexander von Humboldt did, he might have looked down his nose at the rustic backwoods quality of that fledgling republic compared with the sophisticated style, flourishing colegios and universities, and luxury goods of Mexico City and Lima. Unaware that the Spanish American empire had but a few years left, he may have concluded that Spanish America was indeed living a Silver Age.

[50] Van Young, "Material Life," p. 53.

[51] In the eighteenth century, they would all have been men. Twenty or thirty years later, in the the first years of the nineteenth century, several remarkable women travelers came out and wrote unforgettable accounts of their experience. Luis González in his wonderful *Pueblo en vilo: microhistoria de San José de Gracia* (Mexico City: El Colegio de Mexico, 1972), ch. 3, employs the device of multiple opinions to better effect than I do.

Another observer, journeying on muleback, away from the colonial cities into the hinterland, would no doubt have noticed how many indigenous ways remained. Several million people in the core areas of Mesoamerica and the Andes still obtained by far the largest part of their daily calories from the ancestral plants of maize and potatoes. People ate from local plates and pots; pulque and chicha were still the favorite consciousness-altering liquids. Clothing was still largely homespun and woven; houses in the small villages and more isolated hamlets – remember that still in the late eighteenth century at least 85 percent of the population lived outside the main cities and towns – were of daub and wattle or adobe and thatch. Nose close to the ground, this traveler might reasonably have concluded that the Iberian overlay was superficial, that "profound" America was still essentially Indian. Perhaps this traveler privately believed that Spanish colonialism had run its course and that those "creoles" (as the local leaders were now called) who talked about separation from the mother country had a point.

A third observer could easily have quibbled with his fellow travelers' views. A true product of the Enlightenment, he would have noticed that after three centuries of European occupation there was present a wider range of plants and animals, the iron ax and plow, and new processing techniques such as mechanical milling, all of which had increased the productivity of agriculture. The introduction of oxen and mules provided traction and carriage to widen the distribution of regional foods. Because there were rarely steady winds in the high plateaus within tropical latitudes, windmills were unreliable. But whenever possible, streams and rivers were dammed, and watermills introduced to reduce to flour the local and European cereals and provide power to stamping mills in the mines.

A fairly wide range of common and even exotic goods might be found in the houses of middling people in most places. The European intrusion, our observer might reasonably have concluded, left its mark on material culture throughout America not only in the households of Europeans or creoles but even among aspiring caciques and kurakas, not to mention within the expanding ethnic layers, then called the castas. In mining centers and on the large rural estates, steel tools of all kinds were adapted to local use; burros and mules replaced human and camelid carriage. Nor would he have been oblivious to the reordering of public and private space, the organization of people around the central plazas of European and Indian towns. His keen eye would surely have discerned that new ritual calendars overlapped with the old. Everywhere were new patterns of consumption. Not one of these opinions, of course, accurately described the material culture of Latin America at the end of the colonial regime, but, taken together, they might stand as a kind of informal, cursory summary of material life in the empire.

Finally, had yet the last of our travelers been able to traverse the entire stretch of the Spanish empire in the late eighteenth century from the Franciscan missions on the upper Rio Grande in present-day New Mexico to the Jesuit outposts in the far south of Chile, she would have been struck not only by the enormous differences now present three hundred years after the European entry, but also by the elements everyone had in common. Certainly, native influence gave different regions a distinctive character, but our traveler would have found the majority of people across this vast expanse speaking at least some Spanish, kneeling down to the same God, and, of course, sharing multiple aspects of a material culture. This was, to say it again, a *colonial* material culture in which the effects of formal, directed changes as well as those brought about as people maneuvered for position within an imposed social hierarchy, all derived from power and ultimately from conquest itself.

In the first decades of the nineteenth century, the overarching structure of the Spanish colonial state and church, which remarkably had more or less effectively held together an array of disparate peoples and interests in a single empire, gave way, leaving a set of impressive ruins suffused with three centuries of cultural residue. Eventually, twenty-two republics emerged out of a painful and contested struggle, led eventually by a liberal creole elite that looked not inward, toward its own people, nor back to its own madre patria of Spain for inspiration, but rather toward the Atlantic powers of France and England for both its culture and its goods. Now, no *formal* directives on dress, no restraints on trade save the tariffs necessary for revenue, no royal decrees on rectangular city planning would shape Latin Americans' consumption. This marvelous social and political construction, "the liberal market," was to be given freer rein – or reign – to allocate the distribution of goods. Yet, the ethnic and class insecurities and anxieties, characteristic perhaps everywhere but particularly of colonial societies, carried over into the postcolonial hierarchy. Are we not really transplanted Europeans? the creoles might ask themselves. Should not the cultural models for the new republics, their reference groups for fashion and consumption, be the "conquering bourgeoisies" of England and France? What social space and new opportunities would the former castas have in the new social free-for-all? New machines and techniques, new houses, clothing, and food, strongly influenced once again from abroad, will be carried along by the tide of modernity within a new hierarchy of postcolonial power.

CHAPTER 5

Modernizing Goods

Material Culture at the Crest
of the First Liberalism

The bourgeoisie, by the rapid improvement of all instruments of production, by the immensely facilitated means of communication, draws all, even the most barbarian, nations into civilization.[1]

Those European customs that . . . have brought us some advantage have caused us on the other hand much trouble. A frenzy for business had not yet invaded us in those bygone days; there was no luxury but there was decency.[2]

The New, Liberal, World of Goods

By the 1830s nearly all of the former Spanish empire in America except for Cuba and Puerto Rico (as well as the distant Philippines) had dissolved into politically independent republics. Making formal a process that had begun earlier and then intensified in the last decades of colonial rule, the leaders of the new American republics established commercial ties with the economic powers of the North Atlantic basin, primarily with Great Britain and France. British and French and North American merchants established themselves in the principle ports and inland cities, merchant bankers extended loans to the new

---

[1] Karl Marx and Friedrich Engles, "The Manifesto of the Communist Path," in Robert C. Tucker, ed., *The Marx-Engles Reader*, 2nd ed. (New York: W. W. Norton, 1978), p. 477.

[2] Manuel Cabral, *Historia de un martyr* (1897), quoted in *Eadweard Muybridge in Guatemala: The Photographer as Social Recorder*, photographs by Eadweard Muybridge, text by E. Bradford Burns (Berkeley: University of California Press, 1986), pp. 71–2.

governments, and an optimistic wave of European investors hoped to revitalize mining and industry. At the same time, hundreds of travelers from all over Europe and the United States flocked into the newly opened ports, eager to explore commercial possibilities. Many published their accounts, which, together with their line drawings and sketches of landscape and people, provide vivid description of the early postcolonial decades.

Along with all this, dressmakers, tailors, perfume shops, hairdressers, and specialty food stores began to promote the fashions and goods of London and Paris in the port towns and main cities. Shortly after Independence, for example, nearly two-thirds of the principle merchants in Valparaiso and Santiago, Chile, were foreigners, mainly British, German, and French. Mme Calderón de la Barca, the Scottish wife of the new Spanish consul posted to Mexico in 1839, noticed in Jalapa, on the road up from Veracruz to Mexico City, some "large and excellent houses, the best as usual belonging to English merchants." We might notice that after three centuries of colonial rule there was still no decent road between Latin America's largest city and its principal port, a distance of a little over 130 miles. Mme Calderón, offered the choice of a seven-day journey by mule-borne litter, chose the five-day bumpy coach ride.[3]

Cotton and woolen fabric made up by far the largest volume of trade in the heady postindependence years. The British alone increased their exports to Latin America from 56 million yards of cloth in 1820 to 279 million in 1840. That would be nearly 10 yards for every man, woman, and child in Latin America that year had the imports been distributed evenly, which of course they were not.[4] Textiles accounted for 95 percent of all imports into Peru during the first decade after independence.

In these early years, the ornery mule must be given a lot of credit for linking the mills of Lancastershire with the Latin American hinterland. Charles Rickets, the enthusiastic British consul in Peru, estimated that in 1825, while the final battles for independence were still raging, some eight thousand mules carried up from Lima to the highland towns over two million pounds of merchandise. They even hauled British carriages and gigs and heavy equipment for the first local fac-

---

[3] J. J. Tschudi, *Travels in Peru*, trans. Thomasina Ross from the German (New York, 1854), p. 23; "Matrícula del comercio de Santiago según el registro de las patentes tomadas en 1849," in *Repertorio nacional* (Santiago, 1850), vol. 2; *Life in Mexico: The Letters of Fanny Calderón de la Barca*, p. 72.

[4] Eric J. Hobsbawm, *The Age of Revolution* (New York: World Publishing, 1962), p. 373.

Figure 5.1. Quinta Waddington, Valparaiso, Chile. The Englishman Joshua Waddington made his fortune in copper mining and trade in the 1830s and 1840s. *Source:* Views of Chile and Peru, The William Letts Oliver Collection. Courtesy, The Bancroft Library, University of California, Berkeley.

tories, pitching and rolling along steep mountain paths. For that matter, when railroad construction began from inland cities, the locomotives and rails themselves were somehow wrestled up from the ports by cart and muleback, as were the engines and disassembled hulls for the first steamboats on Lake Titicaca. Mules hauled German pianos up to Bogotá from the last steamer port on the Magdalena River, while in even more remote Popayán the same instrument was carried "on the backs of Negroes over the mountains." In the absence of carriages, mule-borne litters, and occasionally human carriers, also transported individual foreign travelers from ports to inland towns.[5]

---

[5] Kruggler, "Consumption Patterns," pp. 34–6; Tulio Halperín Donghi, *The Aftermath of Revolution in Latin America*, trans. Josephine Bunsen from the Spanish (New York, 1973), p. 88.

That prices of imported British textiles were actually competitive with local cloth demonstrates a number of things. First, and remarkably, that colonial obrajes owners had not, in the three centuries of their existence, in lands of abundant sheep and potential markets, been able to modernize their mills. Second, that the costs of maritime transport were negligible compared with terrestrial rates; and, finally, that if prices were more or less comparable, consumers inevitably preferred foreign over local goods. There are striking examples of high terrestrial transport costs. In the 1840s merchants on Costa Rica's Pacific piedmont found it cheaper to ship their sacks of coffee eight thousand miles around Cape Horn to European markets rather than traverse the three hundred miles of mountain trails across the narrow country to the Atlantic port of Limón. As another example, the cost to Colombian artisans of shipping their textiles from the then thriving artisan center of Socorro over the mountain to the Venezuelan town of Cúcuta was twice as much as British maritime rates from London to Maracaibo. In 1864 local suppliers and British merchants, coming from very different distances, landed their goods in the inland towns of Venezuela at almost exactly the same price.[6] Despite these early successes, British and North American merchants, persuaded that once the "shackles of Spanish rule" were removed a vast demand would present itself for their goods, overestimated the purchasing power of Latin American customers, who were, after all, still mainly rural and poor.

Only a trickle of Lancastershire cotton cloth, thread and ribbon, inexpensive laces, and simple knives and shears found their way through itinerant peddlars to the hacienda store or mining camp to the popular masses. Cloth, thread, a few pins, a handful of indigo, and three and a half pounds of Brazilian sugar, for example, are the only items for sale on a large Chilean estate in the mid-nineteenth century.[7] Because only a small part of salaries anywhere in rural Latin America in the nineteenth century were actually paid in money, goods together with daily rations of maize or flour and the various "firewaters" (*aguardientes*) were commonly advanced against the promise of labor. Consequently, despite modest success, the high hopes that European merchants originally held for a mass market, did not materialize. Within two or three

---

[6] David Church Johnson, *Santander siglo XIX: cambios socioeconómicos* (Bogotá: Carlos Valencia Editors, 1984), p. 155.

[7] "Tienda de Cunaco," in Arnold J. Bauer, *La sociedad rural chilena desde la conquista española a nuestros días*, trans. Paulina Matta from the English (Santiago: Andrés Bello, 1994), app. v.

decades the early market for textiles was saturated; further trade would require investment in transportation and, above all, sources of earnings to pay for foreign goods.

We must keep in mind that Latin American provincial towns and even the national capital cities were small from today's perspective and certainly not grand in the eyes of mid-nineteenth-century travelers who came out from Paris or London. Paris in midcentury had some 1.2 million inhabitants; London counted twice that number. In midcentury, the two largest cities in Latin America, by contrast, were Mexico City with just under 200,000, Rio de Janeiro's 180,000, and Havana with nearly 110,000. Santiago de Chile, now over 4 million had then but 90,000, Buenos Aires a few less, Lima but 72,000, Bogotá only 40,000. Away from the capital cities one came to provincial towns, not one in Peru, for example over 25,000, or a single one in Colombia over 15,000.[8] Still, where the entrepreneurial spirit was high, where city folk began to have a bit more money in their pockets, and the hinterland towns were within reach of mule trains, cart roads, or later, of course, railroads, the flow of goods from the Atlantic economy slowly became apparent in local stores. In the Peruvian town of Huaráz, for example, French and English hosiery, linens, broadcloth, and cutlery were offered for sale while a place like Huánuco, close by the mining center of Cerro de Pasco, had, already in the 1850s, silk handkerchiefs, hats, and quite a wide range of other European imports. So, although the urban market for local or imported goods was scant, from midcentury onward between the sophisticated tastes of the urban-dwelling landowner, merchant and mining elite and the 85 percent of the population still rural, a small but ever expanding layer of middling consumers emerged in the cities and provincial towns.[9]

Often insecure and tentative about their niche in the developing republican social scheme, these new clusters of people that later will be called – and, later yet, call themselves – a middle class sought through consumption and behavior to distinguish themselves from the unwashed rural mass while groping for marriage and membership in the still essentially white elite. The new scramble for place occurred in the quickening economic currents of the Atlantic economy and amid the working out of new ideologies, as the Latin Americans who

---

[8] Richard Morse, ed., *The Urban Development of Latin America, 1750–1920* (Stanford, Calif.: Latin American Center, 1971).

[9] Kruggler, "Consumption Patterns," p. 34.

emerged as leaders in the new republics undertook the business of liberal modernization and nation building.

This ambitious project required that the *barbarie* unleashed by the destruction of colonial rule be tamed and that a new citizenry be formed in accordance with the "civilized" standards of Western bourgeois models. Moreover, daily life in the towns and cities began to change. New opportunities and challenges appeared every day for even the provincial urban dweller. Social activity crept out from the dark and musty thick-walled houses into the streets and plazas, into theaters and cafés, to racetracks, restaurants, and tea-dance salons where business-men, housewives, middling professionals, and property owners, them-selves in uncertain relations with the traditional elite, might, worse yet, be mistaken for a dressed up rustic or honest worker.

The fear of confusion was clearly present since midcentury cities still had a rural air. Every morning the streets filled with crowds of vendors from nearly farms. There were "peons from the country with panniers and baskets of fowl, fruit, and vegetables; bakers and milk-women, droves of water-vendors selling their daily supplies from the turbid foun-tains, men enveloped up to their nostrils in bundles of alfalfa."[10] At the top of the social order stood a self-styled creole aristocracy clustered in a dozen square blocks hard by the plaza mayor. Often claiming descent from late colonial landowners and noble families, the republican elite was nevertheless guardedly open to new talent and money. How were the new middling but *decente* town and city folk to navigate these uncharted social waters?

Among a handful of other manuals and books of etiquette, a remark-able guide to urbane manners appeared exactly when it was most needed. Manuel Antonio Carreño's *Manual de urbanidad y buenas maneras*, is surely one of the books, if not *the* book, most widely sold to Latin Americans in the history of Latin America. First available in Caracas in 1853, by the 1870s it had gone through seventeen (Spanish-language) editions published in Paris. In New York City, by the end of the nineteenth century, the same Spanish-language text ran through twenty-five editions. My own volume (Mexico: Editorial Patria, 1987) is from the forty-first edition.[11] Nearly all other Latin American coun-

---

[10] J. M. Gillis, *The U.S. Naval Astronomical Expedition to the Southern Hemisphere during the Years 1849–50–51–52* (Washington, D.C., 1855), vol. 1 (Chile).

[11] Manuel Antonio Carreño, *Manual de urbanidad y buenas maneras*, 41st ed. (Mexico City: Editorial Patria, 1987).

tries brought out their own countless editions, sometimes simplified for childrens' use, sometimes updated in later editions to demonstrate the appropriate "buenas maneras" in such places as elevators and streetcars, not known in Carreño's day.

Carreño himself (1812–74), was the son of a well-known musician and composer and for a time earned his living as a piano teacher and translator of English. Devoted to his daughter for whom he sought out the best music instructors, and perhaps also impatient with the "gross, uncivil, disgusting, and repugnant" manners of the class he tried to avoid in Venezuela, he moved to New York in 1862 and died in Paris twelve years later.

The Manual is clearly aimed at the incipient "middle sectors." There is no mention of peasants or rural villagers or any instruction for "others of greater respectability than us." Curiously similar to the behavioral prescriptions we earlier saw laid down by Bishop Talavera to the new converts of Granada if they were to be acceptable to "los Cristianos de nación," Carreño provides rules for membership in the new, modernizing liberal order. He tells his compatriots how to attend to personal cleanliness; how to eat, walk, speak, and move the body; whose glance to catch; when to look away. He employs his favorite adjectives – disgusting, intolerable, gross, vulgar, repugnant – to condemn a long list of repellent bodily functions such as sneezing, snoring, stretching, blowing one's nose, yawning, belching, biting one's nails, applauding, spitting, scratching (particularly under one's clothes), or gazing at others.

The Manual reflects the material world of midcentury. We see, because Carreño can't bear it, that his neighbors use toothpicks: "a ridiculous custom, inappropriate for refined people."[12] They also brush their teeth – or at least they're supposed to. They always have a handkerchief handy and have elaborate table settings with a variety of knives and forks (four-pronged "good," three-, "uncivil"). Clothes should be changed at least "twice a week, underwear more often," and "people of society always wear clean and polished shoes." Men should wear tie and jacket, socks and shoes indoors, and never go about in shirtsleeves, which must help explain his constant preoccupation with

[12] Only two decades earlier, on Wednesday, November 13, 1839, after the most elegant, aristocratic dinner in Havana, Fanny Calderón de la Barca noticed that "toothpicks were handed round to the guests, ladies and gentlemen; coffee, etc." Life in Mexico: Letters, p. 21. One wonders how workers made handmade toothpicks.

Figure 5.2. "Los hacendados de Bocas," a nineteenth-century family aspiring to the "decencia" advocated by Manuel Antonio Carreño. *Source:* Painting by Antonio Becerra Diaz. Photograph by Rafael Doniz. Fomento Cultural Banamex, A.C. Courtesy, Colección: Casa de la cultura de San Luís Potosí.

sweat and the attempts to remove it, which always "excite an invincible disgust in others." A slight quickening of the midcentury commercial pace can also be discerned. Although men and women are to carry themselves in the streets with decorum and moderation, businessmen, *los hombres de negocio*, may step out a bit during working hours. Nor is anyone merely to drop by a business office to chat idly. Time is beginning to be money.

Writing at time when most houses still kept to the Mediterranean design of interior patios with tall, deep, grillwork windows that gave directly onto the street, Carreño devotes several pages to that private space because "the window is one of the places in which we must manage ourselves with the greatest circumspection." His strictures are directed to the females of the household. They should not sit in the windows except in late afternoon or evening; speak only in a low voice; exhibit only modest laughter; do nothing that might lower one's dignity. At no time is it "decent" nor well seen that a woman appear in the window talking to a man not her relative. Nor should she read in the window lest people interpret this as ostentatious display or a false interest in literature. "All affectation," as Cervantes also put it, "is bad."

In the end, the *Manual de urbanidad y buenas maneras* is a catechism for the still small urban middle sectors – in the mid-nineteenth century, a class in formation. Its primary values are moderation, decorum, and, particularly, *decencia*. Judging from the hundreds of thousands of copies sold, these values obviously struck a resounding chord among the emerging ninteenth-century bourgeoisie and, in fact, have endured until recent years. Like Domingo Sarmiento's better-known *Facundo* (1845), Manuel Antonio Carreño's book aims to set out the "central axiom of modernization, the passage from barbarie to civilization."[13]

Latin American exports of food, fiber, and minerals began to flourish from the 1870s on with the subsequent increase in local investment and generally higher salaries and wages among those sectors connected to the export economy. Consequently, the list of manufactured imports lengthened along with an increased demand for local produce. Dramatically reduced freight costs, brought about by the appearance of rail and steam, help explain the faster pace of economic activity. Even though railroad construction was in the beginning sporadic and discontinuous, its effect was quickly felt and, together with falling maritime rates, made imported goods of all sorts more readily available, particularly in the cities and provincial towns. State and private investors, at first, insisted that railroads run from mines and plantations or estancias outward to export the copper, tin, coffee, sugar, wool, wheat, and beef for the world market. These lines therefore were

---

[13] Beatriz González Stephan, "Escritura y modernización: la domesticación de la barbarie," *Revista Iberoamericana* 60 (Jan.–June 1994): 1–22. I have drawn heavily from Ms. González's excellent article in this section. For biographical details, see *Diccionario de historia de Venezuela* (Caracas: Editorial ExLibris, 1988), 3:587.

frequently not suitable for the carriage of imports *into* the older interior cities and their agricultural hinterlands. Ox carts, mule trains, and human carriers consequently remained important, picking up goods at the railheads where the trains left off well into the twentieth century.

Inventories in Peruvian stores now included hardware and tools, many previously handmade; steam engines and machinery; specialty food items that now included tinned fish and French wine, English beer, all manner of cloth and clothing, pins and needles, curtains, and the first ready-made shoes and boots from England, Italy, and the United States, as well as shoe polish, looking glasses, building timbers, marble, and glass. Some of these items show up in store inventories as early as the 1860s, even in such fairly remote towns as Jauja and Cerro de Pasco. Two decades later the list expands, and we see not only bicycles, typewriters, rifles, and pistols but coaches, buggies, diligences, and shays.

Cycles became something of a rage in the later nineteenth century. Actually, the first were tricycles, the French velocipede, imported from Paris, and a similar machine from Boston into Mexico City in 1869. By 1880, the high-wheeled bicycles, "famed for the headers taken by riders when they were hurled over the handlebars," came in from the United States. Thereafter cycling clubs and racing teams spread through the main cities of the country, popular among the still small urban sector but "sneered at" by what a journalist member of the Porfirian elite called "the lower part of the population." The bicycle, another symbol of modernity in the blossoming belle epoque of Porfirian Mexico nudged along a certain transformation of women's fashion. Young women "looked upon the sport as an opportunity for a freer life," riding off in the company of an up-to-date gentleman, leaving their chaperons behind, dressed in clothing more appropriate for riding, including the "daring bloomer costume."[14]

A great many consumers goods used in daily life are not so visible to the ordinary citizen as bicycles and bloomers. Any good hardware store today carries literally thousands of different items that only trade specialists such as carpenters, plumbers, or appliance repair people might ever be concered with. The rise of a mechanical culture requires the use of steel cables or wire in place of leather straps, nails and bolts in place of wooden pegs, rivets for steam boilers, hinges and locks, all

[14] William H. Beezley, *Judas at the Jockey Club* (Lincoln: University of Nebraska Press, 1987), pp. 44, 50–1.

kinds of special tools, drillbits, screws – one might go on infinitely. All of these things, invisible to most people, began to stream into the new *ferreterías*, whose name itself reflects the passage from colonial leather and wood to the iron age. The Colombian writer, statesman, and visionary Miguel Samper noticed all these little things in stores during his walks through Bogotá in the later 1860s and wondered why they couldn't be made in Colombia at a third the price of imports. Did he not wonder even more why Colombians, long experienced in agriculture and the use of horses, imported their axes, machetes, hoes, rude plows, and scythes as well as their spurs and fetters?[15]

Most of these new manufactured goods, from bicycles and bloomers to hardware and plows, were the result of the inventiveness and productive capacity of the already industrialized nations of northwestern Europe and the United States. They ended up in the hands of a still quite narrow band of consumers; residents of port cities or those cities linked to the outside world by rail or fluvial transport, such as Lima, Bogotá, Mexico City, Santiago, or Buenos Aires, absorbed most of the new imports. Smaller towns usually had but two or three substantial dry goods or general stores (*lencerías y mercerías*) often owned by foreigners. Local merchants had their own stores and laid out their goods in the inevitable retail stalls in arcades around the main squares. Luis Valcárcel reminds us in his evocative *Memorias* that even in such an important provincial capital as Cusco as late as 1905 potable water was carried from a league away; there were no sewers, no gas or electric lights; and only six or seven of the central streets had kerosene lamps, lit at dusk and extinguished at nine or ten in the evening. At the turn of the century Cusco had fewer than twenty thousand people, less than half of whom spoke Spanish as a first language. Here the rare Viennese chair or sofa, the odd piano, perfumes, and fine cloth were still brought by mule train (the railroad came in 1908). The small Cusco elite now and then displayed a treasured English ham, dark German beer or Champagne, or canned fruit, which only came out at fancy dinners and banquets.[16]

We can see that the new commerical relations with the industrial countries of the North Atlantic enabled Latin Americans to import

---

[15] Miguel Samper, "Bogotá in the Nineteenth Century," trans. Sharon Kellum from the Spanish, in Gil Joseph and Mark Szuchman, eds., *I Saw a City Invisible: Urban Portraits of Latin America* (Wilmington, Del.: S&R Books, 1996), p. 115.

[16] Luis E. Valcárcel, *Memorias* (Lima: Instituto de Estudios Peruanos, 1981), pp. 35–46.

goods unimagined a century earlier and to encourage an appetite for European models of consumption, but it is also true that the beginning of foreign and local investment permitted the import of capital equipment and the infrastructure to manufacture locally a lengthening list of goods, which now began to appear in stores and markets alongside imports. With the increasing world demand for Latin American commodities in the last third of the century, export earnings led to increased local investment and the further development of local industry.

Until fairly recently, lack of research on one hand and the ideological requirements of the "dependency" theorists on the other encouraged the idea that the global depression of 1930 marked the dividing line in Latin American industrial development. Before that time, many believed, free-trade policies with undue emphasis on "development toward the outside" had provided little encouragement for local entrepreneurs. In this view, not until the collapse, or at least the severe setback, of world capitalism after 1930 did tariff protection, public investment, monetary policies, and a number of other measures provide an appropriate environment for industrial growth. But recent study has altered this picture. Although the attraction of "free trade" was strong in principle, the need for customshouse revenue, the political weight of local artisanal groups, and the insistence on tariff protections or special concessions by enterprising Latin Americans themselves meant that complete free trade was never fully attained in practice. So, in fact, there was a gradual, light-industrial development, beginning in the middle of the nineteenth century, which gained a certain momentum toward the end of the century. Consequently, the policy of export-led development from the 1870s into the 1920s was not necessarily opposed to the internal growth of manufacturing; rather, export earnings often made it possible. Thus, at the crest of the first liberalism, a still fairly limited segment of Latin American consumers could pick through the goods available not just from import houses but from stores selling the products of local workshops and factories as well.

Cotton textiles made up the largest part of industrial output in Latin American countries. Mexico's first industrialists installed mechanical spinning and weaving machinery by the 1830s. A half century later, some one hundred factories put out over a hundred million meters of cotton cloth. The largest, the Compañía Industrial de Orizaba, employed over four thousand workers. A smaller but still impressive three-block-long Porfirian mill, in Uruapan, Michoacán, still limps along finding a narrow niche for speciality cloth in the modern economy. With its rows and rows of now mostly idle mechanical looms and carding and spinning machines, all imported from Great Britain in the 1880s, the "Antigua Fabrica de San Pedro," looks like a ghostly survivor from Lancastershire.

Mexico's cloth manufacture in fact, was impressive. Brazil, with 7.2 million people, had a textile sector about a third its size. The Peruvians, known for a sizable colonial industry and for that matter famed for cloth making centuries before the sixteenth-century European invasion, were slow to develop modern textile manufacturing. In 1861, for example, the wealthy Garmendia and Nadal families of Cuzco had French machinery for a new textile mill hauled up from Islay on the Pacific to their hacienda in Quispicanchis near Cusco. This was the first modern factory in the south highlands and aimed to compete with the coarse woolens made by the local Indian peasants for local markets. The former colonial obrajes seem not to be competitive at all. Soon after, imported machinery for textile manufacture appeared in nearly all other Latin American countries to offer some competition in the market that lay between imports and the diminishing homespuns.[17] New mills near Concepción in southern Chile or those that arose under Palestinian guidance in Bolivia are examples that could be repeated elsewhere after the turn of the century.

The opening of internal markets by the extension of railroads changed the geography of production. Iron rails lay behind the appearance of more modern national textile and flour milling industries, and because railroads carried coal for steam engines in the new factories and mills, neither were dependent, as they had been, on hydraulic sources for power. Producers of furniture, housewares, and food-processing plants, including the manufacturers of noodles and various pastas, came into existence. Spaniards, who were primarily wine drinkers, introduced beer in the very beginning of the colonial period. But native Americans and their mixed offspring preferred their own chichas or pulque or the innumerable cheap aguardientes that became popular in the eighteenth century. Moreover, beer is perishable and until refrigeration and reliable transport were worked out in the last third of the nineteenth century, breweries were small and supplied a restricted

---

[17] See Stephen H. Haber, *Industry and Underdevelopment: The Industrialization of Mexico, 1890–1940* (Stanford, Calif.: Stanford University Press, 1989). I visited the Antigua Fábrica de San Pedro on August 9, 1999, as the guest of its owner, Mr. Walter Ilsley. Kruggler, "Consumption Patterns," p. 36.

Figure 5.3. Cervercería Cuauhtémoc. Late-nineteenth-century brewery in Monterrey, Mexico. *Source:* Courtesy, Cervercería Cuauhtémoc. Monterrey, Nuevo León, Mexico.

radius of consumers. Mexico, for example, had fairly small-scale breweries in several cities – twenty-nine in all by 1901 – but with the help of German brewmasters, refrigeration, better roads, and heavy capital investment, three giant operations, the Cervercerías Moctezuma, Cuauhtémoc, and Modelo, came to dominate the industry. In a similar manner the breweries at "Quilmes" and "Lomas de Zamora" outside Buenos Aires or the "Antártica" in São Paulo, grew with the spectacular population growth of those cities and by World War I were among the largest breweries in the world. As many of us delightfully remember, long before the North American Free Trade Agreement (NAFTA) of 1994, the superior quality of their beer enabled Mexicans to place such brands as Dos Equis, Bohemia, and Tecate in the U.S. market, a rare example of the successful export of a manufactured commodity to this country.[18]

Railroads not only provided better transport, they inspired some entrepreneurs to industrial activity. In Chile, local foundries made hundreds of trolleys and, more impressively, in 1887 made thirty freight cars and six locomotives that, in the eyes of an enthusiastic contemporary, "would be creditable to any maker in the United States of England." So, although the years before 1930 reveal a certain degree of industrialization, this was mostly to produce consumer, not capital goods. For example, the fact that only 3 percent of the Columbian work force before 1930 was engaged in industry reminds us that in many regions development was scant.[19]

Export earnings also led to the import of machines and tools for the modernization of the sugar and coffee export sectors and enabled some landowners to consider the new range of agricultural equipment – harvesters, threshers, mowers, plows – now available from the industrialized countries. Sugar production underwent a fundamental change after 1870 as English and German technology, developed for beet sugar in their countries, was applied to cane in the tropics. This revolutionized the industry from the Brazilian Northeast, to Salta, Argentina, along the Peruvian north coast to Morelos and throughout the Caribbean and led to ever greater concentration into enormous *central* mills together with a large demand for seasonal workers. By the 1920s, Cuba, with its

---

[18] Haber, *Industry and Underdevelopment*, pp. 4, 85–6.

[19] Cited in Oscar Muñoz, *Crecimiento industrial de Chile, 1914–1965* (Santiago, 1968), p. 17. Colin M. Lewis, "Industry in Latin America before 1930," in Leslie Bethell, ed., *The Cambridge History of Latin America* (Cambridge: Cambridge University Press, 1986), 4:267–324, provides a useful overview of this subject.

huge American- and Cuban-owned mills, produced over 20 percent of the world's sugar and drew thousands of Haitian and Dominican cane cutters into a precarious existence in the countryside.

Agricultural mechanization proceeded much more slowly. Although *agricultores progresistas* in several countries introduced reapers and mechanical threshers as early as the 1850s, they were reluctant to invest in equipment prone to break down, because spare parts were scarce and, above all, a mechanical culture among rural workers was largely absent. With the exception of Argentina, not until the 1920s does one find very many of the mechanical innovations, long common in western Europe and the United States. All of this – factories, ports, railroads, steam transport on river and lake, agricultural machinery – changed the structure of supply for those items of material culture we have been following in this essay. As one moved out from the larger towns and cities into the countryside, which to a new urban generation now appeared ever more rustic, the volume and variety of goods imported from the burgeoning Atlantic economy or drawn from local industry or from artisans, who tended to cluster in the larger cities, became less and less available.

The change from colony to republic had only scant effect on the diet of millions of ordinary rural people who still made up some 80 to 85 percent of the total population of Latin America into the last third of the nineteenth century. In the low thatch and adobe buildings of hundreds of villages, in the rustic shacks clustered in the shadow of the large estates, in scattered rancherías, or in the isolated dwelling on the vast pampas, men, women, and their families continued silently to eat their ancestral meals, centered on tubers in the Andes, manioc on the tropical littoral, and maize in Mexico and central America. The large mass of villagers, estate workers, and smallholders as well as the large number of *jornaleros* and *albañiles* (day workers and construction workers) who followed the harvests and construction sites kept fundamentally to their diet, present for at least two millennia in Mesoamerica, of maize, beans, chile, and pulque; potatoes, coca, and chicha in the Andes; and manioc on the tropical littoral.

Supplemented from time to time with a portion of other vegetables and fruit, in some cases small amounts of *mote* (soaked wheat) or barley gruel, occasional animal protein from backyard chickens, pigs, guinea pigs, and charqui, and the inevitable aguardiente on feast days, these made up the foundation of an ordinary rural person's diet. In fact, there is evidence to suggest that maize and potatoes made up a larger proportion of the ordinary Mexican, Guatemalan, or Andean meal in 1900 than it did in pre-Hispanic times. Obviously some items of Asian and European provenance found their way into native food regimes; still, a careful study of the several hundred workers on El Maguey hacienda in Zacatecas between 1820 and 1880 shows that 75 percent of the basic human energy needs came from maize. Because this was a livestock estate, mainly sheep, more meat than one normally sees, was present in the peon diet.[20]

The weight of custom can be seen in late-nineteenth-century Chiapas where German coffee plantation owners tried, with scant success, to persuade the migrant Maya peasantry to eat tortillas made by the very first *molinos de nixtamal* rather than the metate-ground, comal-baked product of their own households. But elsewhere in central Mexico, hacendados bowed to custom and even hired a *tlacualero*, or food carrier, to make the rounds of individual village households, gather from each woman the tortillas she herself made, and deliver them to her husband or son in the fields.[21]

In Peru and Bolivia it is hard to find any important effect of the entire cycle of liberal import economy on ordinary rural diet. A detailed study of agricultural workers on the Bogotá plain at the end of the century laments a decline in variety from the eighteenth century. *Mazamorra*, here a potato and onion stew thickened with cornmeal, and huge jars of maize chicha provided nearly all the caloric intake of common peons. Ordinary Chilean campesinos, reflecting the Mediterranean overlay in that temperate land, continued their daily intake of *harina tostada*, maize, and *porotos* well into the twentieth century.[22] Obviously, one can find exceptions to this conventional picture. Even ordinary people along the track of the new railroads or on the fringe of the spreading towns and cities found ways to supplement a plain diet with occasional sugar, coffee, and chocolate. Exceptions can be also

[20] Harry Cross, "Living Standards in Nineteenth Century Mexico," *Journal of Latin American Studies* 10 (1978): 8–9.
[21] Karl Kaerger, *Agricultura y colonización en México en 1900*, trans. Pedro Lewin and Dudrum Dohrmann from the German, introd. Roberto Melville (Mexico, 1986), pp. 164, 251. This work was orginally published in two volumes in Leipzig in 1900; Oscar Lewis, "Social and Economic Change in a Mexican Village," *América Indígena* 4, no. 4 (Oct. 1944): 304.
[22] Manuel Cotes, *Régimen alimenticio de los jornaleros de la Sabana de Bogotá* (Bogotá, 1893): pp. 31–2; Bauer, *Sociedad rural chilena*, pp. 181–92.

found among those workers recruited into the new banana or sugar plantations throughout tropical America. Exporters often found it cost-effective to supplement their workers' diet with tinned fruit or sacks of flour brought from Boston or New Orleans on the return journey rather than rely on uncertain local supply.

Attire was a different matter. From the eighteenth century when British and French ships began to unload a few bales of cloth onto the docks at Veracruz, Callao, and a dozen other ports, Latin Americans revealed their vulnerability to both the advanced textile industries of western Europe and an accelerating enthusiasm for fashion. This meant, to the delight of the new merchants, that not only were better-off men and women attracted to new dictates of fashion from abroad but, more important, they accepted a pattern of periodically changing styles, then less common but now a sacred annual ritual for early-twenty-first-century consumers. With independence, the trickle of imported textiles became a flood as the relentless tide of Lancastershire cottons at first met little competition from local manufacturers. Foreign cloth filtered into the countryside through local markets, itinerant peddlers, and the stores present at the larger mines or on most larger haciendas. Deep in the provinces where they were protected by the high cost of carriage, local spinners and weavers made cloth for their own households and laid out the surplus for exchange in local markets.

The infamous colonial obrajes, introduced by the Spaniards in the sixteenth century from Querétaro to Quito, some of which employed hundreds of workers, had already been dealt a blow by eighteenth-century French and British imports. By the 1840s they simply faded away like colonial ghosts in the glare of the new commercial sunrise. English cloth moved quickly through the cities and provincial towns and, to an extent, into the countryside. Even the Mexican woman's shawl or *rebozo*, by the late nineteenth century an indispensable possession, was made from imported cloth, inevitably dyed blue or gray. At the same time British factories strained to imitate and sell traditional garb such as the sarapes of Saltillo or Argentine ponchos. Looms of the old obrajes near Cuzco, says a character in a local novel set in the 1840s, "only served as hen roosts." By the 1860s, a keen French observer noticed that even humble women in the Chilean countryside had begun to "cover themselves with the cotton cloth the foreigners – above all the English – bring in at low prices." This pattern for cotton textile imports and a bit later for woolens as well, can be confidently extended across Spanish America.[23]

The effect of the new roads and railroads and the imports they carried, together with the new textile factories established nearly everywhere in Latin America in the course of the later nineteenth century, was widely felt on consumers and producers. Prices fell across the board, bringing cheap cloth, indeed, a range of new fabrics, within reach of all but the poorest, but at the same time a great many local spinners and weavers lost their trade. In the central provinces of Chile, for example, they numbered 35,068 in the 1854 census but only 4,431 in 1895. The falling prices of British imports also dealt a reeling blow to the female hatters and weavers of Santander, Colombia. Deeper in the provinces, households employing one to four looms operated by the uncalculated cost of family workers were protected from imports by the absence of rail or cart roads and the poverty of markets. These spinners and weavers continued to hang on, making a coarse woolen cloth for local use. In remote villages in Azángaro province in highland Peru, for example, neither imported cloth nor ready-made goods found a market. The cheapest cloth was made in small domestic clothing workshops, while the handful of better-off families "continued to rely on seamstresses and tailors for their dresses and suits." Other local artisans continued to make specialty items such as traditional dresses and hats, a narrow market that offered scant attraction to factory producers.[24]

Visual evidence, seen in the sketches and paintings and then in the photographs, which tend to replace them in the 1860s, show a variety of dress throughout village and countryside so great that it resists easy classification. The loose shirt and trousers of unbleached cotton adopted in the first colonial century remained the classic dress of Mexican campesinos. By the nineteenth century, they aimed to wear the most expensive hats they could afford, at best a heavy, hot, felt sombrero; and, if not, a straw substitute. "Whatever the material, the

[23] Kruggler, "Consumption Patterns," p. 56, citing the novel by Narciso Aréstegui, *El padre Horán* (Cusco, 1848); for Chile, Claudio Gay, *Historia física y política de Chile: Agricultura* (Paris, 1862–5), 1:163.

[24] Arnold J. Bauer, "Industry and the Missing Bourgeoisie: Consumption and Development in Chile, 1850–1950," *Hispanic American Historical Review* 70, no. 2 (May 1970): 232–3; Johnson, *Santander*, pp. 143–58; Nils Jacobsen, *Mirages of Transition: The Peruvian Altiplano, 1780–1930* (Berkeley: University of California Press, 1993), p. 170.

broader the brim and the taller the crown, the more admired the som-brero."[25] Indian peasants of the Andes covered themselves with the inevitable poncho, some of gay colors, others drab. In the high eleva-tions they generally preferred the wool, pullover cap with ear flaps against the cold, although pockets of people such as the Tarabuqueños (close by Sucre, in Bolivia) continued to wear their distinctive helmet hat, an apparent remnant of the immediate postconquest era. Some Aymara women adopted the characteristic *hongo* hat, still worn in many places in the twentieth century.

Many ordinary people wore sandals made of rawhide or fiber. This footwear was so easily made that many poor people made their own footwear. Even in Mexico City as late as the 1920s, an observer believed that among its 400,000 inhabitants, only 50,000 wore shoes, the rest sandals. In the Andes, the rustic sandals or *ojotas*, originally made from llama or sheep pelt and by the 1920s from discarded auto-mobile tires, marked their owners as the rural poor, usually Indian. At the same time increasing numbers of rural people made their way into mining camps, towns, and cities.

Luis Valcárcel, in early-twentieth-century Cusco, noticed that Indians, particularly women, stuck with their country dress but that mestizos quickly adopted city fashions beginning with long narrow trousers and loose shirts in place of ponchos. Indeed, mestizos strained to avoid any semblance of indigenous style in order to show, "in the clearest way possible" their difference from Indians.[26] Footwear con-tinued in the nineteenth century to be a key marker of ethnic and class status. Early-twentieth-century, urban mestizos not only insisted on shoes, but *shined* shoes, to set themselves off from their rustic brothers. With the growth of cities and shifts in ethnic identity, the demand for shoes and shoe polish offered encouragement to eager North Ameri-can and European commercial agents keen to promote ready-made shoes and clothes.

There is little evidence among the many travelers' sketches and early photographs that either the rural houses of ordinary people or their fur-nishings in the nineteenth century were different from those of the colonial period. The main dwelling was inevitably of one story and often one-room, dirt-floored, and windowless. Adobe and thatch were used throughout the higher elevations of Mexico and in the Andes,

---

[25] Beezley, *Judas at the Jockey Club*, p. 71.
[26] Valcárcel, *Memorias*, p. 105.

giving way to bamboo or palm-thatch in the tropics. In Mexico there were rarely stoves, fireplaces, or kitchens, although at times a lean-to off to the side contained a charcoal fire. Charcoal smoked less than wood fires – one reason why Mexicans constructed fewer chimneys, a shocking deprivation for Anglo-American observers who believed the absence of the hearth was a great obstacle to family reunions and the missing chimney a sign of sure primitiveness. Ordinary Andean people faced with a colder climate and little charcoal had better and more fuel-efficient stoves. A few mats, blankets, clay pots, and simple religious icons and images on the walls made up the furnishings. As a rule there were neither chairs, tables, nor beds. After dark only pine-resin torches or the rancid and smoky tallow candles flickered to keep the night at bay. The better-off and wealthier churches might afford beeswax candles. Men slept wrapped in their blankets, women curled in their clothes. Because a person "usually only owned the clothes he wore, wardrobes were unnecessary." In the Peruvian south highlands, where "civilization had not yet extended its enlightening rays," the walls or a common peasant hut were "embellished with smoke-dried pictures representing the beheadings, crucifixions and burning of martyrs."[27]

In the eyes of people who had a larger store of goods, better houses, and a richer diet, the scant possessions of the more isolated Indian population had always been explained by their "inveterate sloth" and "natural inclination to laziness." This refrain runs all through the colonial period into the present. The opinion was behind the various *repartos de mercancías* practiced in eighteenth-century Mexico and Peru, which obliged native people to buy, in effect, on an installment plan such things as cloth, mules, and iron goods, and justified the imposition of the tribute or head tax as well. Contrary to the present orthodoxy that *reduced* taxes will inspire us to *greater* industry, colonial and nineteenth-century officials – and a great many ordinary burghers as well – were persuaded that the requirement *to pay taxes* encouraged Indians to *work harder* and would eventually lead them to appreciate the consumer goods that the industrial age might provide. Otherwise, because Indians defined their "needs" at such a low level, they would work only to acquire the most basic elements of food, clothing, and shelter.

[27] Beezley, *Judas at the Jockey Club*, pp. 68–9; Kruggler, "Consumption Patterns," citing Paul Marcoy, *Travels in South America: From the Pacific Ocean to the Atlantic Ocean* (London: Blackie and Sons, 1875), 1:42.

This unfortunate attitude, many believed, inhibited the entry of such countries as Peru into the company of modern and progressive nations and diminished the potential income of aspiring hombres de negocio. Anyone could see that the desire for consumer goods is an incentive for more work, which in turn drives commerce and production. "If Indians were so ignorant or stubborn as to ignore this simple principle," the modern state had the right to make clear "the civilizing effects of consumption by force."[28] These opinions were directed particularly at the more hermetic Indian communities; in many other places in Mesoamerica and the Andes, such as the Mantaro Valley in Peru, or villages in the orbit of mines and larger cities, native people earned cash wages and were more integrated into a market economy.

In Lima, Santiago, Buenos Aires, Rio de Janeiro, Mexico, and a handful of other cities, gas and electric lights, paved streets, trolley cars, indoor plumbing, and a range of new goods that filled the elegant new two- and three-story department stores rapidly separated the material cultures of the countryside from that of urban life. Among local manufactures, the flood of imports, and a diminished but still present artisanal sector, Latin America consumers made their choices. Let us now follow in more detail the patterns of consumption that arose among members of the new elite who rode with a certain provincial panache the high tide of liberal development until its ignominious collapse in the 1920s.

EXTRANJERIZACION: THE SELF-ESTRANGEMENT OF THE BELLE EPOQUE ELITE

Because most members of the Latin American elite who led the movement to independence persuaded themselves that everything backward in the colonial era had been due to Spanish control, and because independence itself had been tenaciously and at times brutally opposed by Spanish arms, and, most important, because London and Paris had become irresistible poles of economic and cultural attraction, the new republican leaders threw themselves with little hesitation into close commercial relations with the burgeoning economies of northwest Europe. New trade, new ideas, new fashions offered, it seemed, a solution to backwardness. Few people then, any more than now, were

[28] Kruggler, "Consumption Patterns," p. 49.

able to anticipate the not wholly blissful consequences of liberal development.

Suppose, for the moment, that we were able to return to any of the main cities in Spanish America, say, in the 1770s. We notice a stranger, respectably dressed, apparently white, standing nearby. We turn to a friend and ask, "Who is that man?" "Pues, es un Español" – why, he's a Spaniard – would be the likely response, but we would not know whether he had recently come from Spain or descended from a family, long resident in America: the term applied to both the European- and American-born whites. As the rift between empire and colony widened during the last third of the eighteenth century, the people who were to lead the independence movement – mostly white, usually educated, and respectably dressed – now came to be known more and more not as "Spaniards" but as "creoles" – that is, as people who were considered by others, and thought of themselves, to be white and essentially European in culture, even though born in America. Most proclaimed a close identification with their American homeland. Once, however, that independence was achieved, the term "creole" tended to disappear in its eighteenth-century sense, because the elite now wished to think of themselves politically in national terms such as "Mexicans," "Peruvians," or "Chileans." They obviously found the eighteenth-century colonial content of the term publicly inconvenient because they aspired to identify with and lead multiethnic republics.

But although *political patriots*, the republican elite *culturally* faced two ways at once: toward the heterogeneous populations in their own countries, which they aspired to lead, but also back across the Atlantic toward their European antecedents, their source of culture and manufactures. Although a few of the more Catholic and conservative members of this new elite remained attached to Hispanic values, even they joined the majority in rushing to embrace the arts, fashions, and manufactures of England and France. Liberals and conservatives alike wanted to see their new republics as part of a universe of nations, and by bringing European fashions to Mexico, Bogotá, Lima, and Buenos Aires, they might embark on the noble mission of bringing change, modernity, and progress to their countries. In these formative years of the early nineteenth century, few members of the Latin America elite turned to their own people with the introspective nationalism of, say, the United States in 1790, or the former African and Asian colonies, newly independent after World War II. Rather, the new Latin

American republics were "uncompromisingly outward looking, avid to learn and imitate anything coming from France or Britain."[29]

At the same time, if the dominant groups in Latin America saw themselves as separate from the masses in race and culture, they were also bound to their lower-class compatriots by these same features. If members of the elite considered themselves whiter than the more mixed populations, they also recognized that they spoke the same language as most of their compatriots and attended Mass with them as well. Thus, precisely because they could be confused with the common people, the upper groups strained to set themselves off by embracing everything European and especially French and English. From the last third of the nineteenth century onward, income generated by the explosive world demand for fertilizers, coffee and sugar, petroleum and copper, wheat and beef enabled those who benefited from trade to import the goods needed to enter the European world of fashion and thus distinguish themselves from their less fortunate citizens.

Indeed, the cachet of foreignness was an important part of the appeal of imported goods and should be taken into account along with other attributes such as availability and cost. This observation is hardly original because imported goods play an important role in many societies today and among even such rudimentary consumers, for example, as the Melanesian people of the Trobriand Islands, where research long ago demonstrated that certain objects were more highly valued precisely because they came from distant lands. Still, the "allure of the foreign" seems to have been disproportionally strong in postcolonial Latin America. In the last third of the nineteenth century the association between foreignness and progress comes up again and again. Many different groups held a belief in the possibility of creating a local version of modernity, in the sense of joining a universal human march toward a future that would be different from, and superior to, a custom-bound past. Foreign goods stood for modernity because of their association with Europe, the very center of modernity, and because of their evident contrast with local practice.[30] This period – from midcentury to 1930 – is conventionally called the era of *export* economies or "outward development." Actually, the term *import* economies might be

---

[29] Out of a large literature on the subject, see Sergio Villalobos, *Origen y ascenso de la burguesía chilena*, pp. 89–90; Claudio Véliz, *The Centralist Tradition in Latin America* (Princeton, N.J.: Princeton University Press, 1980), pp. 163–88.

[30] Benjamin Orlove and Arnold J. Bauer, "Giving Importance to Imports," in Orlove, *Allure of the Foreign*, p. 13.

equally emphasized because in exchange for a narrow range of export commodities, Latin Americans received a wide selection of socially and culturally transforming goods.

In the beginning, into the Indian world of the sixteenth century, as we have seen, the Spanish conquistadors and the subsequent colonial political and social leaders introduced a metropolitan material culture. This drew on the rich mixtures of the Mediterranean, Islamic, and Asian worlds. They aimed to establish their difference from native inhabitants and the lower-caste mestizos and mulattoes as well, through food, dress, and architecture. Of course, they also sought through a display of abundance – larger mansions, bigger banquets, lavish gifts and ceremonies – to establish their dominance of a multicultural, multiethnic society. Three hundred years later, in the small, upper-class world of Lima, Mexico City, and other major cities in the later nineteenth century, men and women saw the bourgeoisies of London and Paris as the appropriate reference group for clothing as they did for urban design, furniture, and food. Like practically everywhere else in the world, under similar circumstances, they endeavored to construct a barrier between themselves and those scratching their way, now rather more insistently, up the social ladder.

Men's suits and ladies's gowns imported from Paris were wielded against *arriviste* pretenders, known by the curious terms *siútico* in Chile, *huachafo* in Lima, or the more general *gente de medio pelo* elsewhere. The tiny elite of provincial Cuzco, unable to purchase directly from France, brought Paris to the Andes in the form of the *Sastreria* "Paris," where a gentleman might order handmade elegant shirts, frock coats, and even a frac or "smoking." Luís Orrego Luco, the Chilean novelist, remembered with a wry smile in the 1940s his "ambitions as a juvenile snob" in the 1890s to dress with "the cravats of Doucet and the suits of Monsieur Pinaud."[31]

We might notice in passing that in contrast to the abundance of our own world where a nearly infinite range of goods serves as indicators

---

[31] Valcárcel, *Memorias*, pp. 38–9; Luís Orrego Luco, *Memorias del viejo tiempo* (Santiago, 1984), 58; Ramón Subercaseaux, *Memorias de 50 años* (Santiago, 1908). *Siútico*, o.o.o. (of obscure origin), is often thought, incorrectly, to be etymologically related to the English "suit," a term supposedly derived from the observation of the dress of English merchants in Valparaíso in the mid-nineteenth century. *Gente de medio pelo*, literally, "mid-haired people," presumably refers to a social layer between the unkempt and the powdered wig-wearing class of the late colonial period. Cf. middle-brow.

of position and identity, there were, in fact, far fewer ways in the colonial era in which a person might display wealth and power. We have
executive suites, luxury cars, vacation homes, "trophy" wives or husbands, sly designer labels, "gourmet" food, a thousand subtle items from
the Sharper Image. The colonial elite had far fewer possessions, but
they were obvious: essentially, land and slaves or dependent workers,
an often squat and ponderous mansion and servants, their ostentatious
endowment of a gilded church chapel, a groaning and generous table.
Once the republican elite moved away from its obvious rural base of
prestige into a more homogeneous urban setting, a new array of possessions was required for distinction. Attire and personal adornment
provided flexible and portable markers of status.

In the material world of the burgeoning Atlantic economy in the
later nineteenth century, the urge for conspicuous consumption became
more intense but few of the goods the Latin American wealthy might
display were available in their own countries. True, one could build a
larger townhouse, drive in elegant carriages, or engage, rather more
subtly, in private rituals of power. Thorstein Veblen discerned this
about the same time among his own compatriots in New York and
Chicago and wrote about it in his quaint and quirky prose: "Conspicuous consumption of valuable goods is a means of reputability to the
gentleman of leisure. As wealth accumulates on his hands, his own
unaided effort will not avail to sufficiently put his opulence in evidence
by this method. The aid of friends and competitors is therefore brought
in by resorting to the giving of valuable presents and expensive feasts
and entertainments."[32]

It is hard to exaggerate the appeal that English manufactures or
Parisian food and fashion held for the belle epoque elite. From the
1870s on, social life moved more and more away from private houses
into public places, into the elegant new cafés and restaurants, to tea
dances, theaters, and the opera. Contemporary photographs and paintings show top-hatted gentlemen and women in long, off-the-shoulder
gowns at fashionable balls and restaurants. By the 1880s French cuisine
became "all the rage," and the city's most elegant restaurants, such as
the Maison Dorée and the Fonda de Recamier, "did not dare open their
doors without a French chef."[33] In 1891, the Mexican millionaire don

---

[32] Veblen, The Theory of the Leisure Class, p. 75.
[33] Colin MacLachlan and William Beezley, El Gran Pueblo: A History of Greater
Mexico (Englewood Cliffs, N.J.: Prentice-Hall, 1994), pp. 132–3; Beezley, Judas
at the Jockey Club, p. 14.

Ignacio de la Torre y Mier persuaded "the celebrated Parisian chef" Sylvain Daumont, to come to Mexico City, creating such a success that within a year M. Daumont opened his own establishment, a near exact copy of a proper French, belle epoque restaurant.

An 1888 banquet in honor of President Porfirio Diaz offered "Consommé à la Graviarre, Truites a la Meuniere, Filet de Boeuf a la Godard, Dindonneau Truffé a l'Anglais," among the eight courses. The menu, in French of course, was accompanied by a modest little Mouton-Rothschild and a Romanée Conté, perhaps the finest of the great *vins bourguignons*, among other wines. And this despite the phylloxera epidemic just then destroying up to 90 percent of French vineyards, which must have made imports exceedingly expensive. "The quest for imported civilty" reached unanticipated heights in 1910, the centennial celebration of independence, when "not a single Mexican dish appeared at any one of the score of dinners dedicated to this patriotic occasion."[34] A contemporary memoir recalls that merely to hear the two words "Dulcería Francesa" was to be filled with joy. The term "evoked in children, fascinating toys; for women the unique *bon-bons* and *petit-fours*; for men, the excellent wines and delicious pastries, all of which were sold in those enchanting stores that on the mornings of birthdays, were filled with members of the best society."[35] The Porfirian elite, never more than some 2 percent of the total Mexican population, imported linens, grand pianos, and European wines and liquors, subscribed to French books and magazines, traveled abroad, and sent their children to European schools and believed that in doing so, they were "sharing the same activities and attitudes of the international gentry." The Parisian *Revue des deux mondes* lay half-open, and most likely unread, in a thousand salons from Mexico City to Buenos Aires.

At the same time, the improvements in terrestrial and maritime transport that permitted Latin Americans to export their products to pay for European imports also encouraged the elite to make the grand tour of England and the Continent. Memoirs and novels discuss these excursions, sometimes undertaken in unconscious comic excess. Large families, tutors, cooks, and wet nurses boarded steamers for Le Harve or Bordeaux. In 1882, one prominent Chilean family, fearful

[34] Jeffrey M. Pilcher, *Qué Vivan los Tamales!* (Albuquerque: University of New Mexico Press, 1998), pp. 64–5.
[35] René Rabell Jara, *La cocina mexicana a través de los siglos*, vol. VI, la *bella epoca* (Mexico City: Clio, 1996), pp. 44, 36. *Dulcería francesa* translates as "French sweetshop."

that the wet nurse would not last the thirty-three-day journey from Valparaiso to Bordeaux (and persuaded of the salutary benefits of equine milk) carried on board a newly fresh female burro and fifty bales of hay.[36]

These descriptions can be applied across the board in Latin American capitals to a small but influencial segment of the elite. Lima's upper class fell over itself to join private golf and horse-racing clubs, while the "highest ambition of a Limeño was to dress in the Parisian style." Even before massive nitrate exports permitted the Chilean elite to indulge in an orgy of luxury imports, the British consul noticed that "the models of elegance are all French."[37] The new, fancy stores such as Gath y Chaves, which opened in 1910, or the Casa Pra provided European goods over its polished wood and glass cases. Eiffel & Company's construction of the Central Railway Station looked like the Gare du Nord had come to Chile. When a controversy arose over the sale of Chilean property to a foreigner, small wonder that a belle epoque dandy slyly wondered, "Why don't we sell the entire country to France and buy ourselves something smaller, close to Paris?"

Fin de siècle Latin Americans were also conscious of the need to inspire proper ideas about their countries abroad. The opportunities came with the various world fairs and expositions where order and progress and the civilized tastes of the Europeanized layer of society might be displayed while leaving behind the still lingering remnants of barbarie. In 1900, the Santiago newspaper, El Porvenir, got wind of a plan that "certain entrepreneurs of spectacles" were preparing to take a group of Araucanians to the Grand Exposition in Paris. "What national interest does it serve," the newspaper wondered, "to cart around, in order to exhibit in Paris as a sample of Chile, a handful of Indians who are almost savage, brutalized, degraded and repugnant in appearance?"[38]

---

[36] Francisco R. Undurraga Vicuña, Recuerdos de 80 años (Santiago, 1943), pp. 86–7.

[37] Manuel Burga and Alberto Flores Galindo, Apogeo y crisis de la república aristó-cratica, 2nd ed. (Lima: Mosca Azul, 1981), pp. 4, 96. Horace Rumbold, Report by Her Majesty's Secretaries . . . on the Manufactures, Commerce, etc. . . . of Chile (London, 1876), pp. 365–6.

[38] Cited in Patrick Barr-Melij, Between Revolution and Reaction: Cultural Politics, Nationalism and the Rise of the Middle Class in Chile (Chapel Hill: University of North Carolina Press, 2001). Mauricio Tenorio, Mexico at the World's Fairs: Crafting a Modern Nation (Berkeley: University of California Press, 1996).

A collection of menus from hundreds of Chilean private and public dinners around the turn of the century, now held in the Museo Histórico in Santiago, like those of contemporary Mexico, are almost entirely in French. Here one sees that guests at public banquets and in private restaurants drank wines from the Clos de Vougeot or Pommard and sipped the "grands crus" of Bordeaux and the heavenly sauternes of Chateau d'Yquem. In fact, in Chile, members of the elite not only made cultural pilgrimages to Paris and imported French goods; several endeavored to construct themselves as bordelais "chateau" owners in Chile.

A powerful model was present in the new vineyards and wineries established by the nouveaux riches in Bordeaux, which came to be called "chateaux" in the aftermath of the French Revolution, which had aimed to destroy the original, real, *ancien regime* castles. Baron Rothschild acquired "Chateau" Lafite in 1868 alongside the other great houses of Latour, Haut-Brion, and Chateau Margaux. Chileans not only went to Bordeaux to bring back cuttings of the famous cabernet sauvignon and merlot rootstock, they also imported state-of-the-art wine making equipment. More ambitiously, they built their own "chateaux" in the Maipo and Aconcagua Valleys, and imported French, Italian, and English landscape artists and architects to lay out such imposing gardens as those seen today at Viña Santa Rita or the Subercaseaux mansion at Pirque, just outside Santiago. With all of this, they aimed to make a "French" wine in Chile and to make clear their cultural link with Europe. Let us not exaggerate. It's also true that a certain consumer nationalism crept in even at the height of the belle epoque. At political events or ceremonies, party leaders made a point of serving Chilean wines at banquets where presidential candidates were announced, for example, at the meeting of Chilean and Argentine presidents in 1899 in a contested border region in the far south on the Strait of Magellan. Further down the consumer scale a far larger acreage of *viñedos del país* produced drinkable wines for ordinary people.[39]

The best tailors and dressmakers brought English and French fashions within reach of the Latin American elite. A concern for clothes began early in life. In 1907 a thirteen-year-old Brazilian boy who signed his note "Paulino Jr." sent his father on a shopping errand with a request

---

[39] Pozo, *Historia del vino chileno*, pp. 65–100.

for clothes: "One coat of white flannel cloth . . . three little collars in the Santos Dumont style and a white tie, to be bought in Casa Colombo and, if it isn't there, from the Torre Eiffel. N.B. If the cloth can't be found in flannel, bring the same cut in drill."[40] Paulino's father probably went shopping in the Avenida Central or the Rua do Ouvidor in Rio de Janeiro, which, until 1906 was the very heart of elite culture and society. This half-mile stretch of Rio, apart from a shrine to European goods, was also a fashionable promenade, a meeting place of the elite, where "everything novel and 'civilized'" made its first appearance in shop windows. Here, modists put their creations together from materials brought from France while other women bought the latest fashions from Paris, paying a small fortune to acquire a Charles Frederick Worth gown along with the appropriate jewelry.

A recent sprightly book scans the illustrated fashion books of the day, tracking the change in women's skirts from the midcentury's vast yardage of rustling crinoline to the bustle, "which rose and fell through the 1870s and 1880s in various festooned exaggerations of the buttocks." By 1900 skirts had evolved into luxurious trains. At every stage, women forced themselves into corsets and wore large numbers of petticoats. In 1914 a local gossip columinist summed it up: "The women dress in long, full, skirts, thick with underskirts displaying tiny wasp waists . . . thrown into relief by corsets. They wear taffeta and merino . . . boots buttoned or tied high and always carry a silk or gauze fan in a well-gloved hand. They wear no makeup. . . . Carioca women are figures of ivory or wax. . . . when they pass in groups they remind one of a procession of cadavers."[41]

If women's fancy clothes were uncomfortable, constricting, and required a learned talent to negotiate a room full of people, men's clothing in belle epoque Rio provide a particularly telling example of the importance of clothing in the construction of identity. Indeed, it demonstrates an utterly absurd adherence to European consumer reference groups without the slightest bow to practicality or comfort.

Whereas women's fashions and fabric came from France, men's hats and cloth were imported from England. Local tailors cut the woolen cloth, usually black, into trousers, vests, and frockcoats. Under these two layers of wool, properly dressed men wore long cotton or linen

---

[40] Cited in Jeffrey Needell, A Tropical Belle Epoque: Elite Culture and Society in Turn-of-Century Rio de Janeiro (Cambridge: Cambridge University Press, 1987), p. 140.
[41] Ibid., pp. 166–8, 170.

Figure 5.4. Rua do Ouvidor, Rio de Janeiro, ca. 1900. The most elegant shopping street in Rio in the belle epoque. Notice the warmly dressed men in the tropics. *Source*: Photograph by Marc Ferrez. Courtesy, Getty Research Institute, 1200 Getty Center Drive, Los Angeles, CA 90049.

underwear and shirts attached with wing collars bound with neckties –
all with "little concession to ease of movement, blood circulation, temperature or economy." None of this might have seemed out of place in
English latitudes were winters were cold and houses poorly heated. But
we are talking about tropical Rio de Janeiro and particularly the Old
City where businessmen spent the hottest hours of the day, working
through the "vaporous, fever-ridden summer in stolid black English
wool." A Parisian journalist in 1890 had this observation: "Under a
killing climate, in a town where the thermometer attains 40 [104
degrees Fahrenheit] in the shade at times, where the rays of the sun
are, in summer, so broiling that one dies in a flash, the Brazilian stub-
bornly continues to live and to dress himself in the European manner.
He works during the hottest hours of the day; he goes to his office from
nine to four o'clock, like the London businessman; he walks about in
a black frockcoat, capped with a top hat, imposing martyrdom on
himself with the most perfect lack of concern."

Why did they do it? Clearly, dark, heavy, distinctly European clothing stood for modernity, civilization, aristocracy. So the largely white
elite, "in black wool topcoats and vests, in narrow corsets and thick
skirts, endured the swelter, satisfyingly European, satisfyingly distinct,
from the darker, cooler, poor who went about half-naked, openly pro-
claiming uncouth inferiority."[42]

Towns and cities in Latin America up to around 1870, generally
kept to the traditional checkerboard plan imposed by the Hapsburgs
in the sixteenth century, when, we recall, the Spaniards envisioned a
standard urban quadrangular plan laid out with "cord and rule" for
all its cities in the Indies, a plan that would persist even as population
increased. In fact, it did up to the 1870s. But then, the rapid growth
of foreign trade forced the modernization of the port cities and
then the older capitals. Cities were given their first sewers and water
supply, Mexico's Alameda got gas lights in 1873; trolleys, the cars at
first pulled on rails by mules (the so-called, ferrocarril de sangre)
appeared everywhere. In short, the main cities, or at least sections of
them, became Europeanized. In bursts of local pride, Guatemalans
or Chileans liked to call their capitals the "Paris of Guatemala" or
the "Paris of Chile," and by 1911, even Georges Clemenceau, the
French Radical parliamentarian, could call Buenos Aires, "a grand

[42] Quotations in ibid., pp. 167, 169.

European city."[43] In Porfirian Mexico, two personalities, José Cavallari and Antonio Rivas Mercado, both products of the Ecole des beaux artes in Paris, were instrumental in giving the new districts of Juárez, Cuauhtémoc, and Roma a cosmopolitan look, "as aristocratic as those of Versailles, Brussles, and London." This ample urban layout gave rise to the construction of "chalés, mansiones y palacetes."[44]

Liberal secularization of society meant that ritual and ceremony began to move away from the older, church-centered plazas to commercial streets, new parks and paseos, and newly built market squares. Church property itself, confiscated by the modernizing state and sold off to private individuals, aided the development of new settlements on the outskirts, soon to be linked with trolley lines and wide avenues to the older core. Not infrequently earthquakes in many older cities provided additional opportunites for new urban plans. And all of this took place at a time when such Europeans as the prefect of the Seine provided bold models for urban renewal, which must not have been lost on progressive and French-worshiping Latin Americans. Baron Haussmann carried out a massive renewal of Paris, pushing through eighty-five miles of new streets, creating wide carriageways and tree-shaded pavement all in straight lines with scant provision for traffic. It was a dramatic if ultimately philistine undertaking that Marx, his contemporary, believed mixed "barbarism and frivolity."[45]

Urban reform in Latin America took place at a time when most Latin American liberal leaders rejected the Hispanic past as a drag on modernity so that the new diagonal avenues stood in symbolic opposition to the old and discredited quadrangular pattern, which now reaked of a Hapsburg, Counter-Reformation orthodoxy. There are multiple examples – the Paseo de la Reforma in Mexico, Havana's Prado, the great new avenues in Buenos Aires, the lengthening of the 18 de Julio Avenue in Montevideo – of the new urban plan with great avenues

---

[43] Cited in, Ramón Gutiérrez, "La ciudad iberoamericana en el siglo xix," in *La ciudad hispanuamericana: sueño de un orden*, p. 261. (*Ferrocarril de sangre* might translate as "flesh and blood streetcar.")

[44] Jorge del Arenal Fenochio, "Ideología y estilo en la architectura de finales del siglo xix," in Fernández, *Herencia*, pp. 463–75.

[45] Roger Magraw, *France, 1815–1914* (Oxford: Oxford University Press, 1986), p. 183; Alfred Cobban, *A History of Modern France* (Baltimore: Pelican, 1965), 2:167–9. Haussmann also promoted the great sewers, luridly described by Victor Hugo in *Les Misérables*.

projecting out from the older cores or slashing through old colonial sectors. The new boulevards that ran out from the older city plazas came to be lined with three- or four-story town houses in neo-Gothic on the mansard-roofed, Second Empire style. Today they still march along the great avenues in Buenos Aires, and others can be seen tucked down among the glass and steel skyscrapers in Bogotá, Santiago, or Mexico City.

At the same time, those suburban property owners able to bear the cost abandoned the one-story, patio-centered Mediterranean complex, with facades flush with the sidewalk, to construct two- and three-story "mansions" and "palaces," surrounded by tall wrought iron fences, set back from the street to show a grander entrance to visitors. The "palacio Cousiño" in Santiago, built in the 1870s, shows its European face to society through the display of Carerra marble, French chandeliers, European landscape paintings, elegant chairs and sofas. There is nothing Chilean about it. The internal organization of living space paralleled the Janus-faced ambiguity of the owners themselves. In a contemporary Rio de Janeiro *palacete*, the drawing room, billiard room, library, and entrance hall were "more carefully Europeanized in their finish and furnishing." Here the owners welcomed visitors and demonstrated their affinity with European culture. The interior rooms turned back, in effect toward Brazil, toward ordinary living quarters, with more causal and comfortable bed and dining rooms and more traditional furnishings. Such rooms in Rio de Janeiro, even in expensive mansions, had hammocks and floor mats. In Rio at least, even the rituals were different in the two sides of the house. Up front, in keeping with the French style, meals were served in sequential order; in the family dining room, all dishes of the meal were served at once.[46]

All of this – food, clothing, shelter – was part of a much larger process, the formation of a world bourgeoisie or at least of a Western bourgeoisie. The avid consumption of European goods, the journeys to Europe, and contact with its intellectuals, artists, and engineers was something more than "vain posturing or following the latest fashions. It was to place one's self at the peak of the historical moment or perhaps – it might be imagined – at the center of all history." It was to be *modern*. The opera, for example, could be enjoyed, "with all its truculence and tenderness" by members of the "conquering bourgeoisie" in

---

[46] Needell, *Tropical Bell Epoque*, pp. 150–1.

Figure 5.5. Municipal theater in Santiago. Modeled on the Paris Opera, the Santiago version originally was built in 1853, burned, and was reopened in 1873. A symbol of modernity and civilization, it appears in this photograph to have been built ahead of demand. *Source: Views of Chile and Peru*, The William Letts Oliver Collection. Courtesy, The Bancroft Library, University of California, Berkeley.

similar and familiar circumstances, across the board, "in La Scala, Covent Garden, the Met, in Manaos or the Municipal Theater in Santiago."[47] We might add even provincial Mexico where in 1903, don Porfirio Diaz himself journeyed by train to Guanajuato to attend a performance of *Aida* at the opening of the elegant Teatro Júarez.

By entering the larger world of fashion, the new elites everywhere, from Budapest to Tolstoy's St. Petersburg to Lima, could "feel European." Although Latin America's relationship with Europe was part of this larger process, the peculiar duality of its elites gave them a double task. On one side, looking back across the ancient Ocean Sea, they sought connection with the powerful states of the North Atlantic in order to bring what they considered to be advanced ideas and progress to their own republics. As part of this they encouraged railroad construction, port renewal, financial policies, and concessions to foreign investors in order to promote the export of food, fiber, and minerals.

Looking inward, toward their own countries, because of the racial and cultural ambiguities that had existed from the beginning, they sought through the consumption of European goods to assert their more "civilized" identity and to set themselves off from their inferior compatriots, for whom, after all, they could quite easily be mistaken. Such a mistake was not likely between, say, the white settlers and the Kikuyu in Kenya or the French planters among the Vietnamese. This ambiguity, the anxiety of being taken for one of "the other castes," no doubt is part of the explanation for the Latin American elite's devotion to consumption and display. This went hand in hand with its enthusiasm for modernity and the hope, not very intense, that in good time their countrymen and women in the lower orders might gradually move from barbarie to civilization.

---

[47] Villalobos, *Origen y ascenso*, p. 78.

CHAPTER 6

Developing Goods

Hay que consumir lo que el país produce.[1]

Latin America's long nineteenth century drew to a close not with a cal-
endrical bang in 1900 nor even in the cannon fire of a distant world
war, but in the confluence of economic, political, and social circum-
stance in the 1920s. During the subsequent forty or fifty years, up
through the 1960s, strong nationalist feelings, state intervention in
economic matters, the rising sentiment of antiimperialism, and experiments in socialism led to substantial changes in material culture
throughout Latin America. Before we turn to a description of the
choices people were to make in the things they eat, wear, and build
along with their consumption of a widening range of unheard of and
even unimagined new goods, let us now move away from the provincial cosmopolitanism of the belle epoque elite into the small town and
rural hinterland of Latin America, in order to track the gradual development of a consumer culture in out-of-the-way places.

Two Towns

At the turn of the twentieth century, the three thousand or four thousand inhabitants in and about the small town of San José de Gracia in
the state of Michoacán represented fairly well the smallholder, mestizo
communities of west-central Mexico. Their experience may help to
understand how ordinary people experience everyday changes in mate-

---

[1] "You have to buy what the country produces." Admonition from Tala Rodríguez,
beloved criada, to the author, Mexico City, October 1954.

rial culture. With certain allowances made for income, ethnicity, and particularly the relatively close proximity to the United States, one can imagine that the goods we see entering into the life of San José are roughly typical of other places of similar size throughout Latin America.[2]

The people of San José de Gracia milked their cows, made cheese, honey, and beeswax for local markets, and grew the ordinary crops of maize, beans, garbanzos, and some wheat and barley for subsistence and occasional sale. Isolated from the state capital and other towns by rutted dirt roads, few people ventured further from their fields than their eye could see from the roof of the small church in the village square. In the first years of the twentieth century, mule drivers occasionally brought tales from Mexico City of electric lights, phonographs, and other marvels. In 1906, the mail began to arrive on horseback, once a week. Three men in the town subscribed to the Mexico City newspaper, El Pais, which told astonishing stories of the flight of men in winged apparatuses, the clattering telegraph, cars, submarines, and electric streetcars.

Some houses in San José around this time got running water; a couple of streets were paved with cobblestones. One day, someone turned up with a camera. A number of people from the town posed for pictures with an expression of "astonished solemnity"; for others, "no power on earth could have got them to face the camera."[3] About the same time, an agent from the Bayer firm introduced the aspirin. In 1905 "a snappy dresser in a little hat showed up. He knocked at the door of the main houses in town. Some people, taking him for a priest, kissed his hand." In fact, he was a traveling salesman from Singer Sewing Machines who managed to interest five families in one of the most transforming mechanical devices of modern times. A month later five shiny machines arrived along with a young woman to demonstrate how they worked. Someone else in these years opened a small general store filled with various fabrics, groceries, and metal pots and pans.

The pace of change accelerated in the 1920s. Gasoline lanterns began to replace tallow candles and pine-resin torches, and now, in

---

[2] The following draws primarily on Luís González's delightful Pueblo en vilo: Microhistoria de San José de Gracia, translated by John Upton as San José de Gracia: Mexican Village in Transition (Austin: University of Texas Press, 1974). The page references are from the Spanish-language version.

[3] González, Pueblo en vilo, p. 156.

Map 6.1. Place-names mentioned in the text. *Source*: Courtesy, Sebastian Araya, California State University at Humboldt.

1926, an enterprising citizen installed the first small electric generator to light a few yellow bulbs in the church and in two dozen of the better houses. Two years later there appeared in San José the first molino de nixtamal, another revolutionary apparatus, destined to transform the lives of millions of Mexican women. The mill ground soaked maize kernels (or, to employ the ancient Náhautl word, *nixtamal*) into damp flour out of which the eternal tortilla, the staff of life for nearly everyone in Mesoamerica, was formed.

In 1938 a lucky man acquired the first battery radio. Power lines and electricity came in 1942, movies in 1944. There were now also, a few magazines. The most popular among the better-off inhabitants of San José was *Selecciones del Readers Digest*, where one could read "stories of men who never gave up hope, the reports of scientific feats, descriptions of other countries, résumés of novels, stories of the generous and heroic side of capitalism and the brutish side of socialism."[4]

The efforts of the development-minded Mexican state to promote "inward growth" and national markets can be seen in the part-gravel, part-black-top "national" highway that brought buses to San José in 1943; now people could read advertising signs promoting local beer, Coca-Cola, shirts and pants, cattle feed, and a multitude of new products, churned out by a rapidly industrializing society. But even then, the annual income of an ordinary ranchero was scant, barely able to cover the cost of food, a little sugar and kerosene, soap and cigarettes, shoes and shirts. Little was left to buy the more expensive goods beginning to flow from what politicians and economists called the new import substitution industries, or ISI.

Roads and newspaper and radio ads also gave young people from San José the "sensation of living in a jail." They wanted something more, "to make money, to meet girls, to do what they felt like doing, and even go to the 'Yunaites' (the United States) or Mexico City."[5] By the 1950s, nine of every ten persons over the age of fifteen in San José had visited either Mexico or Guadalajara; thousands sought work for dollars in Texas and California.

In the 1950s and 1960s, as the industry-led growth of the "Mexican Miracle," trickled outward to such places as San José, the age-old

---

[4] Ibid., p. 259.
[5] Ibid., p. 262.

Indian campesino dress of loose white cotton shirt and trousers gave way to regular pants and colored shirts; shoes replaced huarache sandals. The cultural influence (and the dollars) brought back from the "Yunaites" could be seen in the change from the adobe, patio-centered dwellings open to the sky and birds, lined with potted flowers, to a more compact, flat concrete and brick house, with toilets, sinks, and tubs, and a gas stove. By 1965, the first television appeared; the more delicate souls used deodorants. That same year, twice a day, jet airplanes crossed over San José de Gracia.

In the north highlands of Peru, some four thousand people in and around the town of Huaylas followed a consumer regime much like that of San José de Gracia under similar circumstances of post-1940 inward economic growth.[6] Like the people of San José, almost all the inhabitants of Huaylas thought of themselves as mestizos; by 1960, only 2 percent identified as Indian. Yet, some 10 percent of all women spoke only Quechua and – very unlike San José, where no one spoke a native language – nearly everyone in Huaylas was bilingual in Spanish and Quechua.[7] The town, in 1960, was connected to the coast by a narrow dirt road, dusty and muddy by season, over which trucks (which doubled as buses) and collective taxis, made the journey to Lima in nine to ten hours.

Ordinary Huaylinos, while drawing on the essential features of Andean food regimes, included in their diet, as did their contemporaries in San José, elements of European and Asian provenance. All meals, except breakfast, started off with soups or stew, thickened by the inevitable Andean potato, vegetables of both Andean and European origin, and, in the better-off households, the odd chunk of beef, chicken, or pork, accompanied by wheat or barley bread. The coastal food-processing industry, a result of the import substitution policies pursued in Peru as in Mexico, supplied canned tuna, packaged rice and noodles, locally elaborated but foreign-sounding Nescafé, and the occasional import, such as Dutch lard or a can of Chilean peaches.

---

[6] This section follows the ethnography carried out in the early 1960s, by Paul L. Doughty, *Huaylas: An Andean District in Search of Progress* (Ithaca, N.Y.: Cornell University Press, 1968).

[7] This calls into question the common practice of defining ethnicity by spoken language.

Figure 6.1. Sewing machine, Bolivia. Invented in the mid-nineteenth century, sewing machines came relatively late to Latin America, around the turn of the century. They utterly transformed the tailor's trade and the clothing industry. *Source:* Photograph: courtesy, Gabriela Romanow and Acción International.

Clothing in Huaylas as in Mexico continued to move away from indigenous modes. Now, even the lower-class men wore clothing tailored in a modern Western style. Some articles were home-sewn; others, such as cotton shirts, were off the rack. There were home-sewn trousers made either of homespun wool or from cotton cloth produced by coastal textile mills. Here as in San José, the sewing machine, by far the most important modern appliance, had worked its magic; 82 percent of the better-off families, 40 percent of the middling groups, and even 14 percent of the "lower class" in Huaylas had such machines among their household possessions. Many women were "skilled at dressmaking"; most clothes were home-sewn, many from patterns copied from old Montgomery Ward or Sears & Roebuck catalogs.[8]

The lack of electricity – only 40 percent of all houses in the Huaylas district had electricity as late as 1963 and far fewer before new installations had arrived just two years before – reduced or practically eliminated such items as radios, phonographs, or blenders, except for battery-driven devices. But sewing machines were driven by foot treadle; indeed, only a dozen of the hundreds of sewing machines in Huaylas were electric. Despite the government's efforts to promote local industry – and by the late 1950s here as in Mexico, the joint enterprise of local and foreign capital had created a wide range of consumer goods – there are still ambivalent feelings about national industries. Even though tariff and transport raised the cost, people with the means were inclined to pay more for imported goods and appliances than buy the local product.

CRECER HACIA ADENTRO: INWARD DIRECTED GROWTH AND CONSUMPTION

The changing consumption patterns of the people in San José de Gracia and Huaylas took place within rapidly changing social and economic circumstances. After a brief global demand in the early 1920s, brought about by the pent-up, post–World War I shortages, prices for such Latin American staples as sugar, coffee, nitrates, food, and fibers began their downward slide. Even before the New York stock market crash in 1929 and the subsequent collapse of the first liberal order throughout the Atlantic world, many Latin Americans had already begun to question the international arrangement of comparative advantage in which they had come to provide raw materials to the industrial countries in exchange for manufactures. As world prices fell, Latin Americans at first tried to compensate for the decrease in price, for example, for a ton of sugar or a sack of coffee, by producing *more* tons and sacks in order to maintain their total earnings. This further depressed prices continuing the vicious cycle.[9]

---

[8] Doughty, *Huaylas*, pp. 72–4.
[9] Victor Bulmer-Thomas, "The Latin American Economies, 1929–1939," in Leslie Bethell, ed., *The Cambridge History of Latin America* (Cambridge: Cambridge University Press, 1994), 6.1:65–116 (hereafter *CHLA*).

Given these circumstances and aiming to diminish their vulnerability to an unpredictable and uncontrollable foreign market, Latin American economic thinkers and political leaders took an urgent interest in a more autonomous development. Foreign and local investors in many Latin American countries had already installed textile mills, food-processing and other light industries, some dating back to the later nineteenth century. But the crisis of the 1930s led the state, in partnership with a segment of the entrepreneurial class, into a more active role to promote industrial development.

A decade later, in 1948, the United Nation's newly formed Economic Commission for Latin America (or CEPAL, in its Spanish acronym) provided the theoretical underpinnings and the statistical data for the new policies. CEPAL – or more precisely, its foremost spokesman, the Argentine economist, Raul Prebisch – endeavored to demonstrate that the theory and practice of comparative advantage favored the industrial "center" of Europe and the United States and worked against the interests of the Latin American "periphery." This, Prebisch and his followers believed, was because greater efficiency in the production of industrial products in the "center" did *not* lead to lower prices for these goods in Santiago or Buenos Aires but rather to higher wages for organized and demanding workers in Detroit. On the other hand, improved agricultural production in Latin America *did* drive its commodity prices down on the world market in part, the theory held, because of an overabundant and consequently inexpensive, still precapitalist, rural work force, not in a position to demand higher wages.

This explained why the *terms of trade* – the number of sacks of coffee, say, necessary to buy a Singer sewing machine – had for the previous half century moved in favor of the exporters of industrial products and against those of raw material or agricultural producers. Latin Americans had to run faster and still lost ground. Indeed, in the example at hand, Latin Americans had to sell only six sacks of coffee or wheat in 1900 to buy a sewing machine, but in 1939 the same machine cost ten sacks. Here then, was a central explanation for Latin America's continued "underdevelopment," a term that gained popularity in the 1940s. The solution was *crecer hacia adentro*, or inward-directed growth, the policy of state-assisted industrialization, or even state-owned industries, behind the high walls of protective tariffs. This was a project designed to produce at home those things previously imported – in the language of the time, import substitution industry. Local industry would thus eventually absorb the underemployed rural population, which would in turn, it was believed, drive up the prices for Latin American raw material exports. These policies, put into effect in all of the major Latin American countries, led to spectacular results in economic output and consumption patterns in the 1950s and 1960s.[10]

Political leaders and others who thought about these matters and were wary of an excessive dependence on the United States had originally hoped for public finance capital, a small version of the Marshall Plan, that had revived Europe after World War II. As it turned out, however, most of the capital for the new industries in Latin America came from European and, primarily, U.S. private investors, either in the form of joint ventures with local capitalists or as corporate subsidiaries, for example, the Volkswagen factory in Brazil and Mexico or Ford and General Motors assembly plants in several countries.

Actually, the branches of all sorts of industries of foreign origin sprang up on the outskirts of the major cities of Latin America, including Purina Feed, soft-drink bottling plants, furniture and kitchen appliance manufacturers, General Electric stoves and refrigerators, Goodyear tire manufacturers, and the products of a wide variety of food-processing industries, which in fact, show up in the 1940s and 1950s in both San José de Gracia and Huaylas. There was even a branch of a large metal fastener works, its plant just outside Santiago innocently advertised in eight-foot-high, painted block letters as, American Screw Chile. The temptation to brush in an "s" to the subject of the verb was irresistible to a generation of young, Chilean, antiimperialists in the 1960s.

As we move through the 1940s, 1950s, and 1960s, the evolution of Latin American industrialization led inexorably to a triple alliance of the state, multinational corporations, and, as junior partners, domestic entrepreneurs. Private investors, mainly from the United States, in turn, required security so that the militant political tendencies that emerged after the war "had to be controlled for adequate business confidence."[11] Latin America's development thus became dependent on foreign capital, which required political "stability." In this process, the Latin American entrepreneurial classes found a

[10] See Joseph Love, "Economic Ideas and Ideologies in Latin America since 1930," in CHLA, 6.1:403–18.

[11] Rosemary Thorp, "The Latin American Economies, 1939–c. 1950," in CHLA, 6.1:134–5.

generally enthusiastic ally in the United States. Along with its nominal support for social tranquility in those countries where its citizens invested their capital, United States policy makers also considered "instability" a "breeding ground" for communism. Consequently, throughout the forty Cold War years following World War II, the United States not only encouraged Latin American governments to keep Marxism at bay but fought tooth and nail against "progressive" social democratic movements as well.

While most Latin American leaders supported the particular kind of industrial development undertaken throughout most of the larger countries in Latin America, opposition arose from various directions. From the beginning, the policies of import substitution were accompanied, by a strong current of economic nationalism and antiimperialism. The expropriation of British and American oil companies into the state-owned Petróleos Mexicanos, or PEMEX (its slogan "Al Servicio de la Patria" suggests the nationalist sentiment surrounding its formation), is an early example, followed by similar nationalizations in Argentina, Brazil (actually a mixed foreign and national capital operation), Peru, and ultimately, Venezuela. Nationalist feeling ran so high in 1953 in Brazil that naturalized Brazilians and even native-born citizens married to foreigners were excluded from owning shares in the newly formed state monopoly, Petrobrás.[12] So at the same time that foreign capital was pouring into the region, many governments expropriated and nationalized foreign-held natural resources or utilities, and created large, state-owned enterprises, such as the steel mills in Brazil, Chile, and Mexico.[13]

In three countries, there eventually developed strong opposition to United States policies and to foreign companies and their domestic allies. Indeed, after encountering intense popular animosity during a "fact-finding" mission to Latin America, in 1969, even Nelson Rockefeller wrote that "a great many and probably a majority of the citizens [in Latin America] regard United States private investment as a form of exploitation or economic colonialism."[14] The Cuban revolutionaries

[12] Rollie Poppino, *Brazil: The Land and the People*, 2nd ed. (New York: Oxford University Press, 1973), pp. 275–6.

[13] Even more paradoxically, the United States occasionally provided the financing (as well, of course, as the designs and machinery) for such enterprises, as, for example, the Brazilian Volta Redonda steel mill. Thorp, "Latin American Economics," pp. 121–2.

[14] Quoted in Thomas O'Brien, *The Century of U.$. Capitalism in Latin America* (Albuquerque: University of New Mexico Press, 1999), p. 141.

beginning in 1959, the Chilean Popular Unity government in 1970–73, and the Sandinistas in Nicaragua in the 1980s, endeavored, through socialist programs, to hold back the tide of capitalist domination.

We cannot, of course, rewind this documentary on Latin American industrialization and run it again with different actors or policies. Had Latin Americans themselves been politically able to develop their own industry on their own terms, perhaps to their own designs, the range of consumer goods available to their citizens might have been quite different, probably narrower, perhaps more original, maybe worse. We cannot know what might have happened, but we can see that the goods promoted in the nineteenth century by commercial agents, and in the twentieth by the imposing models of consumption visible everywhere from billboards to television commercials, assured that Latin Americans in Huaylas and San José – indeed, across the entire continent and a half – would buy pickups, beds, stoves, pots and pans, wrenches, motors, sheet rock, and cattle feed more or less identical to those sold in Denver or Dallas. At the same time, most Latin Americans were surely pleased to have available for purchase such a widening array of goods, often giving little importance to their national origin.

The mention of San José de Gracia and Huaylas suggests a feature of Latin America's material culture that extends back to the arrival of the first Europeans. We notice that nearly every new *mechanical* item (with one important exception that we shall come to) in these two villages is of foreign provenance – that is, either directly imported from foreign counties or originally designed abroad and now made in Latin America by imported machinery and largely foreign capital. As we move out from those two villages into the mines and agricultural hinterland, or back to the new industries with North American or European names that ring the major Latin American cities, through the streets of towns and cities, we find hardware and appliance stores, motors, pumps, screws, bolts and nuts, the innumerable repair shops, and clothing stores. There are a hundred usually unnoticed items such as hooks, snaps, see-through plastic T-square rulers. Those individual houses with electricity now have pots, pans, blenders, gas stoves, tubs, and sinks. Their cupboards are stocked with gouda cheese and corn flakes.

At first sight, a visitor or tourist from Germany or the United States, noticing all the familiar brand names, might be surprised at the apparent "foreignness" of Latin America's material culture. But by the 1950s and 1960s, goods had begun to lose their national identity. Is "Quáquer Oats" made in Mexico by Mexican workers an American cereal? Do not Chileans feel that LAN Chile is their *national* airline, even though the planes are made by Boeing and serviced in San Francisco? When wine is made in Chile from French cabernet sauvignon and merlot grapes in a winery made possible by California capital, do we have "Chilean" wine? North Americans in Chicago certainly believe that tacos and enchiladas made from local ingredients are "Mexican food"; but no Argentine thinks that a *baby bife* or *T-bone* from an Angus or Hereford steer raised in the Pampa is British. Some things – Coca-Cola, an obvious example – are deathlessly symbolic of North American cultural imperialism to many (but, at the same time, eagerly consumed by the millions). American workers in Detroit who apply baseball bats to Toyotas made in Tennessee presumably believe they are Japanese cars. As I write, there are widespread demonstrations in France against McDonald's hamburgers, or *McDomination*. The American company replies that the several hundred franchises in France are French-owned, the company hires only French men and women in France, all the ingredients are produced in France, and the customers are French, so what's all the fuss? There is no way out of these contradictions; clearly goods – clothes, food, airplanes – carry a heavy symbolic weight at the levels of personal and national identity. Equally obvious is the fact that the *national* quality of a good exists more in our head than in any analysis of brand name, foreign ownership, or national origin of ingredients.[15]

At the same time that industrial policies attracted new workers, population growth and migration from the countryside accelerated the expansion of cities. Urban growth created not only the possibility of larger markets for local products but also brought thousands of new participants onto the political stage. Between 1930 and 1990, Latin America's total population increased from 110 to 448 million, nearly twice the rate of North America, which went from 134 to 276 million. Cities grew like mad. In the six major countries of Latin America, for

---

[15] A rather precious but eventually worthwhile discussion of food and nationalism in the Dominican Republic may be found in Lauren Derby, "Gringo Chicken with Worms," in Gilbert Joseph, Catherine LeGrand, and Richard Salvatore, eds., *Close Encounters of Empire* (Durham, N.C.: Duke University Press, 1998), pp. 451–93.

example, only 37 percent of the total population was considered urban in 1940. In a single, long generation, by 1980, this percentage had nearly doubled. The urban increase can be seen particularly in the larger cities. By 1980, around 73 million of the 272 million people in these six countries lived in just a few large metropolises of over 2 million people.[16]

From the beginning, from the first decades after separation from Spain and Portugal, the requirements of property, literacy, and gender meant that before 1940, only a small percentage, usually around 10 percent, of all Latin Americans, voted in congressional or presidential elections. Uruguay had the most open electorate and was the first country to permit female suffrage (in 1932), which meant that some 20 percent of the total population voted in the 1934 presidential election. But Chile, for example, where universal male suffrage dates from the 1870s, no more than 8.4 percent of the total population voted as late as 1945.[17] Nor, in the face of isolation, exclusion, or repression, had ordinary citizens been able effectively to influence state policy indirectly through strikes or demonstrations. But as urban populations grew so did their political consciousness and public demands. At the same time, with the commitment to industrial growth in the 1940s, 1950s, and 1960s, the leaders of all Latin American countries, military and civilian alike, saw the need to incorporate heretofore marginal groups into the nation and to broaden political support in order to expand and consolidate the state. Voter participation shot up rapidly from the late 1940s on.

The new politics occasionally took the form of revolutions, as in Mexico from the 1920s on and in Cuba after 1959. More commonly, across the board and most notably in Argentina, Chile, Brazil, Colombia, Venezuela, Peru, and Costa Rica, military leaders and elected "populists" formed new political parties and attracted support

---

[16] Orlandina de Oliveira and Bryan Roberts, "Urban Growth and Urban Social Structure in Latin America, 1930–1990," in *CHLA*, 6.1:253–324, particularly pp. 257, 319–24. The six countries are Argentina, Brazil, Chile, Colombia, Mexico, and Peru. "Urban" is defined as places of more than two thousand inhabitants.

[17] Jonathan Hartlyn and Arturo Valenzuela, "Democracy in Latin America since 1930," in *CHLA*, 6.2:99–162, particularly pp. 130–2; Karen Remmer, *Party Competition in Argentina and Chile* (Lincoln: University of Nebraska Press, 1984), p. 84. Except for Uruguay and Brazil (1932), women were not enfranchised until after World War II.

through policies of income distribution. They promoted economic and cultural nationalism. New roads and electrification projects were meant to encourage a *national* market; schools, radios, *national* soccer leagues, *national* birds and flowers came into existence. That the resources designed to bind together a national market and encourage nationalist sentiment depended largely on foreign investment was an irony largely overlooked because the system seemed to work.

A MESTIZO ASCENDANCY

There was also a marked ethnic dimension to industrial development and new political organization. The great majority of the men, women, and children crowding into the cities and the exploding metropolitan centers after the 1930s grew out of the centuries-long intermingling of Europeans and native Americans. To these had been added large numbers of Africans in the Caribbean and circum-Caribbean. The long process of Latin America mestizaje had begun with the first contact following 1492 and then accelerated in the subsequent centuries. Throughout Latin America from the eighteenth century on, there had emerged rapidly growing mixed populations. This was not a uniform process. In the central and north of Mexico where the conquistadors implanted themselves in the very heartland of the Aztec world and zealous friars moved quickly to introduce Christianity, mestizaje began early and by the later colonial period was well advanced. Oaxaca, Chiapas, and the Guatemala highlands were marginal to the European invasion and retained much more intact their indigenous culture and modes of consumption than did the more Hispanized regions.

Native opposition to the conquest and the Spaniards' consequent decision to establish their vice-regal capital of Lima on the desert coast rather than in the densely settled Sierra contributed to a more enduring ethnic separation in Peru. By the mid-twentieth century, for example, 47 percent of all Peruvians were defined by national census takers, mainly on linguistic grounds, as "Indian" compared with only 8 percent of all Mexicans.[18] In Chile and the Argentine interior the

---

[18] Florencia Mallon, "Indian Communities, Political Cultures and the State in Latin America," *Journal of Latin American Studies* 24 (1992): 35–54; Alan Knight, "Racism, Revolution, and Indigenismo: Mexico, 1910–1940," in Richard Graham, ed., *The Idea of Race in Latin America, 1870–1940* (Austin: University of Texas Press, 1990), pp. 71–113. Knight points out on p. 74, the "difficulty of slicing a continuum in two or more discrete parts."

native population in the eighteenth and nineteenth centuries was either obliterated by the European advance, pushed into refuge zones, or steadily absorbed into the dominant culture; the Argentine littoral received large numbers of Italian and Spanish immigrants. Colombia, Venezuela, and Central America south of Guatemala, followed a pace of mestizaje that falls somewhere between the Chilean and central Andean pattern.

A glance out the window can tell us that we construct, or have constructed for us, our ethnic identities. In the case at hand, from the first, Spaniards and Portuguese shattered the native hierarchies of power and prestige and introduced into their colonies new values and power relationships. They "created a world turned upside down," as a native Peruvian chronicler lamented in the early seventeenth century, in which there were important privileges and disadvantages in being declared or held by others to be of a certain ethnicity. Because of the baroque proliferation of racial types that emerged as time went on, ethnicity was less determined by physical appearance and language than by consumption. Different kinds of food, dress, and housing took on heavy symbolic meaning. As a result, over the subsequent centuries millions of people went to great extremes, "abandoning native languages, dress, eating habits, religion and sometimes kin, to deflect the negative consequences of being recognized as *indios* while constructing their own identities as mestizo or white."[19]

This pressure continued in the twentieth century. Various states promoted *indigenísmo*, a project that professed a sometimes genuine respect for the distant pre-Columbian culture but at the same time carried out policies that aimed gradually to occidentalize, or incorporate, the "Indian on-the-ground," into a national, Western culture. By the mid-twentieth century, mixed populations were in most countries numerically dominant and arched across the entire spectrum of social classes. Most people thought of themselves, and were considered by others, to be neither European nor Indian but something in-between or, in official parlance, mestizo (from the Latin adjective *mixticiu*).

The explicit manifestations of mestizo politics can be seen, for example, in the Mexican revolutionary decades of the 1920s and 1930s; in the Guatemalan and Bolivian revolutions in the 1950s; in sectors of

[19] Jorge Klor de Alva, "Colonialism and Post Colonialism as (Latin) American Mirages," *Colonial Latin American Review* 1, nos. 1–2 (1992): 3–24, especially pp. 3–5.

Figure 6.2. Calendar art. This ordinary bit of calendar art nicely depicts the ideals of the 1930s and 1940s. The Aztec past in the eagle and serpent and progress in the form of schoolbooks and modern but local dress are elements of Mexican mestizo nationalism. Mestizaje itself is symbolized by the mixture of maize and wheat. Intensely religious – the Virgin and the Holy Family dominate the scene – it is also relentlessly secular. While the state is present in the two monuments, the church and the cross are nowhere represented. In the original, the "Virgin" wears the red, white, and green colors of the flag.

the Peruvian Popular Revolutionary Alliance and again in the Velasco Alvarado regime of 1968.[20] All of these movements created (not without dissenting voices) a sense of themselves – a "mainstream narrative" – in which, out of the painful sixteenth-century encounter between Indians and Spaniards, a new ethnonationalism emerged triumphant. By mid-twentieth century, if not before, most Latin American political leaders, writers, and artists recognized the demographic reality of their countries and began to define themselves culturally as mestizo. This is especially the case in Mesoamerica and the Andes and less so in countries that received relatively large numbers of migrants from Europe in the late nineteenth and twentieth centuries, such as Argentina, Uruguay, and Chile. The analog in the Caribbean was the emphasis on negritude or the recognition of the African past. Others imagined that the "white" and "black" categories imposed by colonial rule would give way to créolité or mestizaje. Frequently proclaimed by politicians, taught in the schools, and commonly expressed in the popular media, "genetic and cultural mixing came to constitute the assumed essence" of most Latin American countries.[21]

An explicit sense of ethnic identity did not create the political movements just mentioned or erupt full blown out of them. But for our purposes here, new forms of popular culture and artistic modes – and along with this, new goods and consumption patterns – began to express themselves and to derive from, the development of mestizo nationalism. Itself a product of the mix of European, African, and native American, the evolving material culture absorbed elements from various quarters of the ethnic spectrum. Not only was the formerly white, creole elite eventually absorbed into the new national identity, even the adjective criollo (creole) itself now came to be appropriated to describe those features of "authentic" or deeply national life – such as the Argentine asado, the Chilean rodeo, or the Mexico charro. Although some poorer mestizos identified with indigenous society, the "overwhelming majority" of mestizos "constituted their cultural practices out of Euro-American models" and for most of the twentieth century they have endeavored to incorporate the native population in a modernizing and Westernizing project.[22]

---

[20] Knight, "Racism," provides a fairly recent and expert summary.

[21] Klor de Alva, "Colonialism," pp. 2–5.

[22] Ibid. In the past fifteen or twenty years, the idea that the nation should be constituted by a more or less homogeneous "race" has been shaken up by a pan-Indianist (not indígenista) discourse that argues for the union of diverse ethnicities within the nation-state.

The gradual, at times nearly imperceptible, development of a mestizo national identity and its corresponding material culture took place under varied social circumstances. It can be seen, for example, in the *mariachi* or *canción ranchera* in Mexico, where the music as well as the musicians' dress is mestizo; in the Chilean *cueca*, a rustic dance that moved from rural taverns to respectable houses of the middle class, or in the transformation of the Chilean service tenant or *inquilino*, long portrayed as a rustic buffoon (and oppressed rural servant of the landowning elite), who, in the 1930s, was reinvented, now as the colorful, proud *huaso*, whose urbanized, folkloric version, a fixture at all patriotic occasions, became representative of an "authentic" criollo Chile. Another manifestation of the gradual change from Euro-centered to local popular culture occurred in Chile: in 1910 a government-sponsored centennial dinner celebrating the separation from Spain was held in downtown Santa Lucia Park, featuring French cuisine while an orchestra played classical music; a quarter century later, in 1935, the Independence Day celebration featured Chileans dancing the cueca at the same spot.[23]

Indeed, the countryside and other social products of its soil, such as the gaucho or charro, were proposed by novelists and social critics as more authentically Argentine or Mexican than the urban elite or immigrant-dominated cities. In Joaquín Edwards Bello's popular Chilean novel, *La chica del Crillón*, winner of the National Literature Prize in 1943, the young Teresa Iturrigorriaga, of aristocratic background, finds her love and salvation not among the foppish youth of the foreignized elite but in the arms of a stalwart, bronze-skinned, explicitly mestizo, man of the soil. Several writers began to point out that real Chileans did not, or should not, feel that they were transplanted Europeans longing for a stroll down the Champs Elysées, but rather the fortunate, mixed offspring of intrepid conquistadors and the indomitable Araucanians.

A generation of Bolivian novelists, writing in the aftermath of the disastrous Chaco War (1932–5) condemned the white elite and sought national regeneration in nationalist, mestizo leaders. Explicit mestizaje became a matter of high principle in revolutionary Mexico of the 1920s

[23] See Barr-Melej, *Between Revolution and Reaction*; and, among a large, older literature, Alberto Cabero, *Chile y los Chilenos*, 3rd ed. (Santiago: Editorial Lyceum, 1948), pp. 80–3, 101–12. The "construction" of the countryside and its inhabitants as the essence and soul of a country is a politically conservative project that is found in many different countries at this time.

and 1930s, enshrined not only in the murals of Diego Rivera and José Clemente Orozco but, later, in the prominent plaque at the newly excavated Templo Mayor, which commemorates the fall of Mexico-Tenochtitlan. Here is engraved the officially correct opinion that the battle was neither a victory nor defeat but the birth of mestizo Mexico.[24] What might be called the "mestizo ascendancy" had implications not only for the political and economic projects it came to promote but also for changes in the ideas and practice of material culture and consumption from the 1930s onward.[25]

The three main categories of material culture that we've endeavored to follow in this book – shelter, clothing, and food – took several paths to modernization in the twentieth century. In the poorer districts, rural people who crowded into the outskirts of the swelling cities at first made do with cardboard and corrugated metal shelter and then often built their own, more stable houses. Sheer poverty inevitably gave these dwellings a similar, common appearance. Under the influence of different construction materials and techniques, the dwellings of ordinary people in small towns and the countryside often evolved from the native-style adobe or the patio-centered Mediterranean models introduced in the sixteenth century into flat-roofed concrete or concrete-block buildings. Housing ministries from the 1940s on, trying to keep pace with the inward flood of migrants, put up large, uniform, subsidized apartment blocks for popular housing, everywhere, from Havana and Caracas to Lima and Rio. Mock Tudor "chalés" or "búngalos," or "ranch-style" houses derived from European or California design, spread out into the better-off suburbs, sometimes even, for example, in the heat of Managua, complete with fireplace and chimney. Apart from spectacular housing experiments such as the wealthy Pedregal development in the south of Mexico City, where the glass and stone construction is integrated into ancient lava beds, it is hard to find many elements of local design that reach back to a deeper cultural root or seek a specific Latin American originality.

Clothing in the post-1930 era followed a tendency toward more variety in cloth and color but within a broadly occidentalized pattern.

---

[24] Mallon, "Indian Communities," p. 35; Marta Irurozqui Victoriano, "La tiranía de los mestizos: electiones y corrupción en Bolivia, 1900–1930" (unpublished essay, 1994, in the author's possession).

[25] Compare the American journalist and writer Stuart Alsop's well-known term, the "Wasp ascendancy."

Both the formal and sometimes flamboyant style of the belle epoque as well as native dress, are compressed into a kind of mestizo conformity. Some native people, notably, for example, the Maya in the highlands of Guatemala and Chiapas or many Quechua or Aymara people in the central Andes, clung to traditional dress. Multiple petticoats, home-made and often elaborate and strikingly beautiful homespun pleated skirts, the shawl or rebozo, and distinctive headwear, were some of the main markers of indigenous and even village identity. But more com-monly, native people, particularly men, in order "to deflect the nega-tive consequences" of being taken for Indian, tended to adopt mestizo or Western-style, shirts, trousers, and shoes. To the extent possible, the ascendant mestizo population aimed to emulate the dress, and with-stand the scorn, of their social betters while at the same time making sure to shed any association with their Indian or village past. A proper middle-class mestizo woman I knew in the 1950s in Mexico remarked that she'd "not be caught dead" wearing a *rebozo*.

Two studies of the same regions of western Guatemala, one researched in 1938–9, the other in 1952–3, reveal the change in mate-rial culture associated with the Guatemalan, mestizo-led revolution after 1944. Although Maya women continued to wear their "age-old" skirts (which, in fact, were just then being reinvented by Indian weavers, mainly from Tononicapán), Indian males "have made drastic changes in their dress," discarding the traditional black-woolen over-garment with open sleeves (the *capishay*) for "ladino-type jackets," T-shirts, and manufactured shoes, "something entirely new among these Indians."[26] Leather shoes or boots were the clearest markers separating urban from rural, or mestizo from Indian, everywhere in Spanish America. By the early twentieth century shoes and shoe polish became a surprisingly important item on the list of new imports. Even today the brilliant luster on Latin Americans' shoes offers a notable contrast to the often dull and dusty footwear of their Anglo-Saxon counterparts.

"Mestizos," noticed Luis Valcárcel in early-twentieth-century Cusco, "never used any article of clothing or adornment in an indigenous way because they wanted to distance themselves in the clearest possible manner from the native people."[27] The widespread household adoption

[26] Morris Segal, "Resistance to Cultural Change in Western Guatemala," *Sociology and Social Research* 25 (1940–41): 414–30; and Segal, "Cultural Change in San Miguel Acatán, Guatemala," *Phylon* 15 (1954): 165–76.

[27] Valcárcel, *Memorias*, p. 105.

of sewing machines, an emblematic mechanical device of the mestizo ascendancy, and the increasing availability of ready-made clothes off the rack, made this easier.

Specialized clothing for work and recreation became increasingly common too, as we move through the twentieth century. The all-purpose loose white cotton garb or homespun wool of early-twentieth-century campesinos and some industrial workers gave way to serge and later denim trousers. Railroad workers and machinists, on the other hand, adopted the coveralls or overalls and striped cap of Britain and United States railway men. Judging from the various photographic collections, mestizos workingmen strove to acquire, for their Sunday best, at least one proper dark suit. Pictures of striking Chilean nitrate workers in 1907, copper workers at Cananea in Sonora, or meat-packers in highland Peru all reveal men dressed in suits, white shirts, ties, and straw or fedora hats. This garb was already common among clerks, businessmen, union leaders, politicians, and so on, a style drawn from the bourgeoisies of western Europe and the United States. And bathing suits for men and women, shorts and shoes for soccer, make their appearance. The result was more variety but within a narrowing band of Occidentalized, mestizo material culture. The models, the "consumer reference groups," were those of western Europe and now, increasingly, of the United States.[28]

NATIONAL CUISINES

Of all the elements that make up a material culture, a people's cuisine is usually the most intimate and personal, the most original, the most rooted in local ingredients, the most conservative, but also the most susceptible of experiment and genial invention. For most poor people, the ordinary fare after 1930 continued to be plates of beans and rice or the deep native staples of maize and potatoes in one form or another, occasionally seasoned by the odd vegetable or an inexpensive chunk of meat. For special occasions, women might prepare a local variation of a meat and vegetable stew, called, depending on the country, *cazuela*,

---

[28] See, for example, the photographs of Martín Chambi devoted to the mestizo culture in and around Cuzco. *Martín Chambi, Photographs, 1920–1950*, foreword by Mario Vargas Llosa, introd. Edward Ranney and Publio López Mondéjar, trans. Margaret Sayers Peden from the Spanish (Washington, D.C.: Smithsonian Institution Press, 1993).

puchero, sancochado, or *mazamorra.* Among the better-off strata, and particularly among the new urban arrivals and the expanding middle classes, the years following 1930 show a more intense incorporation of European, African, and Asian ingredients into the underlying native food regimes. In other cases, one sees the emergence of more elaborate native dishes in which imported elements are subordinate. In either case, the general tendency is toward a mestizo – in some places called a criollo – cuisine.

In the previous chapter, we saw the enthusiasm demonstrated by a fairly thin stratum of the Latin American upper class for French cooks, *la grande cuisine,* and the disdain of the aspiring middle classes for Indian food. At the climax of the first liberalism, during the centennial cele-brations of 1910 in Mexico, not a "single Mexican dish appeared at any of the score of dinners dedicated to the patriotic occasion. The Sylvain Daumont Restaurant served most of the food and G. H. Mumm pro-vided all the Champagne."[29] Along with admiration for European food, several Porfirian intellectuals condemned corn itself, the very basis of the popular diet, as an inferior cereal, at least partly responsible for the lamentable condition of the lower orders. One luminary, the well-known intellectual, engineer, and senator, Francisco Bulnes, advanced the theory that cereals shaped the course of history: wheat eaters were superior, the rice eaters next, and the corn eaters condemned to under-nourished indolence. If Mexico were to be modern, the national diet would have to be modernized too. Just as European immigration might serve to uplift society, so the modernizing foods would come from the outside, not out of indigenous practice.[30]

Although we must not mistake the tastes and opinion of a handful of people for universal belief, it is true that in the nineteenth century Indian popular foods were a source of embarrassment to some of the elite and to a great many mestizos as well, even though they no doubt found irresistible the *taquitos,* or a tamal, or an occasional mole in street-side stalls. The non-Indian population ate wheat bread when possible, even though it generally cost more than twice as much as maize, and generally sought, not always successfully, to consume the roasts, stews, fruit and vegetables, and the beer and occasional wine typical of an ordinary Mediterranean diet.

[29] Pilcher, *Qué Vivan los Tamales,* p. 65.
[30] Ibid., p. 77.

The changing consciousness of the ascendant mestizos and the energies released by the Revolution of 1910 in Mexico changed all that. Whatever they may have privately longed to eat or drink, the victorious revolutionaries had little public sympathy for the cosmopolitan pretension of the old Porfirian elite. In the 1920s and 1930s, as part of the project of "indigenísmo," Mexicans began to promote the virtues of native dishes. The great muralists devoted space to native plants and food; tacos and tamales moved from street-side stalls into more and more private kitchens; people became interested in their culinary past. Long-neglected native foods suddenly became fashionable among wealthy society women while enterprising restaurateurs began to feature "authentic Mexican food" for the burgeoning tourist trade.

By 1946 Josefina Velázquez de León had put together the first collection of the country's varied cuisines in a widely sold cookbook, which exalted "popular foods as the gastronomic expression of the national identity."[31] In the course of these decades, "Corn lost the stigma of its Indian origins," the formerly "repellent foods" of maguey worms and grasshopper – *gusanos* and *chapulines* – fried in garlic became chic and were perhaps the most exotic examples of the way peasant food became incorporated into Mexico's national mestizo cuisine. More commonly, native and imported elements were combined. Mexican cooks found a way to wrap *huitlacoche*, to foreign eyes a generally unappealing corn fungus with an unfortunate Náhuatl name, in crepes. In season, huitlacoche can be found today on the menu of the elegant San Angel Inn. Chiles were stuffed with ground meat and covered with a nut sauce and pomegranate seeds to make an older dish, chiles en salsa nogada, newly popular; another chef, combined a butterflied beef filet with green enchiladas to create *carne asada a la tampiqueña*, wildly popular among the Mexican middle class in the 1940s. The exquisite *mole verde* enhanced the ancient Castilian roast pork, and mole poblano, with more foreign than native ingredients, was occasionally touted as the national dish.[32] A dozen combinations of tacos, tamales,

---

[31] Josefina Velázquez de León, *Platillos regionales de la República Mexicana* (Mexico City, 1946).

[32] This section follows Pilcher's admirable, *Qué Vivan los Tamales*, pp. 129–34. (One of the best places for chiles en salsa nogada is the timeless Hostería Santo Domingo in Mexico City.) Many elegant writers such as Alfonso Reyes, *Memorias de cocina y bodega*, and Paco Ignacio Taibo, *Breviario del mole poblano* (Mexico City: Editorial Terra Nova, 1981), wrote enthusiastic accounts of mole poblano.

and enchiladas became widely accepted food in Mexico City and, joined by the implausible burritos and chimichangas, soon crossed the border northward to pass as "Mexican food" throughout the United States. Pulque did not find its way into the new mestizo middle class; it stayed in the countryside or in the poorer districts of the cities.

Not yet having available the later delights of Pizza Hut and Kentucky Fried Chicken, Mexicans all along the social and ethnic spectrum sat down at night to a plate of black beans and tortillas. The indigenous hominy stew *pozole*, once the secret of the indigenous classes, became the symbol of Guadalajara's "mariachi cuisine."[33] These dishes, frequently served in clay pots and plates made by popular artisans rather than bone china, lay side by side on Mexican tables with conventional foods of European and Asian provenance in exuberant mestizo combination. Mexican beer, introduced by German brewmasters, made imported beer unnecessary. After World War II, all this was often accompanied by the inevitable Orange Crush or Pepsi and even the unspeakable Pan Bimbo. By the 1950s, then, the kinds of meals eaten by the vast majority of non-Indian Mexicans had been fundamentally transformed. By incorporating the peasant food of indigenous Mexico – while remaining ambivalent about the still marginalized Indians themselves – a national cuisine deliberately meant to unify the distinct regions and social classes had emerged, a cultural triumph of the mestizo "cosmic race."

Before the 1930 almost all production of the finely ground, dampened maize flour (*masa*) that forms the basis for tortillas and tamales was carried out by long-suffering women in individual households. Two remarkable machines made the native cuisine of Mexico available to the increasing millions of urban inhabitants. They represent the blending of indigenous techniques and European mechanical culture, a mestizo solution to a national conundrum. The invention and development arose out of local genius of machines appropriate to local circumstances.

For at least four thousand years, the people – or more accurately, the women – of present-day Mexico and Guatemala had, every day of their lives, shelled kernels of maize off the cob by hand, washed them in a perforated clay pot, soaked them in a more or less 1 percent lime solution, and then heated (but did not boil) them for twenty to forty

---

[33] Pilcher, *Qué Vivan los Tamales*, p. 131. Mariachi music and the canción ranchera are both quintessential elements of Mexican mestizo culture.

Figure 6.3. The Eternal Tortillera. After at least four thousand years, women's backbreaking labor on the *metate* was replaced by mechanical mills in the 1930s and 1940s.

minutes. The soaked and softened maize kernels, now called by the Náhuatl term, *nixtamal*, were then laboriously ground and reground on the "bitter, black stone with three feet called the metate."[34] By all accounts this was backbreaking work; women typically spent five or six hours every morning, making masa for tortillas. In 1839, one Miguel María Azcárate, a retired army colonel, carried out a statistical study in which he wrote that 312,500 women, out of a total population of 5 million Mexicans, were required to provide the daily consumption of tortillas. He later reconsidered the figure, taking into account the fact that "the parish priests, landowners, rancheros and many private houses have women with no other task than to provide hot tortillas breakfast, noon, and night," so perhaps the number was closer to a million and a half women.[35]

Toward the end of the nineteenth century the first rattlings of a mechanical revolution in tortilla making began to be felt, and by the 1920s improved nixtamal mills, powered, first by gasoline and later by electric motors, appeared even in the smaller towns. The first molino de nixtamal arrived in the small town of Tepoztlán, just south of Mexico City, in 1925 and, as we have seen, in San José de Gracia in 1928. As state projects made electricity available, mills could be found everywhere, almost always operated by mestizo men. In one five-year period, from 1935 to 1940, the number of mills increased from 927 to nearly 6,000 and in the following decade they spread rapidly into neighboring Guatemala. One might wonder why the invention of the molino de nixtamal occurred two full millennia after the development of wheat and barley flour mills in the Mediterranean and four hundred years after Mexicans could see for themselves water-powered mills as well as the windmills that drove don Quixote to distraction, both introduced by the Spaniards. But European machines for grinding the small cereals dry were never adapted to nixtamal, the soaked maize kernels, essential for tortillas and tamales. Apparently the wet maize kernels clogged the burrs and did not produce a flour sufficiently fine for tortillas. The molino de nixtamal was followed by several attempts to work out an automatic tortilla-making machine, or *tortilladora*. The technological breakthrough for this was made in 1954 by one Alfonso Gándara, an

---

[34] Ibid., p. 99. Archaeologists associate the spread of the tortilla with the extraordinarily worn shoulder and arm bones of women.

[35] Azcárate's work is cited in Sonia Concuera de Mancera, *Entre gula y templanza* (Mexico City: Fondo de Cultura Económica, 1990), p. 59.

engineering student at the National Polytechnic Institute. Between 1960 and 1980, the largest manufacturer sold some forty-two thousand machines, twice as many as his largest competitor.[36]

Gender conflict arose over the use of mechanical mills. Household tortilla making had deep roots in traditional domestic culture where men might in rare instances help shell but *never* grind corn. After the advent of the molino de nixtamal, for a man to be seen even carrying corn to the mill was "a great humiliation."[37] On the contrary, men were long accustomed to tortillas made by their women. Often, a special runner in the employ of an hacienda, for example, gathered cloth-wrapped packets of tortillas from individual village houses and distributed them to the corresponding workers in the field. For some families, the slight cost of mill-ground nixtamal was prohibitive. Men in Tepoztlan complained that the flavor of mechanical tortillas was inferior, and on more than one occasion men stoutly opposed the molino de nixtamal in the 1930s and 1940s on the grounds that it would draw women out of the house into public view, thus providing temptations for gossip and idleness and, so it was believed, even infidelity.

Because of their growing awareness of the benefits of a molino de nixtamal, women became engaged in the political ferment released in the revolutionary decade of the 1930s. Political leaders fell over themselves to be pro-molino. Senator Rubén Ortiz proposed that molinos de nixtamal be made a public utility guaranteed by the Lázaro Cárdenas administration. Indeed, a kind of "nixtamal cacique" in the person of Gabino Vázquez emerged in Coahuila, organizing women's leagues and arranging for loans for mills through the Banco Ejidatario. Cárdenas himself used grants of molinos de nixtamal to enlist new party members. In the end the acceptance of the new tortilla-making technology and the consequent freedom of women from their "slavery to the metate," came about as part of the revolutionary transformation of rural life.[38]

The increase in mixed population together with popular nationalism brought culinary change elsewhere in Latin America. Rice accompanied the sixteenth-century conquest, but not until the arrival of Chinese and Japanese immigrants from the mid-nineteenth century on

[36] Ramón Sánchez Flores, *Historia de la tecnología y la invención en México* (Mexico City: Fomento Cultural Banamex, 1980), pp. 389–94, 604–5.

[37] Lewis, *Tepoztlan: Village in Mexico*, p. 25.

[38] Pilcher, *Qué Vivan los Tamales*, pp. 100–10; Bauer, "Millers and Grinders," pp. 1–17.

did Asian ingredients and cooking find their way to the table of Peruvian mestizos. Moreover, from the last third of the nineteenth century onward, the rich variety of pasta from Italy invaded kitchens and restaurants across Latin America. In nearly every country, as part of the rise of a later-nineteenth-century food-processing industry, pasta factories appeared, putting out noodles, tallarines, and raviolis for popular consumption. This foreign addition to Latin America cooking was, perhaps, the most important since the Spanish conquest and until the later twentieth century invasion of North American fast-food.

In Peru, Pizarro's determination to found the capital on the coast divided the colony between Lima and the high sierra, and also split the cuisine between a Hispano-African – and, from the later nineteenth century, an Asian – coast and the highland provinces. Even though there was less mestizaje in Peru than in central Mexico and a more obvious coastal-highlands breach and mutual antagonism between Europeanized and native culture, the various culinary elements from five continents have come together to create the most impressive cuisine in the Western Hemisphere. Earlier in the twentieth century regional differences were strong; such native staples as *chuño*, *chicha*, *coca*, and *charqui* or *cuy* remained largely beyond the pale of coastal mestizo cuisine. While the small Lima elite in the later nineteenth century thought, like its Porfirian counterparts, that French cooking was most appropriate to their status, nationalist intellectuals such as Gonzalez Prada or Mariátegui noticed with approval that *anticuchos*, *papas a la Huancaína*, or *ceviche* had become more common in the 1920s. A wide variety of local dishes, "the result of Hispano-Andino mestizaje," included the *sancochado*, "the single dish that occupied first place among Limeños." This was a thin lamb- or beef-based stew that accounted for the relatively large amount of animal protein in the diet on the Peruvian coast.[39]

Luis Valcárcel gives us a detailed picture of the emerging mestizo diet in the first years of the twentieth century in provincial Cuzco. Although he tells us that race – "the color of skin" – was the defining characteristic of social relations, the customers in the fifty or so chicha bars or *chicharías* in a total population of nineteen thousand seem intent on borrowing and mixing. In the poorest taverns, Indian peasants sat

---

[39] Burga and Flores Galindo, *Apogeo*, p. 181, Augusto Ruiz Zevallos, "Dieta popular y conflicto en Lima de principios del siglo," *Histórica* (Lima) 16, no. 2 (Dec. 1992): 204–6.

Figure 6.4. Señoritas en la chichería. Cuzco, Peru, 1927. Young mestiza women drinking chicha. *Source:* Photograph by Martín Chambi. Courtesy, Martín Chambi heirs, Cuzco, Peru.

on the dirt floor "drowning their frustrations in chicha." A cut above were better-lit, cleaner places, given a certain prestige by the young, adventurous "gente decente" who frequented them. Here, one ordered chicha in Quechua and ate "in native style" snacks of potatoes with ground ají, bits of skewered lamb, and broad beans with *mote* and more substantial dishes of *papa lisa* or *ollucu* or even roast rabbits or guinea pig. Martin Chambi's marvelous photographs of the 1930s and 1940s provide a vivid picture of Cuzco's mestizo culture.[40]

The more conventional of the Cusco middle class took tea, beer, or ice cream in several respectable shops in the center of town. In Valcárcel's own house, meals began with a *chupe* or broth with vegetables and chopped ears of corn, followed by a meat stew, always with rice, and a baked corn, quínoa, or vegetable pastry, and finally fruit and hot chocolate. Chupe, the inevitable opening dish, according to Valcarcel, was strongly associated in peoples' minds with the creative and life-giving qualities of women.[41] Nevertheless, in contrast to Mexico, Peruvian cuisine like its nationalism, was more fragmented. Lower rates of mestizaje and less enthusiasm on the part of Peruvian mestizos to integrate the Indians into a national project are part of the explanation. Riding the crest of a social revolution in the 1920s and 1930s, and facing less profound historical and geographical divisions than in Peru, "indigenismo came more easily to Mexican (mestizo) elites" than to Peruvians, "for whom the threat of caste war and reversion to barbarism seemed truly present."[42]

By and large, Peruvian mestizos leaned toward the European side of the "criollo" culinary spectrum; and while the highland Indians had from the beginning incorporated barley and wheat, broad beans, and mutton into their food regimes, an integrative, national cuisine so obviously drawn from the indigenous base as in Mexico did not emerge in Peru. Or perhaps that can be put another way: Peru's food regimes drew from so many more sources that by the 1940s and 1950s no single contribution could appear dominant.

In Chile, a less deeply rooted indigenous culture was either exterminated or pushed into the rainy forests and brilliant lake regions of the south. The relatively few survivors in central Chile were absorbed into Hispanic society so that most Chileans, or at least the ones who

---

[40] *Martin Chambi*, pp. 52, 55, 58, 69, etc.
[41] Valcárcel, *Memorias*, p. 97.
[42] Knight, "Racism," p. 77.

Figure 6.5. Railroad employees on the Cuzco-Santa Ana line, 1926. The specialized clothing is characteristic of railroad men everywhere. *Source:* Photograph by Martín Chambi. Courtesy, Martín Chambi heirs, Cuzco, Peru.

Figure 6.6. Ezequiel Arce family with potato harvest. Cuzco, Peru, 1934. Footwear and other clothing sets off mestizo from Indian. *Source:* Photograph by Martín Chambi. Courtesy, Martín Chambi heirs.

thought about it in the later nineteenth century, liked to imagine themselves to be essentially transplanted Spaniards, intermingled to some degree with a handful of middle-class immigrants from western Europe and the United States. In the south, below the city of Concepción and the Bio Bio River, a Mapuche minority clung to its ethnic identity even after the steamrolling "pacification" carried out by the Chilean army in the 1880s and the subsequent occupation of Mapuche land. Battered by the turmoil of the 1960s and 1970s, the Mapuche have reasserted themselves in the 1990s. Until this fairly recent turn, however, the discourse of difference in Chile has generally emphasized class over ethnicity. In effect, Chileans were a hybrid society, and by the early twentieth century, as an expanding number of mestizos moved onto the social and political stage, symbols of a Chilean mestizo or criollo culture began subtly to emerge.

The culinary manifestations of this can be tracked through the several hundred menus, now held in the Museo Histórico in Santiago, from private and public banquets. The menus not only feature imported French Bordeaux and Burgundy wines, but, from around the 1880s, the menus themselves are in French. By the period 1905–10, this affectation faded away, at about the same time that nationalist and criollo (i.e., mestizo) writers assailed the *extranjerizado*, or "foreignized," elite as a "squandering" and wasteful class. The modest *cazuela de ave* or *pastel de choclo*, a peasant dish of mixed national origins – chicken, maize, olives baked in a shallow clay pot produced locally – became representatives of the "authentic" Chile. In the early 1970s, before the flood of Burger Kings and shopping mall food, Salvador Allende, leader of a self-proclaimed "creole socialism," could appeal to the patriotic gastronomy of Chileans across class lines by calling for a revolution with "*empanadas* and *vino tinto*."[43]

Although not all Argentines in the 1920s and 1930s agreed that an "authentic" Argentina could be found in its gaucho past, many more believed that the quintessential gaucho food, the *asado*, described as criollo, represented its culinary soul. Cookbooks permit some insight into culinary values. *La cocina del gaucho* provides a tour of rustic gastronomy through Argentina's provinces so that we are introduced not only to *charqui*, *churrasco* and the abundance of roast meats but also to hybrid stews such as *sanguillo* or the various *locros* with *chuchoca*, whose

---

[43] Hernán Eyzaguirre Lyon, *Sabor y saber de la cocina chilena*, 2nd ed. (Santiago: Editorial Andrés Bello, 1987).

names reveal their Quechua origin. Many recipes employ manioc flour and the fruit of local trees and plants. Doña Petrona Carrizo de Gandulfo's *El libro de doña Petrona*, Argentina's best-selling cookbook, first published in the 1930s, had gone through seventy-four editions by 1980, selling more copies than either *Martín Fierro* or the Bible; it is a monument to the more refined criollo cooking of the Atlantic littoral. It contains some eighteen hundred individual recipes, only six of which, including *salsa sumac micanqui* and *chipá* (a fundamental ingredient is manioc), are based on native American foods. There are five pages of *cóctel* – cocktail – formulas including the "Bloody Mary," "Bronx," "My Hat," "Manhattan," and the "Lloyd George."[44] In Brazil, the dense and nearly overwhelming *feijoada*, with ingredients from Europe, Africa, and America, rose from its slave food origins in the Northeast to become an accepted dish on middle-class tables in Rio and São Paulo in the first decades of the twentieth century. For some of the new generation of nationalists, its combination of local black beans, *farinha de mandioca*, dende oil, and chorizo could be seen as the perfect alimentary expression of "Luso-tropicalism."

For food to have a socially integrative effect in a country, there must be, if not a national cuisine, at least some dishes that make the consumer feel as if he or she is part of a national culinary communion. As practiced in the United States for at least a hundred years, the Thanksgiving Day meal may provide North American readers with a familiar example of the way food and national feeling merge in a single dish. Perhaps less affected by native food than any other country in the Western Hemisphere, the vast majority of the white population nevertheless clings tenaciously to the "tradition," invented in the mid-nineteenth century, of eating food thought to be of Indian origin on Thanksgiving Day. The centerpiece is the roast turkey, immortalized in the paintings of Norman Rockwell on the cover of the *Saturday Evening Post* in the 1950s, and solemnly consumed *en famille*, across the land. Moreover, from the time it became logistically possible, the armed forces bent every effort to provide its soldiers and sailors in the most distant trench or pitching warship with a gravy-covered slice of the national Host. It is no exaggeration to say that if somehow cracked crab or lasagna had been offered in place of turkey, millions of American

---

[44] *La cocina del gaucho* (Buenos Aires: Ediciones Gastronómicas, El gato que pesca, 1978), pp. 44, 132, 148. Petrona Carrizo de Gandulfo, *El libro de doña Petrona*, 74th ed. (Buenos Aires: Talleres gráficos, 1980).

men and women would have felt utterly abandoned, a fundamental link to the larger society at least temporarily shattered.

Separated by the divisive practices of material culture inherent in colonial societies, the people of Spanish America were generally slow to develop national cuisines. The impetus for Mexico's incorporation of Indian peasant foods as the primary elements of a national cuisine came from below, promoted with the energy of a nationalist, mestizo revolution. The people of Ecuador, Peru, and Bolivia, fragmented geographically and socially, have strong regional culinary specialties and have been more resistant to gastronomic nationalism. In other places, such as Chile, Argentina, and Uruguay, the increase of immigrant and mixed population, from the last third of the nineteenth century on, often led to disdain (but continued emulation) of the "foreignized" elite's culinary pretensions, a somewhat bemused interest in native dishes, and eventually, the development of a criollo cuisine.

By the 1970s, the cycle of *crecer hacia adentro* or "inward directed growth" initiated in the 1930s together with the associated practices of material culture was winding down. The high annual growth rates in manufacturing that ran around 7 percent in the 1950s and 1960s, fell to less than 4 percent in the 1970s and plummeted to 0.3 in the 1980s. A combination of circumstances including a fourfold increase in petroleum prices in the early 1970s, heavy borrowing from abroad, a still shallow domestic market (a consequence of persistent unequal income distribution within Latin America) all contributed to a stagnant manufacturing sector that often produced inferior goods at high prices. High, even runaway, inflation rates everywhere wrenched the economies out of kilter and increased the cost of imported consumer goods.[45] The CEPAL model of economic and social development had endeavored to lead Latin Americans away from an excessive dependence on the industrial powers of the North Atlantic, to buy locally what had previously been imported. To the extent possible, consumers were encouraged to edge toward models of consumption that might draw on their own recipes, designs, and architecture.

In the 1970s, Latin Americans had come to a garden of forking paths. Populist policies of income distribution, it seemed to many, had

---

[45] Ricardo Ffrench-Davis, Oscar Muñoz, and José Gabriel Palma, "The Latin Amerian Economies," in *CHLA*, 6.1:159–252; on manufacturing growth rates, see table 4.6, p. 198.

swollen the bureaucracy, led to inflation, but had not relieved inequality. To the left lay Cuba, the only country in Latin America that put its energies squarely on the side of the poorest people. The Cubans had managed, in the face of implacable U.S. hostility, to develop admirable public health and education systems and greater equality of opportunity for its people. This was bought at the expense of liberal political freedoms and eventually led to a dwarf and apathetic civil society and lifeless economy. In Chile, Salvador Allende's Popular Unity *had* taken the left-hand fork – here called, the "Chilean road to socialism" – and again, faced with U.S. opposition as well as that of the majority of Chile's own citizens, ran the economy into the ground. The Sandinista movement in Nicaragua, opposed by an American-backed, murderous counterrevolution, turned out to be both tragedy *and* farce.

Powerful models appeared in the Pacific. In the 1980s, the flourishing "Asian tigers" provided an attractive model for capitalist development. Between 1980 and 1992, for example, their per capita gross domestic product grew at an annual rate of nearly 7 percent, while Latin America's actually fell by 0.5 a year. Closer to home, the neoliberal "shock treatment" implanted by the Pinochet capitalist dictatorship in 1973 began to show positive results in the economic realm growing at 6 percent a year from 1983 into the late 1990s.[46] Finally, at the end of the 1980s, almost at a touch, the socialist states of eastern Europe and the Soviet Union collapsed, ending, at least for the present, the main alternative model to capitalism. Socialism, or at least the idea of socialism, had existed for a century and a half; now, even the Chinese Communists developed industrial free-zones and encouraged market forces. Lacking any realistic alternative to the growing dominance of the United States in the emerging global economy, under strong-arm tactics of the International Monetary Fund and international banks, every Latin American state, with the exception of Cuba, now went down the road toward neoliberalism. It seemed in many ways – under different conditions, of course – a return to the past.

[46] Gary Gereffi and Lynn Hempel, "Latin America in the Global Economy," *NACLA: Report on the Americas* 29, no. 4 (Jan.–Feb. 1996): 20, 21.

CHAPTER 7

GLOBAL GOODS

LIBERALISM REDUX

If it doesn't get all over the place it doesn't belong in your face.[1]

In the 1980s the sea change of economic and social ideas associated with neoliberalism swept away the long period of populist distributional policies. The state withdrew from many of its recent activities; faith in the government was replaced by faith in the market, as the ideological basis for the new regimes. This soon to be orthodoxy promoted a now familiar trilogy: economies open to international trade; privatization of public enterprises; and deregulation – all designed to make the region "market friendly" for foreign investors and to unleash entrepreneurial energies.[2] Tariff walls tumbled; public companies were sold off, often at bargain rates; foreign investment rose to flood proportions. Latin American leaders and their ministers of finance and economy, with substantial popular support, thrust themselves and dragged others into the global economy. This has often led to a new business spirit, an abundance of imported consumer goods, a startlingly unequal distribution of income, a high-riding new rich, high rates of unemployment, widespread poverty, and unprecedented crime in the major cities. In the year 2000, it is not clear whether the turn toward free markets and unrestrained consumerism is the incoming tide of a new, more

---

[1] Popular advertisement in the United States for a hamburger whose ketchup, mayonaise, and fat drips onto the happy eater's blouse and shoes.

[2] Compared with the previous ISI phase, a much larger share of investment now went to produce manufactured goods for export. Although two-thirds of Latin America's exports still derived from agriculture and mining, in Mexico and Brazil manufactured goods account for more than half of total exports (Gereffi and Hempel, "Global Economy," pp. 18–21).

prosperous era or the last, desperate, and savage tsunami of an exhausted capitalist mode, dominant only because there is no imaginable alternative. However it may turn out, neoliberalism in the past ten or fifteen years has revolutionized the material culture of Spanish America.

At the onset of the first liberalism 140 years ago, an acute observer noticed that "on one hand, there have started into life industrial and scientific forces which no epoch of human history had ever suspected. On the other hand, there exist symptoms of decay far surpassing the horrors of the Roman Empire. . . . the new-fangled sources of wealth by some strange weird spell, are turned into sources of want. The victories of art seem bought by the loss of character. This antagonism between modern industry and science on the one hand, modern misery and dissolution on the other hand . . . is a fact, palpable, overwhelming."[3] However familiar this judgment may appear in our own time, along with similarities, there are important differences between the first and the present liberalism.

In both cases, foreign models have provided an important reference for consumption. A century ago, a fairly narrow elite was fascinated by the expensive furniture, elegantly tailored clothes, and the fine wines of London and Paris. Today the pole of attraction is mainly the popular material culture of the United States, and the appeal of these goods reaches much deeper into Latin American society than before. All manner of things from the global market, but especially from the United States, wash into the new shopping centers and trickle even into the most remote niches of rural Latin America. Along with a previously unimagined range of useful and often inexpensive goods, the grossest excesses of American popular culture are available and made irresistible. Cultural critics complain that our culture of guns and violence draws millions of people into movie theaters and video stores; that big-budget Hollywood flics have largely smothered a once promising Latin American film industry. Cable television enables Venezuelan or Mexican fans to follow the Dallas Cowboys, while in the most remote district of Bolivia one can find sports jackets and T-shirts displaying the logo of North American teams. Blue jeans, baseball caps, Nikes and Reeboks are standard gear, present among young people everywhere. "Fat-free" foods and "diet" Pepsi, designed for sale in the

---

[3] Karl Marx, "Speech at the Anniversary of the Peoples' Paper," in Tucker, *The Marx-Engles Reader*, pp. 577–8.

Figure 7.1. Nikes in Cuzco, Peru, 1984. *Source*: Private collection. Courtesy, Mary Altier.

Figure 7.2. Comida lite. Light food. *Source:* Courtesy, Editorial Clío, Libros y Videos. Miguel Angel de Quevedo 783, Coyoacan, Mexico City, 04330.

United States where excess weight is understandably a national obsession, are made available to the malnutritioned in the poorest barrios of Latin American cities.

In a world more and more technologically unified, radio and television penetrate into nearly every household, while widespread electronic mail, scanners, and the Internet are not far behind. Advertisements put out by the most sophisticated American agencies are present on gigantic billboards and hammer away on television. In contrast to the efforts of commercial agents or traveling salesmen with their simple flyers and plain catalogs, the persuasive power of today's media is, of course, astonishing. The nineteenth-century elites had only the distant bourgeoisies of London and Paris for their reference groups; the broad masses of people now are besieged in their own homes by television offering a bewildering array of "choice" but actually making every effort possible that consumer patterns present in the United States will be duplicated in Latin America.

In the last fifteen years of the twentieth century the penetration into Latin America of Burger King and Pizza Hut franchises has increased a hundredfold; the new commercial districts of major cities are "carpeted with Kentucky Fried Chicken, Denny's and McDonald's outlets." Standardization is one of the charms of fast food. One can be confident of finding precisely the same kind of potato in the French fries, the same fat content in the patty, whether in Guadalajara or São Paulo. Perfect Idaho potatoes, mechanically peeled and sliced, are frozen and air-freighted to burger franchises in Chile. A single Wal-Mart store sells more that $1 million worth of goods in a single day in Mexico City. "Even low-paid office workers are indentured to their credit cards and auto loans," writes Alma Guillermoprieto. "In the smog-darkened center of Mexico City, or in its monstrous, ticky-tacky suburban spokes . . . progress has hit Mexico in the form of devastation, some of it ecological, much of it aesthetic."[4]

"The unmistakable scent of the Whopper wafts from the Burger King. A Radio Shack employee drums up business by putting a remote-controlled car through its paces. The song, 'The Night They Drove Old Dixie Down' plays over the loudspeakers." This takes place not in an ordinary United States suburb, but in the Alto Las Condes shopping mall in Santiago, Chile, November 1996.[5] In fact, there is talk in Latin America of the "mall decade." Commerce and people have moved out from the former central plazas of major cities to such places as Botogá's new suburban Unicentro Mall with its 360 stores. Surrounding this are more malls where signs promise "elevators with panoramic views, fast food patios, ample parking." The Colombian supermarket features "imports from the United States such as Nach-Olé Tortilla Chips, Betty Crocker Super Moist Fudge Marble Cake Mix and Pedigree Puppy Dog Food."

At the Plaza de la Cultura in San José, Costa Rica, the people can now enjoy the convenience and perhaps even the taste of McDonald's, Archies, Burger King, and Taco Bell. There's even an upscale Japanese supermarket where the citizens of a country that exports mangos can buy canned mango juice from Taiwan and Israel. On the edge of town, the new Multi Plaza holds 200 stores and another, the Mall San Pedro, has a stall for Victoria's Secret and 259 other temptations. In Quito, there are now eight malls, the largest has 400 stores; apart from clothing, hardly anything else sold there is made in Ecuador. At the malls, Latin Americans go *shopping*, one of the most commonly used English words in Spanish in the hemisphere. Imported goods are the attraction. "People would not flock to malls to gawk at – and

[4] Alma Guillermoprieto, *The Heart That Bleeds* (New York: Alfred A. Knopf, 1994), p. 238.
[5] Alejandro Reuss, "Consume and Be Consumed," *Dollars and Sense*, no. 212 (July–Aug. 1997): 7.

purchase – locally produced consumer goods." Indeed, there are fewer of them.[6]

In 1876 Horace Rumbold, the British counsul in Chile, was impressed by the long quiet streets of private houses, "most built after the fashion of the Parisian petit hotel . . . the clatter of a smart brougham or well-appointed barouche that might figure with credit in the Bois de Boulogne." Rumbold noticed the well-dressed, refined looking women gliding along the well-swept pavement: "the models of elegance are all French." But Santiago, he thought, looked as if "slices of Paris had been dropped down here and there in the midst of a huge, straggling Indian village."[7] There are no firm, reliable quantitative data on income distribution in the nineteenth century, but almost all observers would agree with Mr. Rumbold that income and wealth were sharply divided along class and ethnic lines. Most would also agree that belle epoque liberal development elevated the landowning and entre-preneurial elite to much greater wealth, and even though the urban middle sectors somewhat expanded, class differences widened. Rural people, by far the majority of the population, lived a most rudimentary material culture, scant even by the standards of humble country people today.[8]

The present turn has produced similar results. The most successful neoliberal regimes have the most unequally distributed income. The wealthiest 10 percent of Brazilians control 51 percent of all household income in their country; the top 10 percent of Chileans enjoy (one hopes) 49 percent of theirs. At the other end of the scale, the poorest 40 percent in Brazil have only 7 percent of all household income; the less fortunate 40 percent in Chile, have but 10 percent of national income.[9] In Mexico today, some forty million people out of ninety million live below "a poverty line"; in Chile, twenty-five years of

---

[6] Forrest D. Colburn, "The Malling of Latin America," *Dissent* 43, no. 1 (Winter 1996): 51–4.

[7] Rumbold, *Report by Her Majesty's Secretaries*, pp. 365–6.

[8] In nineteenth-century Latin America and today as well, there is a close associa-tion between social class and ethnicity. Regarding income distribution, there *are* figures taken from *rural* property tax roles that demonstrate extreme inequality in land distribution but we have only estimates for income.

[9] Markos Mamalakis, "Income Distribution," in Tenenbaum, *Encyclopedia*, 3:251–9. A pattern of growing inequality has of course, developed in the United States as well. In Chile, the percentage of impoverished has somewhat dimin-ished, from 32 percent in the late 1970s to the present 28 percent.

export-led growth has reduced the percentage of people in the category of "poverty" from 32 to 28 percent. The wealth of the single richest man in Mexico is said to exceed the annual income of fourteen million of his poorest compatriots.[10]

Despite the growing inequality of income in Latin America and the persistence of extreme poverty among at least a third of the population, products from the global economy may be found in the most remote corners of Latin America. Nowhere have the great multinational soft drink companies had more extraordinary success in convincing millions of consumers, including some of the poorest people in the world, that status, convenience, and "being with it" are more important than nutrition. Fast-food franchises, still limited mainly to the automobile-driving middle class, are not far behind. Coca Cola and Big Macs are only two – although highly visible – commodities presently coursing through the global economy. Let's not imagine that Coke and American franchise hamburgers occupy a central place in the consciousness of most Latin Americans. The historical development, however, of these two commonplace products, emblematic of both American genius and vulgarity, may serve to illustrate important tendencies in the revolutionary consumption patterns presently sweeping through Latin America.

COKE AND BURGERS

Coca-Cola, successfully promoted beyond the wildest dreams of its founders as a sign of youthful, effervescent modernity, has long ago been elevated to cliché status as a symbol of American imperialism. Coke began in the back room of a certain John Pemberton's Atlanta drugstore in 1880. Here, he cooked up in a copper vat over a wood fire, an odd mixture of herbs, seeds, sugar, caffeine, and coca leaves. Originally offered as a cure for headache, depression, and hangovers, when accidentally mixed with soda water, the concoction passed from a medicinal drink to one found pleasurable. But, alas, by only a few hundred

---

[10] If a head of household with five dependants, earns $1.00 an hour, eight hours equals $8.00, three hundred working days equals an annual gross income of $2,400. Divided by the five dependants, each person has an annual income of $480. Multiplied by 14 million, our *Forbes* billionaire need only "be worth," $6.7 billion, a paltry sum these days, to equal the income of all those poor compatriots. Comparing capital with income, of course, may be misleading. Still the figures suggest a certain inequality.

customers. Mr. Pembleton sold out to Asa Candler, a more visionary entrepreneur. His first act was to hire Pembleton's former accountant, (the man responsible for the calligraphic label) and then to found the Coca-Cola Company in 1892. Ten years later, nearly 80 bottling plants were up and running and by 1904, over 3.5 million liters of the condensed formula were sold throughout the country. Exotically named competition such as Takola Ring, Coca Conga, Coca Gola, Coca Kola sprang up overnight. Mr. Candler worried that an ordinary, thirsty customer might grab any one of these similar-sounding drinks, which led one of his partners to hit upon a genial solution. The trick was to design a bottle that might be recognized at the merest glance or even blindfolded. In 1913, the company offered a reward for the best design and soon an obscure student, known in the official history only as "a certain Edwards," came up with what is perhaps the most widely known icon on the planet. Searching through the *Encyclopedia Britannica* for the *coca* plant, whose leaves *are* part of the Coke formula, he apparently strayed to a sketch of the hand-grenade-textured pod of the *cacao* tree, which, being the source of chocolate, has nothing whatever to do with it. Starting with the model of a bulging pod, he molded a base onto the plaster model, stretched out the bottle neck, and drew vertical, grooves down the side to suggest a woman dressed in flowing clothes. In fact, the curvy bottle suggests more than anything the full-figured Gibson Girl of the epoch in a hobble skirt. The red and white lettering was drawn from the American flag. A year later, in 1914, a single share of the Coca-Cola company, originally issued at $100 dollars was worth $1,700. In 1919, Candler's heirs sold their shares for $25 million, then the largest transaction in the history of North American industry.[11]

Coca-Cola flourished in the Prohibition era (1920–33) in the United States under the leadership of Robert Woodruff, the largest shareholder of the company. Known as "Mr. Coke," the official "hero" of the company, Woodruff promoted a key feature that has never been abandoned. Neither, say, an American traveling in Japan nor an Italian in Mexico should note even the slightest difference in the taste or presentation of Coke. Whatever the local water, the concentrate had to be the same everywhere on the planet. And Woodruff had the wit to see that both the curlicued script and the Gibson-girl bottle would

---

[11] This follows the Argentine writer, Osvaldo Soriano, "Coca-Cola es así," *Debate* (Lima) 11, no. 57 (Sept.–Oct. 1989): 36–43.

become recognized worldwide. His advertising slogan, worked up in 1929, "The Pause That Refreshes" is still with us, now in eighty languages.

Faced with the possibilities in 1941 of wartime restrictions on domestic consumption, Woodruff developed two strategies. He managed to convert Coke into a patriotic emblem, to put the bottles in "the front and not the rear guard of the war," ready to bolster the moral of the troops. Men and women at war should to be able to buy a Coke for five cents wherever they might be. The drink, he proclaimed, should evoke in the soldier's heart the memory of his distant country, to know that his girlfriend or mother at the very same moment might also be enjoying a Coke. In a brilliant move, the company managed to link the troops fighting on a distant front with solidarity at home. Through Coke, soldiers abroad and family at home were united in the same Communion. Special handling equipment was designed so that Coke bottles might be carried in tanks, planes, jeeps, and trucks without breaking. In June 1943, General Eisenhower, the supreme commander of the Allied forces in Europe, made an urgent request of Coca-Cola headquarters in Atlanta that 3 million bottles be sent to the North African front. A year later, the company broke all previous sales records; by 1948 it spent $20 million a year on advertising, an amount unthinkable for any other industry.[12] The second strategy, with Europe still at war, was to move into the Latin American market.

Coca-Cola bottling plants opened in Guatemala and Honduras in 1926 and in Mexico and Columbia the following year, but serious penetration of the Latin American market began with the advent of World War II. The company installed its first bottling plants in 1942 in Argentina with unanticipated success. By the early 1970s, Buenos Aires became the single largest urban market in the world, surpassing New York City. In the postwar years, American soft drink companies invested heavily in Latin America and the full force of advertising power was turned onto the millions of potential consumers. Huge Coke "bottles" danced in bullrings, literally millions of lighted signs, umbrellas, scoreboards, blank walls, napkins – anything "that might

---

[12] Ibid., p. 43. Osvaldo Soriano, "Historia de un símbolo del capitalismo moderno," *Araucaria de Chile* (Pamplona, Spain) 35 (1986): 49–59, especially 53. See also Mark Pendergrast, *For God, Country and Coca-Cola* (New York: Charles Scribner's Sons, 1993).

be seen by more that one pair of eyes at the same time" – carried the
Coke logo.[13]

The Latin American market rapidly increased. When Coca-Cola
encountered local competition – as in Brazil from the popular Guaraná,
which, in fact, long predated the arrival of Coke in 1942, or the more
recent and regional *tubaínas* – the company undercut their prices or
offered local bottlers an entire marketing package that was hard to
compete with, particularly, when Coca-Cola was able to spend
$800,000 in order to identify a motherly female kangaroo as the adver-
tising device most likely to appeal to women, who ring up 80 percent
of its sales in Brazil. In 1993 Coca-Cola had 60 percent of the Brazilian market, Pepsi another 13 percent, leaving local producers to scramble for the leftovers.[14] In Peru, from 1935, when the drink was invented,
Inka Kola was put forth as a nationalist alternative to imported soft
drinks. Many Peruvians saw Inka Kola as a symbol of national pride,
the perfect complement to the country's rich cuisine. By 1995 the Peruvian company was still able to keep pace with Coca Cola, essentially
sharing the relatively small annual market of some 75 million gallons
of soft drinks (about fifty cans or bottles per person). In the late 1990s,
however, Coca Cola acquired a 50 percent interest in the Peruvian
company.[15]

Mexicans are Latin America's most enthusiastic soft-drink consumers and are, in fact, second only to residents of the United States
in per capita and overall consumption in the world. Although faced
with some competition from local producers but particularly from Pepsi,
Coca Cola alone sold 1.6 billion cases in 1998. This works out to an
annual, per-capita consumption of about 426, or more than one Coke
a day, for every Mexican man, woman, and child. Twenty years earlier,
Mexico's annual soft-drink intake was around 250 bottles per person.[16]
Taking advantage of deregulation, the elimination of a pre-NAFTA
40 percent tax on foreign soft-drinks, both Pepsi and Coke pour

---

[13] Soriano, "Historia," p. 57.

[14] "Coke Taps Maternal Instinct with New Latin American Ads," *Advertising Age*
68, no. 2 (Jan. 1997): 13.

[15] "Peru's Pride That Refreshes: Kola of a Local Color," *New York Times*, Dec. 26,
1995, p. A4. "Coca Cola Buys Half of Peru's Inka Kola," *Beverage Industry* 90,
no. 4 (Apr. 1999): 13.

[16] A case equals twenty-four twelve-ounce cans or bottles. J. C. Louis and Harvey
Z. Yazijian, *The Cola Wars* (New York: Everest House, 1980); *The Coca-Cola
Company*, Annual Report, 1998.

billions of dollars into the country and recently have begun to buy up soft-drink companies in Mexico. Coca Cola now has about 65 percent of the Mexican soft-drink market, up from 40 percent in the early 1980s.[17]

Despite Guaraná, Inka Kola, Barrilitos, and other fruit-flavored local soft drinks promoted locally as more healthful and as nationalist alternatives to Coke – and even as Coca-Cola consolidated its position as the foremost symbol of American imperialism – more and more Latin Americans chose, and are choosing, Mr. Pemberton's delightful concoction. Coca-Cola's appeal reaches far down the social scale where the company's advertising targets kids and the poor, a practice one nutrition expert called "commerciogenic malnutrition."[18]

To return to the question that opened this book, Why do we acquire the things we do? Why do Latin Americans drink so much Coke? The first answer might be that it's safer than water; another, that it's fairly cheap. This may be true for the middle classes but a twelve-ounce can might cost nearly an hour's wage for ordinary people, much more than bottled water. Others must simply like the taste or find a bottled drink convenient. But Coca-Cola is something more than a soft drink. Its advertising has always identified Coke with modernity and the "good life," including rock bands. High-powered promotion fits soft drinks into new domestic rituals, which themselves have been created by advertising. When a task is finished or the family is together, it's time to reach for "the pause that refreshes." Courtship, dances, rock concerts, and sporting events are made impossible without a Coke. Finally, its very foreignness is an asset. Coke, neatly packaged in ice chests, carried in impressive, specialized trucks, all bearing the familiar logo, is modern, urban, worldly – words once synonymous with "civilized."

Although seen by some as yet another shallow representation of arrogant imperialism, to many more, perhaps only subconsciously, Coke enables its drinkers to associate with the larger world, not unlike the way an eighteenth-century mestizo mason in Mexico may have felt while breaking open a loaf of wheat bread, or perhaps the way a belle

---

[17] Sonia Martínez, "Due South: U.S. Beverage Trends Are Migrating to Mexico," *Beverage Industry* (May 1997): 36–8. An example is the subsidiary of the Monterrey-based FEMSA corporation. See "Coca-Cola to Buy Stake in Mexico Firm," *Los Angeles Times*, Apr. 27, 1993, business section, p. D2.

[18] Richard J. Barnet and Ronald E. Muller, *Global Reach: The Power of the Multinational Corporations* (New York: Simon and Schuster, 1974), p. 184.

Figure 7.3. Coke and Pepsi in Pisac, Peru. *Source*: Private collection. Courtesy, Mary Altier.

epoque Rio dandy felt while preening in a new suit of English tweed. In all three cases, consumption derives in part from power – not today from viceregal decrees or the elegant models of a distant Savile row, but the direct, relentless images created by advertising. Why Coke and not Pepsi? Why does "todo va mejor" with Coke? Perhaps because old Pemberton's accountant had the inspiration to draw out, in his expert calligraphy, the unforgettable original logo, or because a "certain Edwards" saw in the buxom Gibson Girl a model for his distinctive bottle design.

McDonald's got a later start in the world than did Coca Cola but now the golden arches march throughout the landscape to lead the way in an extraordinary explosion of fast-food restaurants throughout Latin America. In 1937 the brothers Richard and Maurice McDonald opened a tiny drive-in café in Pasadena, California. Encouraged by success, they acquired another, larger place, in a flourishing working-class town fifty miles east of Los Angeles. By the mid-1950s, thanks to their Ford-like hamburger assembly line organization, they were raking in $350,000 a year. This caught the eye of one Ray Kroc who made his living selling electrical mixing equipment to the food industry. Others had proposed that their method might be extended to other restaurants but the brothers McDonald lacked ambition: "we don't even manage to spend the money we make now," they pointed out. Mr. Kroc was more persuasive. Richard and Maurice joined up with him and then agreed to sell their name, the right to name concessionaires, and their system itself, for a pittance. By 1961 Big Macs were frying under the Golden Arches in 250 restaurants across the country and the brothers McDonald had been booted overboard.

To insure uniformity of product, Kroc established his own "university," which a competitor compared with the Marine Corps, to train administrators and workers. By 1987, three years after Mr. Kroc's death, the McDonald's chain had 9,900 outlets and the company's sales reached $14.3 billion dollars. At that time, McDonald's 9,900 restaurants also sold 5 percent of all the Coca-Cola sold in the world. Every day of that year, in the United States alone, customers devoured five hundred tons of ground beef; today more than twice that amount. Already in 1987, the company spent $600 million on advertising, $325 million in television alone. This was $50 million more than General Motors and twice as much as its nearest hamburger competitor, Burger King. Like other purveyors of fast and junk food,

McDonald's advertising targeted kids. Their agency created an agreeable clown, "Ronald McDonald," who was shown skating, riding a bike, swimming, and playing ball. "Ronald" was the kids' buddy. The tactics paid off. McDonald's, in the late 1980s, was getting 42 percent of under-seven customers, 10 percent more than the fast-food industry in general.[19]

McDonald's made its first incursions abroad in 1970 at a time when fast food was relatively unknown in foreign markets, although by then already common in the United States. Even so, the company had to adapt its menu to local tastes. At the beginning, business was slow; penetration of Canada required a 20 percent price reduction, and there were no profits at all for the first six years. But thereafter business took off. By 1987 there were over two thousand McDonald's abroad producing 20 percent of all sales.

The company came late to Argentina, a country where much of the middle class and even part of the working class had long been accustomed to eating out several times a month. But by 1985, when McDonald's first implanted its golden arches, together with a native version of its happy clown, income distributional patterns were taking the familiar, modern, unequal shape. Demand for restaurant food contracted and became polarized. "Upscale" places catered to the new elite, while the large numbers of people, who before were able to "sit down with tablecloth and napkins, to consume two different dishes along with a bottle of wine, desert and coffee," now found themselves reduced to the occasional Big Mac and fries.[20]

But Argentina, where even the working class can afford McDonald's or other fast food, is an exception. So far, fast food is a snack for the better-off. In Mexico, where McDonald's opened the same year, only "well-dressed" patrons were in line to taste the first Quarter Pounders. Cars jammed the drive-in Auto-Mac window. The store claimed sales of ten thousand hamburgers the first day of business.[21] In Brazil as well, McDonald's sales do not yet reach very far below the urban middle classes, but even so, with over 180 million people and a large part of the urban population concentrated in Rio de Janeiro and São Paulo, the company has had here its greatest success in Latin America. From

[19] This follows, Eliseo Giai, "Las transnacionales agroalimentarias de la comida rápida: McDonald's en la Argentina," *Realidad Económica* (Buenos Aires) 89 (1989): 104–23.

[20] Ibid., pp. 119–20.

[21] *Los Angeles Times*, Dec. 20, 1985, business section, p. D1.

its first outlet established in Copacabana in 1979, McDonald's, in twenty years, made Brazil its seventh-largest market in the world, installing nearly one thousand restaurants and stands.[22] In late 1997 the company announced that it would invest $1 billion more to double the number of outlets in Latin America in order to offset slowing sales in the United States. Spreading rapidly through the still relatively small but growing automobile-driving, mall-going segment of the Latin American population, the transnational food companies also provide a wide range of delights such as Fruit Loops, Doritos, Cocoa Krispies, Ruffles, and Pizzarolas. Pepsico, for example, is the largest salty-snack and cookie processor in Mexico.[23] Entering the twenty-first century, we may confidently predict that the golden arches, giant plastic clowns, enormous flickering hot dogs, and engaging Kentucky colonels will spread the advanced culinary regime of the United States ever more widely among the eager consumers of Latin America.

While the onrush of neoliberalism tends to push aside local producers and purvey a uniform, industrial product, the growth of artisanal production in Mexico provides a remarkable counterpoint to standardization. Even as Mexico embarked on a forced-draft industrialization in the 1950s and continuing into the post-NAFTA years (1994 to the present), arts and crafts have flourished; in fact, there are more craftsmen and -women than ever. Around 1980, for example, some six million people – then 10 percent of the population – were engaged in arts and crafts. How does artisanal production survive and even increase in the countries of Latin America that have a large Indian component, under conditions of capitalist expansion?

There is a straightforward explanation. Population growth together with land scarcity leads the poorer rural inhabitants to seek additional income so they turn to work deep in their tradition. They make cloth and clothes, pottery and many different arts and crafts. The Mexican state itself supported this effort in the 1960s through FONART (The National Fund for the Promotion of Arts and Crafts) as part of the policy of import substitution industry and to further the ideological aim

---

[22] www.mcdonalds.com.br. "McDonald's No Brasil." Brazil ranks seventh, after the United States, Japan, Canada, Germany, England, and Australia. In 1999, McDonalds had twenty-one thousand outlets in the world.

[23] *New York Times*, Oct. 1997, p. D4; Charles Handy and Suchada Langley, "Food Processing in Mexico Attracts U.S. Investments," 16, no. 1 (Jan.–Apr. 1991): 20–5; Brad Miller, "Pass the Fruit Loops, Por Favor: U.S. Junk Food Invades Mexico," *Progressive* 55 (Feb. 1991): 30–2.

of internal social unification, state formation, and nation building. The encouragement offered by the state was also intended to slow rural-to-urban migration and contribute to social stability. In this sense, it can be argued that arts and crafts, far from being a contradiction, actually fit into the overall picture of capitalist hegemony because they contribute to social cohesion and the ability of the society to reproduce itself.[24]

Mexican arts and crafts also depend on the important flow of Mexican and foreign tourists who have their own reasons to buy artisanal work. In a world in which the good consumed is more and more separate from its production, many people it seems want "to establish symbolic relations with simpler life-styles," to seek a closer connection with nature and with the "Indian artisans who represent that lost closeness." Thus, millions of visitors (2 million went to the Mexican state of Michoacán alone in 1977) will eschew the large, convenient FONART store in the capital cities, or even the more convenient large outlets now present in the United States, to buy directly from the village craftsman or -woman. Artifacts from Erongaríguaro placed in the living room in Milwaukee also "vouches for the trip abroad" (and the socioeconomic and leisure time implied) and demonstrates that one is sufficiently "cultured" to embrace such exotic goods. Then too, in an ever more uniform world, "advertising whispers secretly to us all" the ways to make our lives different from others.[25]

But, one might ask, how can we talk of an "ever more uniform world" of goods if we are awash in variety? Are we not offered a stunning array of "choice" at every turn? If one imagines the variety and amount of goods, say, in a township of Kansas farmsteads or the material possessions of a proper bourgeois household in the Mexico City suburb of Tacubaya in 1940, with those present today, we'd no doubt be struck by the drab uniformity of gallused overalls in the first case and the more or less similar "Mexican modern" household furnishings in the second. But both these places then were very different from a middle-class suburb in Chicago. Today, the material culture in all three places would be strikingly similar. Different *brands* of refrigerators, televisions, cars, or T-shirts, to be sure, but near identical *categories* of goods. Regional

---

[24] This is the argument of Néstor García Canclini's fascinating study, *Transforming Modernity: Popular Culture in Mexico*, trans. Lidia Lozano from the Spanish (Austin: University of Texas Press, 1993), particularly ch. 3.

[25] Ibid., pp. 40–1.

and national differences are being leveled out, subsumed into global patterns.

In the specific case of Michoacán, the logic of interrelation between globalizing capitalism and traditional arts and crafts drives a twofold movement in the realm of consumption. The artisans themselves wear less hand-made clothing and use fewer clay pots, wooden spoons, or reed chairs. They are being replaced by manufactured goods "that are cheaper or more attractive because of their design or modern connotation." At the same time, their own artisanal production is revived and even thrives because of a demand for the unusual, the exotic, in Mexican cities and abroad.[26]

By Way of Conclusion

The practice of material culture, of course, is not static and never has been. One generation's innovation is the next's tradition. So what we see in the present – Cokes, Whoppers, Purépecha pots – will be modified, appropriated, given new meaning, fall out of fashion. We have seen from the beginning how people accepted new elements of material culture, resisted some, and transformed others. Long before Columbus, people from the central Andes worked maize and exotic llamas into their agriculture. Later, millions of people incorporated fireworks and fiestas into their lives, drawing from the rituals of the powerful new organizing whole of a once alien Christianity. Many native Americans and their offspring saw the obvious value of sheep and iron tools and were happy to have them. Millions more insisted on tortillas or chicha, present for millennia, as essential items in their diets. Ingenious cooks combined Asian spices with chocolate and local fowl to produce the exquisite mole poblano; Mexican mechanics adapted European mills to grind the nixtamal of ancient Mexico; postmodern ranchera singers dress in Jean Paul Gaultier–like cone-shaped bras and belt out anti-NAFTA songs. But still, during the Christmas season, in Mexican "houses rich and poor, throughout the republic and among immigrants to the United States, women prepare tens or even hundreds of dozens of tamales to feed their networks of family and friends."[27]

For millennia in Latin America people have been sorting through a mixed heap of goods to find those objects considered less expensive or

[26] Ibid., p. 41; Guillermoprieto, *Heart*, p. 248.
[27] Pilcher, *Qué Vivan los Tamales*, p. 161.

more stylish, nourishing, or comfortable. Some help create new identities or maintain older ones; people choose other goods that "make
and maintain social relationships" or give material substance to the
rituals, private and tiny, public and grand, that punctuate their lives.
Since the sixteenth century until fairly recent times, goods have also
been seen, both by the Eurocentric emissaries who imposed them and
the local consumers who sought them, as "civilizing goods." All this
was a long, sporadic, discontinuous and contested process that gave
way, in the course of the first liberalism, to "modernizing goods," followed in turn in the last half of the present century, by an effort at
"developing goods."

Now, Latin Americans are caught up in the "global goods" of an
expanding world market powered by capital mobility, the Internet,
media-constructed demand, and their own desire for convenience and
abundance. This has also required the resignation – so far at least – on
the part of the people who do the work, to accept underemployment
and low wages. To those today who remember, however faintly, the
responsible elites, the bourgeois restraint, or even the modesty and
decorum among country people, the present excess of a narrow stratum
of high consumers alongside the poverty of ordinary people might seem
as if an "uncivilizing process" is underway. Others who can buy quart-
sized jars of Dijon mustard and frozen Jimmy Dean sausages at the Wal-
Mart or inexpensive and stylish Liz Claibourne blouses made in the
United Arab Emirates, or the beleaguered housewives who buy supermarket tortillas or escape the daily routine by taking their kids to Carl's
Jr. – even if the ketchup occasionally drips on their shoes – may be
understandably impatient with those who harp about the vulgarity of
consumerism.

Dropping down from these lofty thoughts to ordinary household
consumers, we return again to the humble tortilla whose recent fate
provides a telling symbol of what the global economy has wrought in
our lives. "Does anyone remember," asks our most brilliant journalist,
"when tortillas did not crumble to bits if reheated? Does anyone
remember when tortillas rarely needed to be reheated, because one of
the rituals of the day was to stand in line at the local tortillería, which
perfumed the midday air for blocks around? Does anyone remember
when tortillas were so delicious that when you came out to the street
with your warm packet of them wrapped in a thick cloth and as soon
as you were home, without further ado, you stood there in the kitchen
and ate one or two with nothing but a little salt?" In the 1990s, giant

corporate industrial mills, using dehydrated corn turn out millions of tons of nixtamal flour and processed tortillas. "The corporations tinkered with the mixture . . . experimented with the proportions, and finally served up to the Mexican people the rounds of grilled cardboard that at present constitute the nation's basic foodstuff." The president of Molinos Azteca, the most important industrial tortilla producer, made Forbes magazine's list of billionaires on July 15, 1996.[28]

Quite apart from one's aesthetic judgment on the globalization of consumer culture, or whether a free market allocates the distribution of goods more humanly equitable than any conceivable alternative, or whether higher levels of consumption can be environmentally sustained, we can be sure of one thing. As we enter this new cycle of economic organization and consumption patterns, the present neoliberal sameness that from the northern reaches of Sonora to southern Chile seems to have fallen over the land, will turn out to be as transitory as all the others.

[28] Alma Guillermoprieto, "In Search of the Real Tortilla," *New Yorker*, Nov. 29, 1999, pp. 46–7. Ms. Guillermoprieto, a descendant of the nineteenth-century Mexican Reform era liberal, Guillermo Prieto, is the author of *The Heart That Bleeds, Samba* (New York: Random House, 1991), and a great many articles on Latin America in the *New Yorker* and the *New York Review of Books*, among other journals.

BIBLIOGRAPHY

MANUSCRIPT SOURCES

Archivo general de Indias. Seville.
  Charcas, legajos, 244, 344, 623.
  Quito, legajos, 172, 211, 403.
  Mexico, legajos, 2463, 2791, 2549
Archivo general de la Nación. Mexico City.
  Conventos, vol. 18.

BOOKS AND ARTICLES

Andrews, Jean. "The Peripatetic Chili Pepper." In Nelson Foster and Linda S. Cordell, eds., *Chilies to Chocolate: Food the Americas Gave the World*, pp. 81–93. Tucson: University of Arizona Press, 1992.

Armella de Aspe, Virginia. "Vestido y evolución de la moda en Michoacán." In Rafael Diego Fernández, ed., *Herencia española en la cultura material de las regiones de México*, pp. 291–324. Zamora, Michoacán: El Colegio de Michoacán, 1993.

Barnet, Richard J., and Ronald E. Muller. *Global Reach: The Power of the Multinational Corporations*. New York: Simon and Schuster, 1974.

Barr-Melij, Patrick. *Between Revolution and Reaction: Cultural Politics, Nationalism and the Rise of the Middle Class in Chile*. Chapel Hill: University of North Carolina Press, 2001.

Bauer, Arnold J. "La cultura material." In Marcello Carmagnini, Alicia Hernández Chávez, and Ruggiero Romano, eds., *Para una historia de América: las estructuras*, pp. 404–97. Mexico City: Fondo de Cultura Económica, 1999.

"La cultura mediterránea en condiciones del nuevo mundo: elementos en la transferencia del trigo a las Indias." *Historia* (Santiago, Chile) 21 (1986): 31–53.

"Industry and the Missing Bourgeoisie: Consumption and Development in Chile, 1850–1950. *Hispanic American Historical Review* 70, no. 2 (May 1970): 227–53.

"Millers and Grinders: Technology and Household Economy in Mesoamerica." *Agricultural History* 64, no. 1 (Winter 1990): 1–17.

La sociedad rural chilena desde la conquista española a nuestros dias. Trans. Paulina Matta from the English. Santiago: Andrés Bello, 1994.

Beezley, William H. *Judas at the Jockey Club.* Lincoln: University of Nebraska Press, 1987.

Borah, Woodrow W. "The Mixing of Populations." In Fredi Chiappelli, ed., *First Images of America,* 2:707–22. Berkeley: University of California Press, 1976.

Price Trends of Royal Tribute in Nueva Galicia, 1557–1598. Ibero-Americana Series, vol. 55. Berkeley: University of California Press, 1991.

Boyd-Bowman, Peter. "Spanish Emigrants to the Indies, 1595–98: A Profile." In Fredi Chiappelli, ed., *First Images of America* 2:723–36. Berkeley: University of California Press, 1976.

Berthe, Jean Pierre, ed. *Las nuevas memorias del Capitán Jean de Monségur.* Mexico City: UNAM, 1994.

Brading, David. "El clero mexicano y el movimiento insurgente de 1810." In Arnold J. Bauer, ed., *La iglesia en la economía de América Latina, siglos xvi al xix,* pp. 129–48. Trans. Paloma Bonfil from the English. Mexico City: INAH, 1986.

Braudel, Fernand. *The Structures of Everyday Life.* Trans. Sian Reynolds from the French. New York: Harper and Row, 1981.

Bruhns, Karen Olsenk. *Ancient South America.* Cambridge: Cambridge University Press, 1994.

Bulmer-Thomas, Victor. "The Latin American Economies, 1929–1939." In Leslie Bethell, ed., *The Cambridge History of Latin America,* 6.1:65–116. Cambridge: Cambridge University Press, 1994.

Burga, Manuel, and Alberto Flores Galindo. *Apogeo y crisis de la república aristocrática.* 2nd ed. Lima: Mosca Azul, 1981.

Burns, Kathyrn. *Colonial Habits: Convents and the Spiritual Economy of Cuzco, Peru.* Durham, N.C.: Duke University Press, 1999.

Cabero, Alberto. *Chile y los chilenos.* Santiago: Editorial Lyceum, 1948.

Cabrera, Luis. *Diccionario de aztequismos.* Mexico City: Oasis, 1980.

Carrasco, Pedro. "Matrimonios hispano-indios en el primer siglo de la colonia." In Alicia Hernández Chávez and Manuel Miño, eds., *Cincuenta años de historia en México,* 1:103–18. Mexico City: Colegio de México, 1991.

Carreño, Manuel Antonio. *Manual de urbanidad y buenas maneras.* 41st ed. Mexico City: Editorial Patria, 1987.

Carrizo de Gandulfo, Petrona. *El libro de doña Petrona.* 7th ed. Buenos Aires: Talleres gráficos, 1980.

Cervantes y Saavedra, Miguel de. *Don Quijote de la Mancha*. Vol. 2. Ed. Martín de Riquer. Barcelona: Editorial Juventud, 1958.

Chambi, Martín. *Photographs, 1920–1950*. Foreword by Mario Vargas Llosa. Introd. Edward Ranney and Publio López Mondéjar. Trans. Margaret Sayers Peden from the Spanish. Washington, D.C.: Smithsonian Institution Press, 1993.

Cieza de León, Pedro. *La crónica del Perú*. Madrid, 1922.

Ciudad hispanoamericana: el sueño de un orden. Madrid: Secretaría de Obras Públicas, 1991.

Cobban, Alfred. *A History of Modern France*. 2 vols. Baltimore: Pelican, 1965.

Cobo, Barnabé. *Obras del P. Barnabé Cobo*. Biblioteca de Autores Españoles, vol. 92. Madrid, 1956.

"Coca-Cola Buys Half of Peru's Inka Kola." *Beverage Industry* 90, no. 4 (April 1999): 13.

Coca-Cola Company. Annual Report. 1998.

"Coca-Cola to Buy Stake in Mexico Firm." *Los Angeles Times*, Apr. 27, 1993, Business section, D2.

La cocina del gaucho. Buenos Aires: Ediciones Gastronómicas, El gato que pesca, 1978.

Coe, Sophie. *America's First Cuisines*. Austin: University of Texas Press, 1994.

Cohen, Leah Hager. *Glass, Paper, Beans: Revelations on the Nature and Value of Ordinary Things*. New York: Doubleday, 1997.

"Coke Taps Maternal Instinct with New Latin American Ads." *Advertising Age* 68, no. 2 (Jan. 1997): 13.

Colburn, Forrest D. "The Malling of Latin America." *Dissent* 43, no. 1 (Winter 1966): 51–4.

Concuera de Mancera, Sonia. *Entre gula y templanza*. Mexico City: Fondo de Cultura Económica, 1990.

El Conquistador Anónimo. *Relación de algunas cosas de la Nueva España y de la gran ciudad de Temestitan*. Mexico City: Editorial América, 1941.

Cook, David Noble. *Born to Die: Disease and the New World Conquest, 1492–1650*. Cambridge: Cambridge University Press, 1998.

Cook, Sherburne F., and Woodrow Borah. "Indian Food Production and Consumption in Central Mexico before and after the Conquest (1550–1650)." In Sherburne Cook and Woodrow Borah, *Essays in Population History: Mexico and California*, 3:129–76. Berkeley: University of California Press, 1979.

Cotes, Manuel. *Régimen alimenticio de los jornaleros de la Sabana de Bogotá*. Bogotá, 1893.

Couturier, Edith. "Micaela Angela Carillo: Widow and Pulque Dealer." In David Sweet and Gary Nash, eds., *Struggle and Survival in Colonial America*, pp. 362–75. Berkeley: University of California Press, 1981.

Crewe, Ryan D. "Unam Fides et una Baptisma: Theological Imperialsm in Granada and Mexico, 1492–1570." Honors thesis. University of California, Davis, 1999.

Cronistas de las culturas precolumbinas. Mexico City: Fondo de Cultura Económica, 1963.

Crosby, Alfred, Jr. The Columbian Exchange: Biological and Cultural Consequences of 1492. Westport, Conn.: Greenwood Press, 1972.

Cross, Harry. "Living Standards in Nineteenth Century Mexico." Journal of Latin American Studies 10 (1978): 1–19.

D'Altroy, Terrance, and Timothy K. Earle. "Staple Finance, Wealth Finance and Storage in the Inka Political Economy." In Terry Y. LeVine, ed., Inka Storage Systems, pp. 41–72. Norman: University of Oklahoma Press, 1992.

D'Altroy, Terrance, and Cristine Hastorf. "The Architecture and Contents of Inka State Storehouses in the Xauxa Region of Peru." In Terry Y. Le Vine, Inka Storage Systems, pp. 259–86. Norman: University of Oklahoma Press, 1992.

David, Elizabeth. Harvest of the Cold Months: The Social History of Ice and Ices. London: Michael Joseph, 1994.

Defourneaux, Marcelin. Daily Life in Spain in the Golden Age. Stanford, Calif.: Stanford University Press, 1979.

Derby, Lauren. "Gringo Chicken with Worms." In Gilbert Joseph, Catherine LeGrand, and Richard Salvatore, eds., Close Encounters of Empire, pp. 451–93. Durham, N.C.: Duke University Press, 1998.

Descola, Jean. Daily Life in Colonial Peru. London: George Allen and Unwin, 1968.

Diamond, Jared. Guns, Germs and Steel: The Fates of Human Societies. New York: Norton, 1997.

Diaz del Castillo, Bernal. Historia de la conquista de Nueva España. Ed. Joaquín Ramírez Cabañas. Mexico City: Editorial Porrua, 1992.

Diccionario de historia de Venezuela. Vol. 3. Caracas: Editorial ExLibris, 1988.

Doughty, Paul. Huaylas: An Andean District in Search of Progress. Ithaca, N.Y.: Cornell University Press, 1968.

Douglas, Mary, and Baron Isherwood. The World of Goods. New York: Basic Books, 1979.

Durston, Alan. "Un régimen urbanístico en la América hispana colonial: el trazado en damero durante los siglos xvi y xvii." Historia (Santiago, Chile) 28 (1994): 59–115.

Eadweard Muybridge in Guatemala: The Photographer as Social Recorder. Photographs by Eadweard Muybridge. Text by E. Bradford Burns. Berkeley: University of California Press, 1986.

Eyzaguirre Lyon, Hernán. Sabor y saber de la cocina chilena. 2nd ed. Santiago: Andrés Bello, 1987.

Febvre, Lucien. A New Kind of History. Ed. Peter Burke. Trans. K. Folca from the French. New York: Harper and Row, 1973.

Fenochio, Jorge del Arenal. "Ideología y estilo en la architectura de finales del siglo xix." In Rafael Diego Fernández, ed., *Herencia Española en la cultura material de las regiones de México*, pp. 463–76. Zamora, Michoacán: El Colegio de Michoacán, 1993.

Ffrench Davis, Ricardo, Oscar Muñoz, and José Gabriel Palma. "The Latin American Economies." In Leslie Bethell, ed., *The Cambridge History of Latin America*, 6.1:159–252. Cambridge: Cambridge University Press, 1994.

Flandrau, Charles. *Viva Mexico!* Urbana: University of Illinois Press, 1964.

Flores Galindo, Alberto. *Aristocracia y plebe: Lima 1760–1830*. Lima: Mosca Azul, 1984.

Foster, George. *Culture and Conquest: America's Spanish Heritage*. New York: Wenner Gren Foundation for Anthropology, 1960.

———. *Tzintzuntzan: Mexican Peasants in a Changing World*. Boston: Little, Brown, 1967.

Foster, Nelson, and Linda Cordell. *Chilies to Chocolate: Food the Americas Gave the World*. Tucson: University of Arizona Press, 1992.

Fraser, Valerie. *The Architecture of Conquest: Building in the Viceroyalty of Peru, 1535–1635*. Cambridge: Cambridge University Press, 1990.

Frezier, Amedée. *Relation du voyage de la mer du Sud aux cotes de Chily et du Perou fait pendant des annés 1712, 1713, & 1714*. Paris: Chez Jean Geoffroy Nyon, 1716.

Garavaglia, Juan Carlos. *Mercado interno y economía colonial*. Mexico City: Grijalbo, 1983.

Garcia Canclini, Néstor. *Transforming Modernity: Popular Culture in Mexico*, ch. 3. Trans. Lidia Lozano from the Spanish. Austin: University of Texas Press, 1993.

García Márquez, Gabriel. *Cien años de soledad*. 9th ed. Buenos Aires: Editorial Sudamericana, 1968.

Garcilaso de la Vega (El Inca). *Obras completas del Inca Garcilaso de la Vega*. Biblioteca de Autores Españoles, vol. 133. Madrid, 1960.

Gay, Claudio. *Historia física y política de Chile: Agricultura*. 2 vols. Paris, 1862–5.

Gereffi, Gary, and Lynn Hempel. "Latin America in the Global Economy." *NACLA. Report on the Americas* 29, no. 4 (Jan.–Feb. 1996): 17–24.

Giai, Eliseo. "Las transnacionales agroalimentarias de la comida rápida: McDonalds en la Argentina." *Realidad Económica* (Buenos Aires) 89 (1989): 104–23.

Gibson, Charles. *The Aztecs under Spanish Rule*. Stanford, Calif.: Stanford University Press, 1964.

Gillis, J. M. *The U.S. Naval Astronomical Expedition to the Southern Hemisphere during the Years 1849–50–51–52*. Vol. 1 (Chile). Washington, D.C., 1855.

Golte, Jurgen. *Repartos y rebeliones*. Lima: Instituto de Estudios Peruanos, 1980.

Gonzalbo Aizpuru, Pilar. "Vestir al desnudo: un acercamiento a la ética y la estética del vestido en el siglo xvi novohispano." In Rafael Diego

Fernández, ed., *Herencia española en la cultura material de las regiones de México*, pp. 329–49. Zamora, Michoacán: El Colegio de Michoacán, 1993.

González, Luis. *Pueblo en vilo: microhistoria de San José de Gracia*. Mexico City: El Colegio de Mexico, 1972.

González Obregón, Luis. *La vida en México en 1810*. 1911. Reprint, Mexico City, 1979.

González Stephan, Beatriz. "Escritura y modernización: la domesticación de la barbarie." *Revista Iberoamericana* 60 (Jan.–June 1994): 1–22.

Gopnik, Adam. *New Yorker*, April 26, 1999, p. 22.

Gruzinski, Serge. *Painting the Conquest: The Mexican Indians and the European Renaissance*. Paris: UNESCO, Flamarion, 1992.

Guillermoprieto, Alma. *The Heart That Bleeds*. New York: Alfred A. Knopf, 1994.

Samba. New York: Random House, 1991.

"In Search of the Real Tortilla." *New Yorker*, Nov. 29, 1999, pp. 46–7.

Gutiérrez, Ramón. "La ciudad iberoamericana en el siglo xix." In *La ciudad hispanoamerica: sueño de un orden*, pp. 252–67. Madrid: Secretaría de Obras Públicas, 1991.

Haber, Stephen H. *Industry and Underdevelopment: The Industrialization of Mexico, 1890–1940*. Stanford, Calif.: Stanford University Press, 1989.

Halperín Donghi, Tulio. *The Aftermath of Revolution in Latin America*. Trans. Josephine Bunsen from the Spanish. New York: Harper and Row, 1973.

Handy, Charles, and Suchada Langley. "Food Processing in Mexico Attracts U.S. Investments." *Food Review* 16, no. 1 (Jan.–Apr. 1991): 20–25.

Haring, C. H. *The Spanish Empire in America*. Oxford: Oxford University Press, 1947.

Hartlyn, Jonathan, and Arturo Valenzuela. "Democracy in Latin America since 1930." In Leslie Bethell, ed., *The Cambridge History of Latin America*, 6.2:99–162. Cambridge: Cambridge University Press, 1994.

Hassig, Ross. *Trade, Tribute and Transportation: The Sixteenth Century Political Economy of the Valley of Mexico*. Norman: University of Oklahoma Press, 1985.

Hermitte, Esther, and Herbert Klein. "Crecimiento y estructura de una comunidad provinciana de tejedores de ponchos: Belém, Argentina, 1678–1869." In *Documentos de trabajo*, no. 78. Buenos Aires: Centro de Investigaciones Sociales, Instituto Torcuato di Tella, 1972.

Hicks, Frederick. "Cloth in the Political Economy of the Aztec State." In Mary Hodge and Michael Smith, eds., *Economies and Polities in the Aztec Realm*, pp. 79–100. Austin: University of Texas Press, 1994.

Hobsbawm, Eric. *The Age of Revolution*. New York: World Publishing, 1962.

Huamán Poma de Ayala, Felipe. *El primer nueva corónica* [sic] *y buen gobierno*. Ed. John V. Murra and Rolena Adorno. Mexico City: Siglo XXI, 1980.

Jacobsen, Nils. *Mirages of Transition: The Peruvian Altiplano, 1780–1930.* Berkeley: University of California Press, 1993.

Johnson, David Church. *Santander siglo xix: cambios socioeconómicos.* Bogotá: Carlos Valencia Editores, 1984.

Joseph, Gil, Catherine LeGrande, and Richard Salvatore, eds. *Close Encounters of Empire.* Durham, N.C.: Duke University Press, 1998.

Joseph, Gil, and Mark Szuchman, eds. *I Saw a City Invisible: Urban Portraits of Latin America.* Wilmington, Del.: S & R Books, 1996.

Juan, Jorge, and Antonio Ulloa. *Relación histórica del viaje a la América meridional.* Vol. 1. Introd. and ed. José P. Merino Navarro and Miguel Rodríguez San Vicente. Madrid: Fundación Universitaria Española, 1978.

Kaerger, Karl. *Agricultura y colonización en México en 1900.* Trans. Pedro Lewin and Dudrum Dohrmann from the German. Introd. Roberto Melville. Mexico, 1986.

Katz, Friedrich. *The Ancient American Civilizations.* New York: Praeger, 1972.

Kizca, John. *Colonial Entrepreneurs: Families and Business in Bourbon Mexico City.* Albuquerque: University of New Mexico Press, 1983.

Klor de Alva, Jorge. "Colonialism and Post Colonialism as (Latin) American Mirages." *Colonial Latin America Review* 1, nos. 1–2 (1992): 3–24.

"*Mestizaje* from New Spain to Aztlán." In *New World Orders: Casta Painting and Colonial Latin America,* pp. 58–72. New York: Americas Society Art Gallery, 1996.

Knight, Alan. "Racism, Revolution and Indigenismo: Mexico, 1910–1940." In Richard Graham, ed., *The Idea of Race in Latin America, 1870–1940,* pp. 71–113. Austin: University of Texas Press, 1990.

Konetzke, Richard. *Colección de documentos para la formación social de Hispanoamerica, 1493–1810.* 3 vols. in 5 ps. Madrid, 1953–62.

Kruggler, Thomas. "Changing Consumption Patterns and Everyday Life in Two Peruvian Regions: Food, Dress and Housing in the Central and Southern Highlands, 1820–1920." In Benjamin Orlove, ed., *The Allure of the Foreign: Imported Goods in Postcolonial Latin America,* pp. 31–66. Ann Arbor: University of Michigan Press, 1997.

Kubler, George. *Mexican Architecture in the Sixteenth Century.* 2 vols. New Haven, Conn.: Yale University Press, 1948.

Ladero Quesada, Miguel Angel. "Spain, circa 1492: Social Values and Structures." In Stuart B. Schwartz, ed., *Implicit Understandings,* pp. 96–133. Cambridge: Cambridge University Press, 1994.

Larson, Brooke. *Colonialism and Agrarian Transformation in Bolivia.* Princeton, N.J.: Princeton University Press, 1988.

León Pinelo, Antonio. *Question* [sic] *moral si el chocolate quebranta el ayuno eclesiástico.* 1636. Prologue by Sonia Concuera de Mancera. Reprint, Mexico City: Condumex, 1994.

LeVine, Terry Y. *Inka Storage Systems*. Norman: University of Oklahoma Press, 1992.

Lewis, Colin M. "Industry in Latin America before 1930." In Leslie Bethell, ed., *The Cambridge History of Latin America*, 4:267–324. Cambridge: Cambridge University Press, 1986.

Lewis, Oscar. "Social and Economic Change in a Mexican Village." *América Indígena* 4, no. 4 (Oct. 1944): 299–316.

Tepoztlan: Village in Mexico. New York: Holt, Rinehart and Winston, 1960.

Life in Mexico: The Letters of Fanny Calderón de la Barca. Ed. Howard T. Fisher and Marion Hall Fisher. New York: Doubleday, 1966.

Lockhart, James. *The Nahuas after the Conquest*. Stanford, Calif.: Stanford University Press, 1992.

"Sightings: Initial Nahua Reactions to Spanish Culture." In Stuart B. Schwartz, ed., *Implicit Understandings*, pp. 218–48. Cambridge: Cambridge University Press, 1994.

Spanish Peru. Madison: University of Wisconsin Press, 1968.

Lockhart, James, and Enrique Otte, eds. *Letters and People of the Spanish Indies*. Cambridge: Cambridge University Press, 1976.

Long, Janet. *La cocina mexicana a través de los siglos*. Mexico City: Clio, 1997.

Louis, J. C., and Harvey Z. Yazijian. *The Cola Wars*. New York: Everest House, 1980.

Love, Joseph. "Economic Ideas and Ideologies in Latin America since 1930." In Leslie Bethell, ed., *The Cambridge History of Latin America*, 6.1:403–48. Cambridge: Cambridge University Press, 1994.

MacLachlan, Colin, and William Beezley. *El Gran Pueblo: A History of Greater Mexico*. Englewood Cliffs, N.J.: Prentice-Hall, 1994.

McNeish, William. "The Origins of New World Civilization." *Scientific American* 211, no. 5 (Nov. 1964): 6–18.

Magraw, Roger. *France, 1815–1914*. Oxford: Oxford University Press, 1986.

Mallon, Florencia. "Indian Communities, Political Cultures and the State in Latin America." *Journal of Latin American Studies* 24 (1992): 35–54.

Mamalakis, Markos. "Income Distribution." In Barbara Tenenbaum, ed., *Encyclopedia of Latin American History and Culture*, 3:251–9. New York: Simon and Schuster Macmillan, 1996.

Martínez, Sonia. "Due South: U.S. Beverage Trends Are Migrating to Mexico." *Beverage Industry* (May 1997): 36–8.

Marx, Karl. "Speech at the Anniversary of the Peoples' Paper." In Robert C. Tucker, ed., *The Marx-Engles Reader*, pp. 577–8. 2nd ed. New York: W. W. Norton, 1978.

Marx, Karl, and Friedrich Engles. "The Manifesto of the Communist Party." In Robert C. Tucker, ed., *The Marx-Engles Reader*, pp. 469–99. 2nd ed. New York: W. W. Norton, 1978.

Mason, J. Alden. *The Ancient Civilizations of Peru*. Rev. ed. New York: Penguin, 1968.

"Matrícula del comercio de Santiago según el rejistro de las patentes tomadas en 1849." In *Repertorio nacional*, vol. 2. Santiago, 1850.

"Memorial, al parecer, de Fray Hernando de Talavera para los moradores del Albaicín." In Antonio Garrido Aranda, ed., *Organización de la iglesia en el reino de Granada y su proyección en Indias*, pp. 307–9. Córdoba: University of Córdoba, 1979.

Metraux, Alfred. "The Revolution of the Ax." *Diogenes*, no. 25 (Spring 1959): 28–40.

Miller, Brad. "Pass the Fruit Loops, Por Favor: U.S. Junk Food Invades Mexico." *Progressive* 55 (Feb. 1991): 30–2.

Miño Grijalva, Manuel. *La protoindustria colonial hispanoamericana*. Mexico City: Fondo de Cultura Económica, 1993.

Mintz, Sidney. *Sweetness and Power*. New York: Viking Penguin, 1991.

Monardes, Nicolás. *Libro que se trata de la nieve y de sus provechos. Biblioteca Monardes*. 1571. Reprint, Seville: Padilla Libros, 1988.

Morris, Craig. "The Wealth of a Native American State: Value, Investment and Mobilization in the Inka Economy." In J. Henderson and Patricia Netherly, eds., *Configurations of Power: Holistic Anthropology in Theory and Practice*, pp. 26–47. Ithaca, N.Y.: Cornell University Press, 1993.

Morse, Richard, ed. *The Urban Development of Latin America, 1750–1920*. Stanford, Calif.: Latin American Center, 1971.

Muñoz, Oscar. *Crecimiento industrial de Chile, 1914–1965*. Santiago, 1968.

Murra, John V. "Cloth and Its Functions in the Inca State." *American Anthropologist* 64, no. 4 (Aug. 1962): 710–28.

"Existieron el tributo y los mercados antes de la invasión europea." In Olivia Harris, Brooke Larson, and Enrique Tandeter, eds., *La participación indígena en los mercados surandinos*, pp. 51–64. La Paz, 1987.

Formaciones económicas y políticas del mundo andino. Lima: Instituto de Estudios Peruanos, 1975.

"Notes on Pre-Columbian Cultivation of Coca Leaf." In Deborah Pacini and Christine Franquemont, eds., *Coca and Cocaine: Effects on People and Policy in Latin America*. Cultural Survival Report, June 23, 1986, pp. 49–52.

"Rite and Crop in the Inca State." In Stanley Diamond, ed., *Culture and History*, pp. 393–407. New York, 1960.

Needell, Jeffrey. *A Tropical Belle Epoque: Elite Culture and Society in Turn-of-Century Rio de Janeiro*. Cambridge: Cambridge University Press, 1987.

Neruda, Pablo. *The Heights of Macchu Picchu*. Trans. Nathaniel Tarn from the Spanish. New York: Farrar, Straus and Giroux, 1974.

Novo, Salvador. *Historia gastronómica de la ciudad de México*. Mexico City: Editorial Porrua, 1997.

O'Brien, Thomas. *The Century of U.$. Capitalism in Latin America.* Albuquerque: University of New Mexico Press, 1999.

Oliveira, Orlandina, and Bryan Roberts. "Urban Growth and Urban Social Structure in Latin America, 1930–1990." In Leslie Bethell, ed., *The Cambridge History of Latin America*, 6.1:253–324. Cambridge: Cambridge University Press, 1994.

O'Phelan Godoy, Scarlett. *Rebellions and Revolts in Eighteenth-Century Peru and Upper Peru.* Cologne: Bohlau Verlag, 1985.

Orlove, Benjamin. "Down to Earth: Race and Substance in the Andes." *Bulletin of Latin America Research* 17, no. 2 (1998): 207–22.

——— "Giving Importance to Imports." With Arnold J. Bauer. In Benjamin Orlove, ed., *The Allure of the Foreign: Imported Goods in Postcolonial Latin America*, pp. 1–30. Ann Arbor: University of Michigan Press, 1997.

——— Ed. *The Allure of the Foreign: Imported Goods in Postcolonial Latin America.* Ann Arbor: University of Michigan Press, 1997.

Orlove, Benjamin, and Arnold J. Bauer. "Chile in the Belle Epoque: Primitive Producers; Civilized Consumers." In Benjamin Orlove, ed., *The Allure of the Foreign: Imported Goods in Postcolonial Latin America*, pp. 113–50. Ann Arbor: University of Michigan Press, 1997.

Orrego Luco, Luís. *Memorias del viejo tiempo.* Santiago, 1984.

Ortiz, Fernando. *Cuban Counterpoint: Tobacco and Sugar.* Introd. Bronislaw Malinowski. Prologue by Herminio Portell Vilá. Trans. Harriet de Onís from the Spanish. New York: Alfred A. Knopf, 1947.

Pareja Ortiz, María del Carmen. *Presencia de la mujer sevillana en Indias: vida cotidiana.* Seville: Excma. Diputación Provincial, 1994.

Parry, J. H., and Robert Keith. *New Iberian World.* 5 vols. New York: Times Books and Hector and Rose, 1982.

Pendergast, Mark. *For God, Country and Coca-Cola.* New York: Charles Scribner's Sons, 1993.

"Peru's Pride that Refreshes: Kola of a Local Color." *New York Times*, Dec. 26, 1995, A4.

Peterson, Willard. "What to Wear? Observations and Participation by Jesuit Missionaries in Late Ming Society." In Stuart B. Schwartz, ed., *Implicit Understandings*, pp. 403–21. Cambridge: Cambridge University Press, 1994.

Phillips, William D., Jr., and Carla Rahn Phillips. *The Worlds of Christopher Columbus.* Cambridge: Cambridge University Press, 1992.

Pilcher, Jeffrey M. *Qué Vivan los Tamales!* Albuquerque: University of New Mexico Press, 1998.

Pizarro, Pedro. *Descubrimiento y conquista de los reinos del Perú.* Biblioteca de Autores Españoles, vol. 168. Madrid, 1965.

Poppino, Rollie. *Brazil: The Land and the People.* 2nd ed. New York: Oxford University Press, 1973.

Pozo, José del. *Historia del vino chileno*. Santiago: Editorial Universitaria, 1998.

Rabell Jara, René. *La cocina mexicana a través de los siglos*. Vol. 6, *La bella época*. Mexico City: Clio, 1996.

Remmer, Karen. *Party Competition in Argentina and Chile*. Lincoln: University of Nebraska Press, 1984.

Reuss, Alejandro. "Consume and Be Consumed." *Dollars and Sense*, no. 212 (July–Aug. 1997): 7.

Rouse, Irving. *The Tainos: Rise and Decline of the People Who Greeted Columbus*. New Haven, Conn.: Yale University Press, 1992.

Ruiz Zevallos, Augusto. "Dieta popular y conflicto en Lima de principios de siglo." *Histórica* (Lima) 16, no. 2 (Dec. 1992): 201–16.

Rumbold, Horace. *Report by Her Majesty's Secretaries on the Manufactures, Commerce, etc. in Chile*. London, 1876.

Salvucci, Richard J. *Textiles and Capitalism in Mexico: An Economic History of the Obrajes, 1539–1840*. Princeton, N.J.: Princeton University Press, 1987.

Sánchez Albornoz, Nicolás. *The Population of Latin America*. Berkeley: University of California Press, 1974.

Sánchez Flores, Ramón. *Historia de la tecnología y la invención en México*. Mexico City: Fomento Cultural Banamex, 1980.

Sauer, Carl Ortwin. *Agricultural Origins and Dispersals*. Cambridge, Mass.: MIT Press, 1952.

———. *The Early Spanish Main*. Berkeley: University of California Press, 1966.

Schivelbusch, Wolfgang. *Tastes of Paradise: A Social History of Spices, Stimulants and Intoxicants*. Trans. David Jacobson from the German. New York: Vintage Books, 1993.

Scott, James. *Seeing Like the State: How Certain Schemes to Improve the Human Condition Have Failed*. New Haven, Conn.: Yale University Press, 1998.

Segal, Morris. "Cultural Change in San Miguel Acatán, Guatemala." *Phylon* 15 (1954): 165–76.

———. "Resistance to Cultural Change in Western Guatemala." *Sociology and Social Research* 25 (1940–41): 414–30.

Shaw, George Bernard. *Androcles and the Lion*. In *Collected Plays with their Prefaces*. London: Max Reinhardt, 1972.

Smith, Adam. *An Inquiry into the Nature and Causes of the Wealth of Nations*. Ed. Edwin Cannan. Introd. by Max Lerner. New York: Modern Library, 1937.

Soriano, Osvaldo. "Coca-Cola es así." *Debate* (Lima) 11, no. 57 (Sept.–Oct. 1989): 36–43.

———. "Historia de un símbolo del capitalismo moderno." *Araucaria de Chile* (Pamplona, Spain) 35 (1986): 49–59.

Soustelle, Jacques. *The Daily Life of the Aztecs*. Stanford, Calif.: Stanford University Press, 1970.

Spalding, Karen. *Huarochirí: An Andean Society under Inca and Spanish Rule.* Stanford, Calif.: Stanford University Press, 1984.

Stavig, Ward. *The World of Tupac Amaru: Conflict, Community and Identity in Colonial Peru.* Lincoln: University of Nebraska Press, 1999.

Subercaseaux, Ramón. *Memorias de 50 años.* Santiago, 1908.

Super, John C. *Food, Conquest and Colonialization in Sixteenth-Century Latin America.* Albuquerque: University of New Mexico Press, 1988.

——— "The Formation of Nutritional Regimes in Colonial Latin America." In John C. Super and Thomas C. Wright, eds., *Food, Politics and Society in Latin America*, pp. 1–23. Lincoln: University of Nebraska Press, 1985.

Taibo, Paco Ignacio. *Breviario del mole poblano.* Mexico City: Editorial Terra Nova, 1981.

Taylor, William. *Drinking, Homicide and Rebellion in Colonial Mexican Villages.* Stanford, Calif.: Stanford University Press, 1979.

Tennenbaum, Barbara. *Encyclopedia of Latin American History and Culture.* 5 vols. New York: Simon and Schuster Macmillian, 1996.

Tenorio, Mauricio. *Mexico at the World's Fairs: Crafting a Modern Nation.* Berkeley: University of California Press, 1996.

Tepaske, John J. *La real hacienda de Nueva España: la real caja de México, 1576–1816.* Mexico City: INAH, 1976.

Thompson, Guy P. C. "The Ceremonial and Political Roles of Village Bands, 1846–1974." In William Beezley, Cheryl Smith, and William French, eds., *Rituals of Rule, Ritual of Resistance*, pp. 307–42. Wilmington, Del.: S & R Books, 1994.

Thorp, Rosemary. "The Latin American Economies, 1939–ca. 1950." In Leslie Bethell, ed., *The Cambridge History of Latin America*, 6.1:117–58. Cambridge: Cambridge University Press, 1994.

Trelles Aréstegui, Efraín. *Lucas Martínez Vegaso: funcionamiento de una encomienda peruana inicial.* Lima: Catholic University Press, 1982.

Tschudi, J. J. *Travels in Peru.* Trans. Thomasina Ross from the German. New York, 1854.

Turrent, Lourdes. *La conquista musical de México.* Mexico City: Fondo de Cultura Económica, 1993.

Ulrich, Laurel Thatcher. "Cloth, Clothing and Early American Social History." *William and Mary Quarterly*, 3rd ser., 53, no. 1 (Jan. 1996): 18–48.

Undurraga Vicuña, Francisco R. *Recuerdos de 80 años.* Santiago, 1876.

Valcárcel, Luís E. *Memorias.* Lima: Instituto de Estudios Peruanos, 1981.

Van Oss, Adriaan C. *Catholic Colonialism: A Parish History of Guatemala, 1524–1821.* Cambridge: Cambridge University Press, 1986.

——— *Inventory of 861 Monuments of Mexican Colonial Architecture.* Amsterdam: CEDLA, 1978.

Van Young, Eric. *Hacienda and Market in Eighteenth-Century Mexico*. Berkeley: University of California Press, 1981.

"Material Life." In Louisa Shell, Huberman and Susan Socolow, eds., *The Countryside in Colonial Latin America*, pp. 49–74. Albuquerque: University of New Mexico Press, 1996.

Veblen, Thorstein. *The Theory of the Leisure Class*. 1899. Reprint, New York: Penguin, 1994.

Velázquez de León, Josefina. *Platillos regionales de la República Mexicana*. Mexico City, 1946.

Veliz, Claudio. *The Centralist Tradition in Latin America*. Princeton, N.J.: Princeton University Press, 1980.

Vicens-Vives, J., ed. *Historia de España y América*. 4, *Burguesía, industrialización, obrerismo: Los Borbones. El siglo xviii en América*. Barcelona: Editorial Vicens-Vives, 1961.

Villalobos, Sergio. *Origen y ascenso de la burguesía chilena*. Santiago: Editorial Universitaria, 1987.

Viola, Herman, and Carolyn Margolis, eds. *Seeds of Change: A Quincentennial Celebration*. Washington, D.C.: Smithsonian Institution Press, 1991.

Warren, J. Benedict. *La administración de los negocios de un encomendero en Michoacán*. Morelia, Michoacán: Secretaría de Educación Pública, 1984.

Xerez, Francisco de. *Verdadera relación de la conquista del Perú y la provincia del Cuzco, llamada Nueva Castilla* Seville, 1534. Reprinted in *Cronistas de las culturas precolombinas*. Mexico City: Fondo de Cultura Económica, 1963.

Index